T0004327

PRESENTED TO

....

BY

....

DATE

....

TWO-A-DAY

DEVOTIONS
FOR MEN

TWO-A-DAY

DEVOTIONS FOR MEN

DAILY WISDOM FOR MORNING & EVENING

BARBOUR
PUBLISHING

© 2023 by Barbour Publishing, Inc.

Editorial assistance by Elijah Adkins

ISBN 978-1-63609-554-7

Please see page 383 for Bible translations used in this book.

Published by Barbour Publishing, Inc., 1810 Barbour Drive, Uhrichsville, Ohio 44683, www.barbourbooks.com

Our mission is to inspire the world with the life-changing message of the Bible.

Member of the
Evangelical Christian
Publishers Association

Printed in China.

TWO-A-DAY

DEVOTIONS FOR MEN

Barbour's *Daily Wisdom for Men* devotionals are consistent bestsellers—now highlights from these annual books have been carefully collected into a "morning and evening" edition.

You'll enjoy these concise readings, two for each day of the year, to inform your mind, lift your spirit, and challenge your behavior—all in pursuit of becoming more like Jesus.

Written by men, for men, these meditations touch on a wide range of topics relevant to Christian living:

- from the nature of God to the hardships of this world
- from sin to salvation
- from spiritual disciplines to the human nature we all battle.

You'll find the twice daily encouragement you need to lift your eyes from this messy world to the heavenly realm, where Christ is seated at the right hand of the Father (Colossians 3:1).

MORNING: FAITH STARTS HERE / *In the beginning God created the heaven and the earth.* Genesis 1:1 KJV / Science has been trying to catch up to this simple statement for thousands of years. And for every astonishing discovery, more questions arise as the complexity of the natural world unfolds. The testimony of God's fingerprints on His works can be found at the level of irreducible complexity—that bottom line that separates nothingness and being.

God alone can cross that line. Every scientist who ever lived is just playing in His sandbox—and the wisest of them acknowledge it.

You can put your trust in the God who designed stars and flowers and the human eye—but who also wired you for belief and community and love. Nothing is impossible for Him.

It all starts with believing Genesis 1:1.

EVENING: FOR GAINING WISDOM / *The proverbs of Solomon son of David, king of Israel: for gaining wisdom and instruction; for understanding words of insight.* Proverbs 1:1–2 NIV / Solomon's wisdom was greater than the wisdom of all the people of the East and all the wisdom of Egypt (1 Kings 4:30). Here, at the beginning of Proverbs, the believer is told that Solomon recorded his wisdom to give the people of God greater insight.

How many times have you worked your way through the book of Proverbs? Can you cite its wisdom on pride, money, discipline, hard work, prudence, inheritance, justice, bitterness, anger, patience, wine, and purity? If it's been awhile since you've studied the book, now is the perfect time to start again.

As you begin working your way through Proverbs, take notes and ask the Lord what He wants you to learn this time through.

MORNING: GOD-HONORING HUMILITY / *Humble yourselves, therefore, under God's mighty hand, that he may lift you up in due time.* 1 Peter 5:6 NIV / It's probably fair to say that pride is at the heart of nearly every sin. Pride causes people to boast about themselves and to tear others down. It deceives them into thinking that they can fulfil God's promises without Him, thus leading to a lack of prayer. Pride creates conflicts, and it keeps us from confessing our sins so that we can be reconciled.

It's no small wonder that God has said, "I hate pride" (Proverbs 8:13)! Instead, God loves humility—the acknowledgment that we have nothing to offer Him apart from what He has already done. So humble yourself before God. Don't seek to be exalted on your own; rather, wait patiently for God to reward you.

EVENING: LOVE DOES NO HARM / *Love does no harm to a neighbor; therefore love is the fulfillment of the law.* Romans 13:10 NKJV / The five books of Moses contain the law of God, and the overwhelming majority of them boiled down to one simple precept: do no harm to your neighbor. The apostle Paul, therefore, explained that loving your neighbor—and thus refusing to harm them—automatically fulfills the law.

As a man, you may balk at the idea of letting anyone push you around—you must be assertive and never show weakness. Love and gentleness may seem soft in comparison.

Not so. You can be gentle to the weak yet tough when the time is right. You can be assertive yet honest and fair. You can act justly without letting anyone push you around. Loving others takes courage and strength, and it proves you're a true man of God.

MORNING: WISE INVESTMENTS / *Lay up for yourselves treasures in heaven*. Matthew 6:20 KJV / When Secretary of State William Seward bought the vast northern territory of Alaska from the Russians back in 1867, many Americans mocked the investment, calling it "Seward's Icebox." In hindsight, however, it was an extremely wise purchase. For a mere $7.2 million ($121 million in today's dollars), 586,412 square miles were added to the nation.

Similarly, Jesus advises all Christians to invest in their eternal future. You do that by having faith in Him, living a godly life, giving generously, and doing good to all men.

Know this, however: people will try to disparage you, insisting that you're wasting your time. But that's because they have no vision for the future. Like Seward's critics, they don't recognize a truly wise investment when they see one.

EVENING: READ YOUR BIBLE! / *Your word is a lamp for my feet, a light on my path*. Psalm 119:105 NIV / Life is busy, isn't it? Between eight-hour workdays, time spent with family and friends, church, and various other activities, it's sometimes hard to squeeze in some alone time with God in prayer and Bible reading.

The author of this evening's verse understood that the Word of God gives us direction and lights our way. But the apostle Paul had even more to say about it: "All Scripture is God-breathed and is useful for teaching, rebuking, correcting and training in righteousness, so that the servant of God may be thoroughly equipped for every good work" (2 Timothy 3:16–17 NIV).

Reading books about the Bible is a good thing, and attending group Bible studies is probably even better. But nothing should ever take the place of spending time alone with God, reading and meditating on His written Word.

MORNING: GOD HONORS HARD WORK / *A sluggard's appetite is never filled, but the desires of the diligent are fully satisfied.* Proverbs 13:4 NIV / It might be hard to believe (especially as your alarm's ringing on Monday morning), but God always intended for man to work. Adam's first assignment in the Garden of Eden was "to work it and take care of it" (Genesis 2:15 NIV).

Sadly, when Adam and Eve sinned, work turned into toil—and it's been that way ever since (Genesis 3). But God still wants each man to work. Laziness, His Word tells us, leads to poverty.

So work hard, approaching your duties with commitment and passion. And as you work, remember the apostle Paul's words: "Whether you eat or drink or whatever you do, do it all for the glory of God" (1 Corinthians 10:31 NIV).

EVENING: LIVING FOR GOD / *So then, each of us will give an account of ourselves to God.* Romans 14:12 NIV / "We must all stand before Christ to be judged. We will each receive whatever we deserve for the good or evil we have done" (2 Corinthians 5:10 NLT).

This verse isn't about the ultimate condemnation of the unsaved (Revelation 20:11–15). Rather, it describes the appearance of Christians before the judgment seat of Christ shortly after His second coming.

The purpose of this accounting is to reward believers for the good—and the bad—that they've done. First Corinthians 3:11–15 makes it clear: although believers themselves will be spared, any selfish works will be burned.

Jesus repeatedly promised that God would reward diligent service for Him, but He also warned that we will give an account for idle words and lives (Matthew 12:36). How you live matters very much—so live for God!

MORNING: FORGIVE YOURSELF! / *Therefore, there is now no condemnation for those who are in Christ Jesus.* Romans 8:1 NIV / Some Christian men haven't quite mastered letting go of the past. They walk around filled with regret and guilt, believing deep down that God still intends to lower the boom on them for prior misdeeds.

Satan, whom the Bible calls "the accuser of our brothers and sisters" (Revelation 12:10 NIV), loves few things more than tormenting believers with reminders of their sinful pasts. But the Bible also says there is no condemnation for those of us who belong to Jesus—our sins are forgiven and buried in a sea of divine forgetfulness (Micah 7:19).

So no matter what awful things you might've done before Jesus found you, you must forgive yourself. Let go of your sinful past and enter the fulfilling life God has given you through the sacrifice of His Son.

EVENING: GAINING WEALTH GOD'S WAY / *Dishonest money dwindles away, but whoever gathers money little by little makes it grow.* Proverbs 13:11 NIV / For many people, getting ahead financially means making false claims on their income tax, overcharging for goods or services, and cutting corners on quality whenever possible. But their dishonesty is eventually exposed, and all that lying comes to naught.

God's way to financial prosperity, however, involves honestly gathering money little by little and diligently setting it aside in a savings account. If you start early enough, you'll eventually earn compound interest. And if you gain enough money, you can earn even more by investing it.

Being faithful day after day is the best way to build a successful life.

DAY 6

MORNING: STRENGTH THROUGH TRIBULATIONS / *Not only so, but we also glory in our sufferings, because we know that suffering produces perseverance.* Romans 5:3 NIV / A quick summary of this morning's verse, which was written by the apostle Paul, would look something like this: What doesn't kill you makes you stronger.

Paul, having endured more than his share of suffering during his ministry, knew as well as anyone that God can use tribulations to strengthen believers and give them the character and drive it takes to endure whatever this hostile world throws at us. Just as an athlete's training regimen tears his body down but later makes it stronger and more fit for competition, tribulation can make us stronger, more Christlike, and better fit for the work God has given us to do.

EVENING: CARING FOR OTHERS / *Don't look out only for your own interests, but take an interest in others, too.* Philippians 2:4 NLT / When the Bible says, "take an interest in others," it's referring to *everyone*. This includes your wife, children, relatives, workmates, acquaintances, and total strangers—anyone who's not looking back at you in the mirror.

Doing this means listening to the cousin whose interests bore you. It includes caring for that elderly relative who seems to be a relic of a bygone century. It includes spending time with your children, laughing at their jokes and sympathizing with their sorrows. To begin, you must discard the notion that your time is too valuable or that the rewards aren't worth the trouble.

Many people aren't willing to put forth the effort to care for others—but the rewards for doing so are great indeed.

MORNING: FEELING SMALL? / *When I consider your heavens. . .what is mankind that you are mindful of them?* Psalm 8:3–4 NIV / According to one story, President Theodore Roosevelt and his good friend William Beebe, a naturalist, went for a walk after dinner one night. Roosevelt pointed skyward and observed, "That is the Spiral Galaxy in Andromeda. It is as large as our Milky Way. It is one of a hundred billion galaxies. It consists of one hundred billion stars, each larger than our sun. Now I think we are small enough. Let's go to bed."

King David, though he had no clue as to the vastness of the created universe, was still astonished by what he could observe. But to him, the most amazing fact was that the God who had created it all could look down from His throne in heaven and love him.

What a wonderful thought!

EVENING: GIVING GENEROUSLY AND WISELY / *Give freely and spontaneously. Don't have a stingy heart. The way you handle matters like this triggers GOD, your God's, blessing in everything you do*. Deuteronomy 15:10 MSG / Often, giving "freely and spontaneously" seems contrary to sound reason. Aren't you supposed to follow a well-thought-out budget and not your impulses? Yes, but God differentiates between selfish personal expenditures and selfless provision for the needy. And He promises to bless you for your generosity.

When God's Spirit speaks to you, you must follow your heart instead of your head. The Bible states clearly, "You shall surely give to him, and your heart should not be grieved when you give" (Deuteronomy 15:10 NKJV). If you know that God wants you to give, then give—even if your natural mind tries to hold you back.

MORNING: A MOST IMPORTANT COMMAND / *Whoever claims to love God yet hates a brother or sister is a liar. For whoever does not love their brother and sister, whom they have seen, cannot love God, whom they have not seen.* 1 John 4:20 NIV / Let's face it: some people are hard to love. They're too loud, too opinionated, too overbearing, too unlearned, too. . . you get the point.

The apostle John, however, had some very strong words about this subject: if you can't love someone who's right in front of you, how can you say you love a God you can't even see? Merely saying we love God but not the people He's placed in our lives makes us *liars*.

Ouch!

So when you encounter "unlovable" people, love them the way Jesus loved, unconditionally and sacrificially. And if they still refuse to change, love them all the more. It's God's job to change people—it's your job to show them His love.

EVENING: SERVICE WITH A SMILE / *Whatever your hand finds to do, do it with your might.* Ecclesiastes 9:10 NKJV / When businesses use slogans such as "We're not satisfied until you are" and "We go the extra mile," it sometimes seems like the world of commerce has grasped the Bible better than Christians.

In Paul's day, slaves were plenteous in the Roman Empire, and he gave them the following advice: "Obey your earthly masters in everything. . . , not only when their eye is on you and to curry their favor, but with sincerity of heart and reverence for the Lord" (Colossians 3:22 NIV).

"Service with a smile" shouldn't stop at our jobs—it should also extend to our families, our friendships, and every other human interaction we have.

MORNING: ONE-ON-ONE INTERVENTIONS / *Better is open rebuke than hidden love. Wounds from a friend can be trusted, but an enemy multiplies kisses*. Proverbs 27:5–6 NIV / Confrontation is uncomfortable for most people. We don't like being told that we're harboring sinful or unhealthy attitudes. And we *definitely* don't want to tell it to another!

But the Bible tells us that if a brother or sister in the Lord is either living with obvious sin or has a spiritual "blind spot," a true friend is willing to risk the friendship and say what needs to be said.

It's easy to decide to just mind your own business when your friend strays from God's standards. But this morning's verse teaches us that being a real friend involves the willingness to speak difficult truth to those you love.

Are you that kind of friend?

EVENING: LIVING WHAT YOU UNDERSTAND / *To him who knows to do good and does not do it, to him it is sin*. James 4:17 NKJV / Situations will arise in which you won't know the correct thing to do until you look through the crystal-clear lens of hindsight. In such cases, you're not held accountable. But most of the Bible's important teachings are very plain. The problem is that they can be difficult to obey.

Mark Twain said, "It ain't those parts of the Bible that I can't understand that bother me, it is the parts that I do understand." Most Christians would agree. Some, for example, might be deeply bothered by Jesus' command to "Love your enemies" (Matthew 5:44 NKJV). "He couldn't have meant that literally!" they reason, and then they use that conclusion as an excuse for retaliation.

However, God knows how well you understand His expectations, and His judgment will always be fair.

MORNING: ESTABLISHING—AND PROTECTING—YOUR REPUTATION / *A good name is more desirable than great riches; to be esteemed is better than silver or gold.* Proverbs 22:1 NIV / The great basketball coach John Wooden once said, "Be more concerned with your character than your reputation, because your character is what you really are, while your reputation is merely what others think you are." A life defined by godly character—fairness, integrity, familial love, and reverence toward God—will almost always lead to a good reputation.

There are few things in life that are worth guarding with great passion, and one of those is a good reputation. The only way to establish and protect a good reputation is by making sure your thoughts, words, and actions please God in every way.

EVENING: FIGHT LIKE MEN / *Keep your eyes open, hold tight to your convictions, give it all you've got, be resolute, and love without stopping.* 1 Corinthians 16:13–14 MSG / When Nehemiah and his men were surrounded by enemies who threatened to overwhelm them, he encouraged them, saying, "Don't be afraid of the enemy! Remember the Lord, who is great and glorious, and fight for your brothers, your sons, your daughters, your wives, and your homes!" (Nehemiah 4:14 NLT).

When problems linger on and on and start morphing into serious threats, they can seem so overwhelming that you feel like throwing up your hands in despair and yelling, "I give up!" But that is precisely when you need to be resolute. Have courage and don't give up the fight.

Certain things are well worth fighting for with every ounce of courage you have. Only then can you win battles and withstand the onslaughts of the enemy.

MORNING: SOLID AND STEADY / *Tell the older men to have self-control and to be serious and sensible. Their faith, love, and patience must never fail.* Titus 2:2 CEV / As they get older, most men naturally become more serious and sensible. In fact, younger guys often complain that old men have even lost their sense of fun and adventure. But while older Christian men should retain a zest for life and occasional levity, God intends them to be steady pillars of their families, societies, and churches.

In order to reach full maturity, a man must exercise a lifetime of self-control. He must remain sexually pure, govern any greedy tendencies, control his temper, and maintain a daily habit of prayer and devotions. Victory won't happen overnight, but it'll be worth it in the long haul.

EVENING: STANDING IN THE GAP / *"So I sought for a man among them who would make a wall, and stand in the gap before Me on behalf of the land, that I should not destroy it; but I found no one."* Ezekiel 22:30 NKJV / During Ezekiel's life, God was looking for a righteous man in Jerusalem who would stand in the gap on behalf of the land so that He wouldn't destroy it. Sadly, He found no one. Apparently, the city had crossed the point of no return with God. The righteous had abandoned the gates. God's judgment was certain.

The act of falling away can be almost unrecognizably subtle. A compromise here. A "small" sin there. And before you know it, you've lost your house and then your city—if not physically then morally.

If God were to look for a man to stand in the gap today, would you be there?

MORNING: SHIFTING OUT OF WORK MODE / *Better to be patient than powerful; better to have self-control than to conquer a city.* Proverbs 16:32 NLT / God designed men as purpose-driven, goal-oriented beings so that they concentrate on their life's mission. Many men, however, focus inordinately on building a career. They're like heat-seeking missiles—locked on target and ignoring all distractions. This can be a good thing. . .except when those "distractions" include family.

That's why a man must learn to leave his work at the office. Otherwise, he'll walk into his house and tune out his family, still trying to solve work problems. He'll become impatient when his wife requires his attention or his children ask him to play.

It takes self-control for a man to keep his mind off work. But the rewards and joys that come from a healthy family life make the effort well worth it.

EVENING: A DIVINE MEETING PLACE / *Judas, who betrayed Him, also knew the place [a garden, over the Brook Kidron—also known as the garden of Gethsemane]; for Jesus often met there with His disciples.* John 18:2 NKJV / Even though Jesus knew that Judas was about to betray Him, He didn't vary His pattern of meeting with His disciples in the Garden of Gethsemane. Judas, being one of those disciples, would have known this pattern well.

We can worship Jesus in spirit and in truth from anywhere; however, whether it's your front porch, a nearby walking trail, or a meditative garden, having a dedicated space to meet with Jesus helps clear away worldly distractions.

Do you have a place where you routinely meet with Jesus? Do your family, your friends, and even your enemies know about this place? If not, find one and begin using it today.

MORNING: HONEST, SINCERE CHRISTIANITY / *The seeds that fell on the good soil represent honest, good-hearted people who hear God's word, cling to it, and patiently produce a huge harvest.* Luke 8:15 NLT / When many people read the parable of the sower, they often focus on the salvation aspect and miss its other important lessons.

The parable does speak of getting saved, but this theme is part of a larger picture. Jesus doesn't offer you a ticket to heaven just so you can shift into cruise mode until you die. Being saved is the beginning of an entirely new lifestyle, where "honest, good-hearted people" who accept the gospel then set out to live it.

You shouldn't stop at hearing God's Word—you must find your spiritual nourishment in it, cling to it, and carefully follow its instructions.

Have you ever wished you knew the secret to a victorious life? Well, this is it!

EVENING: SUFFERING FOR CHRIST / *For to you it has been granted on behalf of Christ, not only to believe in Him, but also to suffer for His sake.* Philippians 1:29 NKJV / Paul knew what it meant to suffer for Christ. He was in constant danger and always in need of food, shelter, and clothing.

Writing from a Roman prison, he wanted the believers in Philippi to understand that they too were called to suffer for Christ. Such suffering had been granted to them by God; it was a privilege.

How can we see it as any less in our own lives? The American church tends to get so caught up in attempts to ward off suffering that it often forgets Paul's words.

None of us are called to seek suffering, but we are called to endure it when it comes.

DAY 14

MORNING: SERVING OTHERS / *He sat down, called the twelve disciples over to him, and said, "Whoever wants to be first must take last place and be the servant of everyone else."* Mark 9:35 NLT / Many men are leery of the concept of servanthood. While they understand the need to love their fellow man, the idea of consistently putting others first and themselves last seems like an alien, unpractical concept.

Jesus' disciples had this mindset too. They had just been arguing about which of them would be greatest in Jesus' coming kingdom when He informed them that if they truly wanted to be first, they must put themselves last. If they served others, God would reward them beyond measure. But if they didn't want to pay such a price, they'd still go to heaven; they just wouldn't be as greatly rewarded.

How badly do *you* want your eternal rewards?

EVENING: BITTER AS WORMWOOD / *For the lips of an immoral woman drip honey, and her mouth is smoother than oil; but in the end she is bitter as wormwood.* Proverbs 5:3–4 NKJV / An immoral woman speaks directly to our carnal nature. She is persuasive and inviting, but in the end, she is as bitter as "wormwood"—a word that also appears in Revelation as the name of a star that turns the waters into a poisonous substance with the power to kill.

Sexual immorality really is that serious. If we do not die physically from disease, we certainly place ourselves on the brink of spiritual death.

Are you currently in the clutches of temptation from an immoral woman? Recognize that she is as bitter as wormwood. She doesn't have your best interest at heart. Turn from her and embrace life instead.

MORNING: REFUSING TO COMPLAIN / *Do not say, "Why were the old days better than these?" For it is not wise to ask such questions.* Ecclesiastes 7:10 NIV / Many older men can remember when the economy was strong and growing. Middle-aged men miss the years before the Great Recession. Young men were just entering the labor pool when the global downturn hit and changed all the rules. Naturally, everyone responds by asking, "Why were the old days better than these?"

The Bible, however, calls this attitude unwise—it's basically just a complaint that betrays a lack of trust in God. No matter how difficult life gets, complaining will only bring defeat. Instead, you must learn to say with Paul, "I have learned the secret of being content in any and every situation. . .whether living in plenty or in want" (Philippians 4:12 NIV).

Contentment and determination lead to victory.

EVENING: FRESH INSIGHTS / *Wise men and women are always learning, always listening for fresh insights.* Proverbs 18:15 MSG / The late cultural critic Neil Postman released a book in 1985 called *Amusing Ourselves to Death: Public Discourse in the Age of Show Business*. His primary concern was the way every aspect of our culture—even religion included—was conditioning us "to tolerate visually entertaining material. . .to the detriment of rational public discourse." Fast-forward a few decades and his premise seems even more persuasive.

Of course, consuming entertaining media is fine, but it will shape our worldview if we neglect consuming other media for knowledge and fresh insights.

Fresh insights aren't just found in media though. Having coffee with a church elder, digesting sermons, or attending Christian social gatherings are invaluable sources as well.

How are you looking for "fresh insights" in compliance with Proverbs 18:15?

MORNING: REGULAR SPIRITUAL CHECKUPS / *But exhort one another daily, while it is called "Today," lest any of you be hardened through the deceitfulness of sin.* Hebrews 3:13 NKJV / Some men stubbornly refuse to see a doctor. Even in the face of worsening symptoms, they persuade themselves that it will somehow just "go away."

Some men act this way toward their spiritual health as well. But God knows how deceitful sin is. It often begins as an innocent thought, which leads to a not-so-harmless thought, which leads to temptation, which leads to sin, which may lead to an entrenched habit that's not easily rooted out. That's why God counsels men to "exhort one another daily."

If you're struggling with a stubborn sin, make yourself accountable to a solid, trusted Christian friend. Then follow up. Faithfully go for your spiritual checkup. You'll be glad you did.

EVENING: THE DISPERSION / *Peter, an apostle of Jesus Christ, to the pilgrims of the Dispersion in Pontus, Galatia, Cappadocia, Asia, and Bithynia.* 1 Peter 1:1 NKJV / Persecution, which caused the "Dispersion" mentioned in this evening's verse, is still going on today.

The Voice of the Martyrs shares the story of ISIS spray-painting the Arabic letter *N*—which stands for *Nasrani*, a derogatory term for Christians—on the homes and businesses of Iraqi believers. They were given a choice: convert to Islam, leave, or die. More than one hundred thousand Christians fled, unwilling to renounce their faith. This has sparked a movement called "I Am N," in which fellow believers from around the world stand with them.

Are you and your family aware of worldwide persecution? Do you pray about it daily? If not, try visiting the Voice of the Martyrs website. They have plenty of resources to help you get started.

MORNING: POWER OVER ENEMIES / *Though they plot evil against you and devise wicked schemes, they cannot succeed.* Psalm 21:11 NIV / Paul asks, "If God is for us, who can be against us?" (Romans 8:31 NIV).

In a glum moment, you might reply, "Lots of people." And that's true. Lots of people could set themselves against you. The Psalms are full of David's pleas for God to deliver him from new enemies. But here's the true question: Who can *effectively* oppose you?

If you're God's child, doing His will and seeking to please Him, your enemies can't succeed. They may utter fearful threats and seem to win for a time, but God is on your side. You will prevail.

Trust God, stay close to Him in the secret place of the Most High, and He will protect you.

EVENING: LOVING THE BRETHREN / *We know that we have passed from death to life, because we love the brethren.* 1 John 3:14 NKJV / In Nebraska in the fall, everything revolves around the Cornhuskers football team. Weddings, birthday parties, retirement celebrations, and anniversaries are scheduled so that everybody can see the game. After the game, conversations about the outcome flood the streets.

Consequently, confused transplants to the region often develop a strong dislike for this culture, sometimes even mocking the team and its fans. But the fans are not fazed. If anything, it strengthens their ties.

Similarly, the world often hates us as Christians. We need not despair, however. This is usually a good indicator that we're on the right path because it proves others can see the difference in us.

Just as we aren't afraid to flaunt our passion for a sports team, we mustn't hide our love for God's people.

MORNING: THE SOURCE OF POWER / *The L*ord *is the. . .Creator of all the earth. He never grows weak or weary. . . . He gives power to the weak and strength to the powerless.* Isaiah 40:28–29 NLT / God, who created the earth and the entire universe full of possibly trillions of stars without breaking a sweat, has absolutely unlimited power. In fact, He still delights in doing the miraculous.

Human beings, however, have definite limitations to their strength. A hard day's work, a ten-minute run, or even a stressful day leaves us exhausted. However, when your batteries are running low—or even if you suffer from permanent disabilities—God can empower you to accomplish things you could never have dreamed of.

As God told Paul in 2 Corinthians 12:9 (NLT), "My grace is all you need. My power works best in weakness."

EVENING: SPIRITUAL GARDENING / *Now he who plants and he who waters are one, and each one will receive his own reward according to his own labor.* 1 Corinthians 3:8 NKJV / Have you ever felt inadequate in your evangelization efforts? For most of us, the ground we're planting in seems dry and unreceptive to the gospel. But the next time you encounter such ground, consider the verse above.

Some of us are called to plant seeds in rough terrain, while others are called to pour a little water. But the two aren't mutually exclusive. You can be a planter who waters on occasion or a waterer who plants on occasion. Both will receive a reward. But do you know what *isn't* an option? Sitting in the pew while others work.

Which gardening role do you naturally gravitate toward? Are you seeking out new ways to garden for God everywhere you go?

MORNING: FOLLOWING GODLY MENTORS / *Remember those who led you, who spoke the word of God to you; and considering the result of their conduct, imitate their faith.* Hebrews 13:7 NASB / Western society puts great emphasis on being an independent, self-made man. It is good to be able to make your own way in this world, but that's not the whole story. There is also tremendous value in heeding the advice of pastors and spiritual leaders. These senior saints have walked the walk for many years and have much to teach.

Some men think submitting to spiritual leadership is a sign of weakness—how wrong they are! Paul said, "Let all who are spiritually mature agree on these things. If you disagree on some point, I believe God will make it plain to you" (Philippians 3:15 NLT).

So don't be afraid to follow the counsel of spiritual leaders and emulate their lifestyle. It's the wise thing to do.

EVENING: LIFTING OTHERS / *Therefore let us not judge one another anymore, but rather resolve this, not to put a stumbling block or a cause to fall in our brother's way.* Romans 14:13 NKJV / It's hard not to look at stronger believers and envy their praying abilities or biblical knowledge. Likewise, we sometimes look down on weaker believers or even contrast ourselves to Christians who appear to be in a similar place spiritually.

The latter two instances are stained with pride and can lead to judgment. Paul wanted the Roman church members to stop judging each other on matters like dietary restrictions or religious holidays. Instead, he wanted them to put their brothers' spiritual well-being first.

Rather than comparing yourself to other believers and then judging them, make their spiritual welfare of utmost importance. Doing so will lead to joy in the Holy Spirit.

MORNING: PUT YOUR TRUST IN GOD / *Trust in the LORD with all your heart. . .in all your ways submit to him, and he will make your paths straight.* Proverbs 3:5–6 NIV / Whatever your level of education, you don't have all the answers. Whether you're facing a strange predicament, an unexpected turn of events, or a tragic loss, you may find yourself grappling in the dark and asking *why*.

God, however, has all the answers. Just submit to Him, praise Him for the successes in your life, turn to Him in times of hardship, and ask Him to direct you in all you do. There's no halfway with following God.

If you make God an integral part of your life, trusting Him completely in every choice you make, He will lead you and help you accomplish His will.

EVENING: DARK NIGHT INSPIRATION / *Ascribe to the LORD the glory due his name; worship the LORD in the splendor of his holiness.* Psalm 29:2 NIV / What inspires you? For some, it's time with family. Others require the quiet glory of a scenic location. For poets and songwriters, experiences and feelings are key.

Francis Scott Key, the poet who authored America's national anthem in the 1800s, didn't get his inspiration from something beautiful, however; he got it from a firsthand perspective of war. The anthem's words are filled with images of chaos, yet they are colored with hope. That's because once the last shot was fired, the ragged American flag still waved in the early morning breeze.

Even in our darkest times, we can be inspired because God walks with us. You may not have Francis Scott Key's lyrical talents, but God wants to hear your own song.

DAY 21

MORNING: FOCUS YOUR HEART ON HIM / *"What good is it for someone to gain the whole world, yet forfeit their soul?"* Mark 8:36 NIV / Reality television has become very popular because viewers can identify with everyday people and their daily routines. Sometimes, however, reality stars are asked to say or do things that may compromise their integrity. They have to decide whether their pursuit of glory means more than their reputation.

You don't have to be famous to face similar decisions. You may want a bigger house, a fancier car, or an exclusive membership at an elite country club, but have you ever considered the moral ramifications of what it might take to get there?

Higher than any corporate ladder, heaven is the greatest position you can ever achieve. If you focus all your energy on God's kingdom, He promises that you will live abundantly now and for eternity.

EVENING: WALK YOUR TALK / *"Prove by the way you live that you have repented of your sins and turned to God."* Matthew 3:8 NLT / Some Jewish leaders followed the Old Testament laws and ancient oral traditions, yet John the Baptist still criticized them. They were hypocrites, he said, for being too legalistic, and they used religion to advance their political power. John the Baptist wanted them to prove their allegiance to God through the way they lived their lives—not through words or rituals.

What about you? Do you go beyond church attendance and Bible readings and truly practice what you preach? Do others see Christ in you everywhere you go? God knows your true intentions. He looks beyond your words and religious practices and will ultimately judge you for your behavior.

Today, make sure you put your Christian faith into practice.

MORNING: A SHINING LIGHT / *Jesus replied, "My light will shine for you just a little longer. . . . Put your trust in the light while there is still time; then you will become children of the light."* John 12:35–36 NLT / When speaking to a crowd in Jerusalem about how He would soon die, Jesus explained that they should take advantage of His presence on earth. Since He was the Light of the world, following Him would lead them out of darkness and into eternal salvation with His Father in heaven.

God wants you as a Christian to bear Jesus' light to the world. Today, get up and start spreading the Word of the Lord. Be a shining light and a blessing for people everywhere to see. Inspire them to come to the Lord by illuminating the world around you.

EVENING: AN OPTION WORTH TAKING / *The only thing that counts is faith expressing itself through love.* Galatians 5:6 NIV / Let's look at forgiveness from the angle of love. Jesus' greatest commands were very simple: love God and then love everyone else. And according to 1 Corinthians 13, forgiveness is an essential part of this process because love keeps no record of wrongs (verse 5).

Refusing to forgive makes a man bitter, easily provoked, and defensive. How could such a person ever obey God's command to love? When faith is expressed through love, bitterness and resentment get an eviction notice.

If love is a choice, then forgiveness is also a choice. You can't blame your negative circumstances—past or present—for your decisions. Forgiveness can remove your burdens, heal old wounds, and even restore broken relationships.

So when the choice to forgive presents itself—take it!

MORNING: THE WANDERING EYE / *Do not lust in your heart after her beauty or let her captivate you with her eyes.* Proverbs 6:25 NIV / Lusting after women is dangerous and can lead to sin, creating separation between you and God. Therefore, if you find yourself attracted to a woman who is married or in a relationship, stay away from her. Ask God to change your desires before you give in. Even if an attractive woman is single, resist the urge to stare at her with lustful intent—God doesn't want your mind preoccupied with sex.

In our society, sex is all around us. However, you can train yourself to have self-control by focusing on controlling your thoughts. Avoid television programming that portrays sex. Stay away from bars and nightclubs. Never look at pornographic material.

By taking these small steps, resisting temptation will become easier each time.

EVENING: NEXT QUESTION / *"Don't bargain with God. Be direct. Ask for what you need. This isn't a cat-and-mouse, hide-and-seek game we're in."* Matthew 7:7 MSG / Scholars have found more than three thousand questions between the pages of Genesis and Revelation. Some questions have obvious answers, while others are more difficult. Some came from a place of great pain, while others were used to clarify. Some were intended to try to trap Jesus, and others Jesus asked to make the hearer think.

Wanting to learn is natural, so God is not frustrated by the questions you have. (In fact, God will sometimes respond with questions of His own. He likes to hear your answers too!)

However, once your answers come, you must always be prepared to change how you think, respond, and live—God's answers are never wrong.

MORNING: BIG ENOUGH TO LISTEN / *"My feet have closely followed his steps; I have kept to his way without turning aside. I have not departed from the commands of his lips; I have treasured the words of his mouth more than my daily bread."* Job 23:11–12 NIV / You can almost hear the astonishment of Job's friends when he declared his innocence. It was clear they didn't believe Job continued to follow God.

Often, God uses suffering to draw clear truth from a broken heart and lead you beyond the pain. You'll probably never have an immediate understanding; sometimes you'll just need to talk through those things you struggle with most and let God deliver comfort.

Don't give up. Don't entertain the idea of rejecting God. And don't be afraid to be honest with Him.

EVENING: DON'T FAIL TO TRUST GOD / *And because the Israelites forsook the LORD and no longer served him, he became angry with them. He sold them into the hands of the Philistines and the Ammonites, who that year shattered and crushed them.* Judges 10:6–8 NIV / Since God has limitless power, and trusting Him plugs you into that power, it's worth asking, "What can cause a disconnect between God and me?"

First of all, trust stems from faith, so you *must* have faith. You must believe not only that God exists but that He's all-powerful. Also, you "must believe. . .that he rewards those who earnestly seek him" (Hebrews 11:6 NIV). You must trust that if you pray, He will answer your prayer. And for that, you must believe that He loves you. It's really that simple.

Put your trust in God—He's the only one who will never let you go.

DAY 25

MORNING: THE WEAK GAIN STRENGTH / *[God said,] My strength comes into its own in your weakness.* 2 Corinthians 12:9 MSG / Years ago, guys would gather on Saturday afternoons at their local theater and purchase tickets to watch the latest western. Cowboys filled the screen, and each roughneck had two gifts: a firearm and the art of self-sufficiency. While they offered help to others, they didn't seem to need help themselves.

Consequently, moviegoers began believing that the quote "God helps those who help themselves" was biblical. Men didn't want to bother God and thought they were doing Him a favor by keeping their problems to themselves. The Bible, however, never tells us to go it alone. Why would we need (or want) a Savior if we could save ourselves?

Let God's strength make up for your weakness.

EVENING: HOMECOMING / *Jesus said, "Let the little children come to me, and do not hinder them, for the kingdom of heaven belongs to such as these."* Matthew 19:14 NIV / Each spring, myriads of swallows fly six thousand miles from Argentina to the American Southwest. Their destination? A 250-year-old structure at San Juan Capistrano.

This building was not built for birds; it was intended as a mission where human visitors could receive comfort, guidance, and love. However, when the swallows arrived, the water and insect supply around the mission just seemed too inviting. Eventually, the leadership of the mission expanded the old stone structure to make room for the swallows when they visited.

Jesus, having given up everything for us, invites the unwelcome and unloved to come to Him. There are no qualifications or exceptions.

Even the swallows seem to know the church is home. Wouldn't it be nice if we all felt the same?

MORNING: BAD COMPANY / *Do not be misled: "Bad company corrupts good character."* 1 Corinthians 15:33 NIV / When you were a child, your parents probably told you to stay away from troublemakers. Mom and Dad didn't want you to follow bad people down the wrong path. Hopefully, as an adult, you've internalized that message and naturally shy away from people who'll lead you into trouble.

Christians certainly should be mindful of the people we surround ourselves with. Be careful not to associate too closely with unbelievers who speak out against Christ—they can fill you with doubt and pry you away from Him. And too many unbelievers live for the pleasure of the moment, unconcerned about one day answering to God.

Be wise in your dealings with these people. Make sure you're influencing them, rather than the opposite.

EVENING: TROUBLED WATERS / *"When you pass through the waters, I will be with you; and when you pass through the rivers, they will not sweep over you."* Isaiah 43:2 NIV / Life is full of good moments. . .and unpleasant ones. Some days feel like a breath of fresh air; others like you've fallen into a manure pit.

Maybe you've received bad news about a loved one, or maybe one of your dreams has been crushed. Whatever your situation, know that it won't last forever—God is in control. The Lord longs for a deep relationship with you, and if you run to Him first, He'll be right there to comfort you and solve the problem. On the other hand, when you have a good moment, be sure to run to God with thanksgiving.

Rely on Him with all your understanding. . .He will see you through.

MORNING: A REASON FOR COURAGE / *"Be strong and coura-geous. Do not be afraid or terrified because of them, for the* Lord *your God goes with you; he will never leave you nor forsake you."* Deuteronomy 31:6 NIV / Moses told the Israelites that the Lord was going to be the first to enter Canaan. "The Lord your God Himself crosses over before you; He will destroy these nations from before you" (Deuteronomy 31:3 NKJV). Knowing that the Almighty would be fighting at the vanguard of their army was good reason not to fear!

In Hebrews 13:5 (NKJV), the author quotes this morning's verse to Christians: "I will never leave you nor forsake you." This inspires them to boldly respond: "The Lord is my helper; I will not fear" (verse 6).

Whatever danger you face, don't give in to fear. Be strong. God will fight for you.

EVENING: THE PENCIL PARABLE / *Looking unto Jesus, the author and finisher of our faith.* Hebrews 12:2 NKJV / The author scanned the various writing implements on his desk. First, he chose a pen, but he tossed it to the side after one mistake. Maybe a highlighter would work? No, they were hard to read. He tried crayons and markers, but nothing suited the author.

That's when he grabbed the pencil. It wasn't as flashy as a marker or as elegant as a pen, but it had a satisfying and familiar scratch, and its eraser could fix a mistake in seconds. It was just what the author needed.

We can be pencils in the hands of the author of life—let's surrender control, allowing God to take our unassuming lives and draft a story He's proud of.

MORNING: *A good man leaves an inheritance to his children's children, but the sinner's wealth is laid up for the righteous.* Proverbs 13:22 ESV / Most people think of their legacy as the money, property, or possessions they pass on after death. Of course, that kind of legacy is important in that it shows our love for our wives, children, and grandchildren. It's something every godly man should want.

But our legacy also includes so much more. It is spiritual, moral, and relational. It's the way we've influenced our loved ones, friends, community, and world. Everyone leaves that kind of legacy—the godly person and the sinner alike.

We should therefore live with our legacy in mind. At every decision point, moment of temptation, and opportunity to serve God and His kingdom, we should evaluate which choice will make our wives, our children, our grandchildren—and most importantly—our God proud of us.

EVENING: HOME SWEET HOME? / *As long as we are at home in the body we are away from the Lord.* 2 Corinthians 5:6 NIV / In 2 Corinthians 5:1–10, Paul spoke about his struggle between life and death. He realized that this physical life in some ways kept him from being "at home" with the Lord.

In a sense, this physical world is our "home." It's the one place in the universe where life flourishes. We were made to live here. But this world as it now exists is not our *true* home. We were never meant for some sin-ravaged and broken planet. We were meant to enjoy limitless intimacy with God (Genesis 3).

"Home" is wherever we feel comfortable and at ease. Therefore, we should always be restless in this sinful culture. It's the only way we'll ever be truly "at home" with Christ.

MORNING: AT THE CORE: VALUES / *I consider everything a loss because of the surpassing worth of knowing Christ Jesus my Lord, for whose sake I have lost all things. I consider them garbage, that I may gain Christ.* Philippians 3:8 NIV / Every day, we are confronted with choices that cause us to consider what we truly value. Often, the greatest challenge is when we must choose between two good things. Is advancing my career more valuable than time with my children? Is work more important than worship? Hobbies more than my wife's happiness? Momentary pleasure more than purpose?

In this morning's verse, Paul expresses his greatest value: knowing Jesus. Nothing else came close—he willingly let go of everything and considered it little more than garbage in comparison.

Are you like Paul, ready to value your relationship with God over your ambitions, pleasure, and possessions?

EVENING: HOLDING ON / *Immediately Jesus reached out his hand and caught him.* Matthew 14:31 NIV / Following the hero's path means both letting go and holding on.

The story of Peter "walking on water" (Matthew 14:22–36) is a perfect example of this truth. Peter "let go" of the safe confines of the boat. But when he began to sink, Christ caught him, and Peter "held on" with all his strength.

Like a trapeze artist, we must let go in order to reach for what's next. Letting go and spinning through the air can be a terrifying, yet exhilarating, experience. The performer, however, knows the "catcher" will be there at the right time to hold on with an iron grip.

We too must hold on with all our strength to God's love that holds us close. Only then will we enjoy soaring free from the limits of our fears and failures.

DAY 30

MORNING: FLOURISHING / *The righteous will flourish like a palm tree*. Psalm 92:12 NIV / Most Christians are familiar with the events of Palm Sunday—Jesus' triumphal entry into Jerusalem as the crowds spread their cloaks in the streets and waved palm fronds. This welcome was fit for a king—and rightly so! That day began the series of events that led to an upper room, a garden, a mock trial, a cross, and the empty tomb. There is no Easter without Palm Sunday.

In Psalm 92:12–15, the palm tree symbolizes the spiritual life Christ made possible for all His children. Like the palm, we can grow, flourish, and live a fruitful life, but only when we draw our life and strength from a deep and nourishing relationship with God.

An uprooted plant doesn't flourish. It dies. Are you rooted in your Savior today?

EVENING: THE CLEAR CHOICE / *The Israelites did just what the* LORD *commanded*. Exodus 12:28 NIV / The first Passover is the story of two peoples and one choice.

After more than four hundred years in Egypt, the Israelites were clearly influenced by their host nation's culture and religions. Getting Israel out of Egypt took a few days, but getting Egypt out of Israel took forty years. In that moment, however, the choice was clear: Israel would obey or disobey. Their firstborn would live or die. They would find freedom or stay in slavery. Before they could cross the Red Sea, they first had to cross the threshold of obedience.

They chose wisely.

We all face moments in which we must decide to either move forward with God or stay where we are. In that moment, life, death, and the fate of us and everyone we love all hang in the balance. What will you choose?

MORNING: AT THE CORE: LOVE / *"A new command I give you: Love one another. As I have loved you, so you must love one another."* John 13:34 NIV / The word "love" has many shades of meaning. So what does it mean to love like Christ?

That isn't an easy question to answer. One practical definition is "always acting in the other person's best interest." Just like Jesus, this kind of love isn't selfish. It's not passive; it's active. It's not emotional; it's biblical. It doesn't cower in fear of the consequences; it's courageous.

But how do you know what's best for someone? When you pray, ask for godly wisdom and the Holy Spirit's leading. What does the Bible teach? If the Bible isn't clear, ask for wise, mature Christian counsel.

The more you follow these steps, the closer your love will match up with Christ's.

EVENING: COMMENDATIONS / *"I commend to you. . ."* Romans 16:1 NIV / It's a stunning list.

At the end of his letter to the Romans, Paul takes time to greet, commend, and thank twenty-five individuals and, in some cases, their congregations. All of them were of vital importance to his life and ministry.

Making this journey alone isn't just difficult; it's impossible. We all need spiritual allies to help us along the way.

Paul's allies were his benefactors, coworkers, and friends. Together, they provided a network of material, emotional, relational, and spiritual support. When Paul suffered, they comforted him. When Paul was discouraged, they encouraged him. When Paul wanted to quit, they challenged him. Paul accomplished great things by standing on their shoulders.

We need to intentionally build this kind of network and work at keeping it healthy and strong. None of us can "go it alone."

MORNING: A CLEAR LINE / *As the time approached for him to be taken up to heaven, Jesus resolutely set out for Jerusalem.* Luke 9:51 NIV / Jesus knew false arrest, torture, crucifixion, and death waited for Him in Jerusalem. But He was determined.

In order to enjoy a fulfilling life in God, each of us must face a painful challenge. This challenge is different for every man. Some of us struggle to confess sin and make amends to those we've harmed. Some of us have to leave behind our careers, friends, or families. Some of us must kill the ambition, pride, selfishness, or lust in our hearts. It will cost everything. . .and we know it.

On our own, we aren't firm, strong, or resolute enough. We will inevitably fail. That's why Christ promises to help (Philippians 4:13).

EVENING: TAKE HOLD / *I press on to take hold of that for which Christ Jesus took hold of me.* Philippians 3:12 NIV / The more we grow in Christ, the more we realize how little we truly know Him. In Philippians 3:12–14, Paul outlined a strategy for taking hold of more and more of God in our lives.

First, don't expect to ever truly reach that goal. Second, remember that the more Christ takes hold of us, the more motivated we are to pursue Him. Third, leave the past—with its mistakes and failures—in the past. Backward focus prevents forward motion. Fourth, press on. Like athletes leaning into the tape at the finish line, we should exert every effort and lean into God.

And, finally, keep your eyes on the prize. What is this prize? "To know the power of [Jesus'] resurrection" (Philippians 3:10 NIV). This expectation should be more than enough to keep us in the race.

MORNING: BREAK THE CYCLE / *As a dog returns to its vomit, so fools repeat their folly.* Proverbs 26:11 NIV / In the movie *Groundhog Day*, Bill Murray plays Phil, an arrogant weatherman who relives the same day over and over until he learns to become a better person. Because it's a movie, you know Phil will learn his lesson and snap the cycle (and even get the girl in the end).

Real life offers no such guarantees. Men, enticed by the world's empty promises, often stray from the faith, getting caught in a never-ending cycle of sin, shame, and disgust—just like a dog eating his own upchuck.

The only true freedom from this cycle is to give your life unreservedly to Jesus. The future He has for you won't be problem-free, but you'll be free of the pressure to conform to the world and its ways.

EVENING: AFTER. . . / *After you have suffered a little while, [God] will himself restore you and make you strong, firm and steadfast.* 1 Peter 5:10 NIV / Peter reminds us that when we are tested, we suffer for "a little while." It doesn't feel that way. Pain stretches time. We feel like our suffering has always been here, and we fear it always will.

But we need to view our pain in light of eternity. Yes, tests are painful, but they won't destroy us. This life is a quickly evaporating vapor. For those who overcome, joy everlasting awaits.

And remember: nothing is out of God's control. The one who loved us from before time also has dominion over all things—even our suffering!

MORNING: GOD'S JEALOUS LOVE FOR YOU / *"Do not worship any other god, for the LORD, whose name is Jealous, is a jealous God."* Exodus 34:14 NIV / Perhaps the thought of a jealous God conjures up images of a toxic relationship. However, the whole of scripture—especially the book of Hosea—portrays God as a heartbroken lover who has been rejected repeatedly by His beloved people. His jealousy isn't pushy or overbearing.

Saint Francis of Assisi once noted that God cares so deeply for us that He has humbly made Himself vulnerable to the point that He allows us to break His heart.

The costly love of God that suffered for our sake on the cross is the same jealous passion that's eloquently summarized in John 3:16 (KJV): "God so loved the world. . ."

Once we understand God's jealous passion for us, our love for Him will naturally follow.

EVENING: RESTORATION AFTER GOD'S REBUKE / *"The LORD your God. . .will no longer rebuke you, but will rejoice over you with singing."* Zephaniah 3:17 NIV / When we fail, we may go through a season of the Lord's discipline. Perhaps we dread such seasons, fearing that we might be cut off from the Lord forever.

Understandable as these fears may be, discipline is always intended to lead us to restoration with God. What parent would ever discipline a beloved child with any other goal than complete restoration? Isn't God's rebuke the ultimate proof that He loves us?

And even if we pass through a season of God's discipline, it's never destined to last forever. We are God's beloved people, the source of His joy and the focus of His song. Once this hard season is over, we'll discover that God has remained with us and has never let us go.

MORNING: HOW TO WAIT ON GOD / *Let all that I am wait quietly before God, for my hope is in him.* Psalm 62:5–6 NLT / Most of us can be nudged into waiting on God, but waiting *quietly* is a whole other matter. We're often tempted to make requests, complain, suggest solutions, and even pray for specific outcomes, as if we know the best way for God to act. When we give in to these temptations, it often takes a tragedy, crisis, or difficult situation to shake us loose. Those who wait quietly, however, have truly surrendered themselves to God's direction and provision.

Placing our trust completely in God does not guarantee smooth sailing. In fact, conflict and trouble are always just around the bend—the question is whether we are truly waiting in expectant silence before God.

EVENING: FREED TO SERVE / *"I, the Lord, have called you in righteousness; I will. . .make you to be a covenant for the people and a light for the Gentiles, to open eyes that are blind. . .and to release from the dungeon those who sit in darkness."* Isaiah 42:6–7 NIV / We all know that God has made us righteous and freed us from sin's power. But what's next?

This evening's passage says that we have been freed in order to liberate others from bondage, both spiritual and physical. If this calling strikes you as intimidating, here's the good news: the life of God is taking hold in your heart and reshaping your desires and thoughts. As God brings liberation into your life, sharing it with others will become irresistible.

Are you open to God's renewal? Do you need to set aside time tonight to allow God's liberty to begin taking hold in your life?

MORNING: ENDURING LOVE / *"You loved Me before the foundation of the world."* John 17:24 NKJV / How often do we mistakenly believe that God's love guarantees that we'll never suffer? When life goes wrong, it's tempting to look for where we've gone wrong. Jesus' prayer before His suffering on the cross jars us out of such notions.

Jesus was certain that God's love had remained in Him even before creation, stretching for years beyond our comprehension into eternity past. Even if the Father didn't spare Him from the great darkness that spread before Him, Jesus never doubted God's love.

A preacher who had lost his eyesight once said, "Never doubt in the darkness what God has shown you in the light." Though God might seem distant now, you can trust that the same God who was present in the past will be there in the future as well.

EVENING: FROM FAILURE TO DELIGHT / *Who is a God like you, who pardons sin and forgives the transgression. . . ? You do not stay angry forever but delight to show mercy.* Micah 7:18 NIV / When you sin, do you imagine God as angry, disappointed, or incredulous that you've failed yet again?

Whether you struggle with habitual sin or worry that you've transgressed beyond God's forgiveness, there is a promise for you: God's mercy extends beyond your imagination. Our Lord is not like the false gods of Micah's day—deities that demanded offerings in order to be placated.

Sin is undoubtedly serious and can alienate us from God. But if we confess it, God delights in forgiving and restoring us. So never try hiding your failures; bring them out before Him so that He can show mercy to you with His pardon.

MORNING: HOW TO SABOTAGE THE GOSPEL / *Do everything without complaining and arguing, so that no one can criticize you.* Philippians 2:14–15 NLT / There is one surefire way to undermine your ability to communicate the gospel: engaging in arguments. When we fight to win arguments and justify our actions, we engage in an entirely self-centered practice that has a nasty tendency to cast blame on others.

While communicating the gospel has the potential to create peace, complaining and arguing will give our listeners reasons to criticize us. Even if we're completely convinced that we deserve to complain or argue, Paul reminds us that such actions will only separate us from our listeners.

When we stop fighting to be "right," we remove a major obstacle and keep as many doors open as possible for the good news to take root and flourish.

EVENING: HOSPITALITY: A LIFE-CHANGING PRACTICE / *Dear friend, you are faithful in what you are doing for the brothers and sisters, even though they are strangers to you. They have told the church about your love.* 3 John 5–6 NIV / John notes that Gaius, the elder addressed in this evening's passage, has recognized unknown ministers as brothers and sisters rather than treating them as strangers. At a time when most people lacked significant resources, Gaius likely went to great lengths to host these traveling preachers in his home.

The ministry of hospitality may be one of the most demanding costs of discipleship. Inviting fellow Christians into our homes prompts us to change our schedules, share our resources, and make space (literally) for others. But along the way, we'll enjoy deeper relationships with our Christian family. . .and even benefit from the blessings and prayers of those who enter our doors.

DAY 38

MORNING: PRAYER THAT'S WORTH THE WAIT / *When your words came, I ate them; they were my joy and my heart's delight, for I bear your name, Lord God Almighty.* Jeremiah 15:16 NIV / Imagine waiting hours for an exquisite meal at a restaurant, growing hungrier by the second. When the steaming food finally arrives, it's beyond your wildest expectations, and you savor each bite. This is how it can feel to wait patiently on God to answer our prayers. And just as the delicious food is worth the wait, so is God's reply.

There is no meal that can restore us quite like God's presence. Even better, as we are nourished by God's Word, we can share our blessings with others so that they can take partake in our joy as well!

EVENING: THE SLOW CREEP OF COMPROMISE / *King Solomon, however, loved many foreign women. . .from nations about which the Lord had told the Israelites, "You must not intermarry with them, because they will surely turn your hearts after their gods."* 1 Kings 11:1–2 NIV / After presenting King Solomon's wealth and wisdom in striking detail, the author of 1 Kings offers a sobering observation: Solomon had married many foreign women who were turning him away from the Lord.

Solomon probably thought that since he lived in the epicenter of worship for Yahweh, surely a few foreign alliances through marriage couldn't change his heart. But sure enough, he gradually drifted further from God as he became more tolerant of foreign gods. Even the wisest king was no match for the slow creep of compromise.

As you examine your heart today, search intently for even the tiniest areas of compromise. Doing so will spare yourself and your family a world of pain.

DAY 39

MORNING: KEEP YOUR WORD! / *Above all, my brothers and sisters, do not swear—not by heaven or by earth or by anything else. All you need to say is a simple "Yes" or "No." Otherwise you will be condemned.* James 5:12 NIV / Ever known a guy who, whenever he said he'd meet you for coffee or help you paint your house, could always be counted on to show up?

That's the kind of friend *we* should strive to be.

Even if you don't take this morning's Bible verse literally (which, in today's world, is virtually impossible to do), James' core principle remains: be a man who can be taken at his word.

In other words, be so dependable, so true to your word, that people never have to ask, "Do you promise?" Be the man whose "yes" or "no" is the strongest guarantee they need.

EVENING: REAL POWER / *"My grace is all you need. My power works best in weakness."* 2 Corinthians 12:9 NLT / When Anthony "Spud" Webb bounced the ball off the glass and threw down a tomahawk slam to win the NBA Slam Dunk Contest on February 8, 1986, the entire crowd forgot he was only five feet seven inches tall—the shortest player ever to win.

Webb's triumph reflects God's favorite method of accomplishing things: using the least likely people. Look at His most famous men: Moses stuttered, Gideon hid in a hole, David was a kid herding sheep, and Paul was a hard-boiled, Christian-hating Pharisee. But after they accepted God's calling, each of them accomplished great things.

If you think you're the least likely person God could ever use, you might be right. But if you're open to God's guidance, your inability will open the door for His ability.

MORNING: RADICAL LOVE / *Husbands, love your wives, just as Christ loved the church and gave himself up for her.* Ephesians 5:25 NIV / Sometimes, when we're trying to fully understand what God is communicating through His written Word, it's helpful to look at the context.

The culture in Paul's day was radically different from ours. Back then, men had total authority over their wives, and women had no choice but to submit unquestioningly to their rule.

Therefore, Paul's command for husbands to love their wives "as Christ loved the church," was a great departure from societal norms. This was a sacrificial love that looked out for the *wife's* needs and desires.

Even today, Paul's instructions are still a radical departure for many married men. Are you willing to stand out and love your wife like God loves you?

EVENING: THE RIGHT THING TO BRAG ON / *"Let not the wise boast of their wisdom or the strong boast of their strength or the rich boast of their riches, but let the one who boasts boast about this: that they have the understanding to know me."* Jeremiah 9:23–24 NIV / God hates a braggadocious attitude. And if you've ever been around a guy who won't shut up about his own possessions or talents, then you probably understand why—what an annoying way to expend one's energy.

Even worse, when we boast about our own accomplishments, we indirectly say our abilities arose from our own efforts, not from God.

God wants us to make sure our words point to Him as our loving benefactor. Our only true boast is in knowing Him.

MORNING: CHARACTER THAT MATTERS: COURAGE / *"Have I not commanded you? Be strong and courageous. . .for the LORD your God will be with you wherever you go."* Joshua 1:9 NIV / Winston Churchill once famously remarked, "Courage is rightly esteemed the first of human qualities. . .because it is the quality that guarantees all the others." Our values don't matter if we don't have the courage to act on them.

As Joshua stood on the edge of the promised land, God told him to "be strong and courageous." But Joshua's resolve was not his own—it rested on the solid foundation of God's promise.

When we follow God's command and honor Him, God fights for us!

So be strong and courageous. When God is on our side, what room is there for fear?

EVENING: SERVING GOD BY SERVING OTHERS / *"The King will reply, 'Truly I tell you, whatever you did for one of the least of these brothers and sisters of mine, you did for me.' "* Matthew 25:40 NIV / This evening's verse seems to imply that serving others is required for salvation. That's a real head-scratcher. Doesn't the Bible teach that salvation comes solely from faith?

When we take a broader look at the Bible, we see that Jesus' words fit the message of salvation perfectly: good works won't "earn" God's eternal salvation, but those who are saved have God's Spirit living within them and will thus be motivated by love to serve.

Have you been wondering what kind of service God has in mind for you? If so, first ask Him to give you the right motivation to serve, and then ask Him to show you how.

Opportunities are all around you—you just need to keep your eyes open!

MORNING: TALKING TO YOURSELF / *Why, my soul, are you downcast? Why so disturbed within me? Put your hope in God, for I will yet praise him, my Savior and my God.* Psalm 42:5 NIV / Do you ever look at the trials in your life and then start talking to yourself? If not, you're probably in the minority. Everyone tends to mutter things like "There's no way out of this. Things aren't going to get better. This isn't fair!"

There are all sorts of voices vying for our attention, but the most treacherous ones—the ones with the greatest chance of drowning out our heavenly Father's voice—might be our own.

So when you find yourself muttering about the unfairness of your situation, turn your attention instead to the Lord—He's more than willing to take control of every storm, no matter how fierce.

EVENING: SPEAKING OF OTHERS. . . / *A gossip betrays a confidence, but a trustworthy person keeps a secret.* Proverbs 11:13 NIV / Most of us have a pretty good handle on avoiding the "biggies" where sin is concerned (murder, adultery, theft, and so on). But let's get real with ourselves—how many of us watch how we talk about other people?

The Bible has plenty to say about gossipers, and none of it is good. Take a look at these descriptors found in the King James Version: backbiter (Psalm 15:3), busybody (1 Timothy 5:13), inventor of evil things (Romans 1:30), talebearer (Proverbs 11:13), and whisperer (Proverbs 16:28).

God takes gossip very seriously, and His Word repeatedly warns us of the serious consequences involved—in both this world and the next.

So if you can't find something good to say about someone, either search harder or keep it to yourself.

MORNING: OUTWARD APPEARANCES / *But the LORD said to Samuel, "Do not consider his appearance or his height, for I have rejected him. . . . People look at the outward appearance, but the LORD looks at the heart."* 1 Samuel 16:7 NIV / Our culture puts a lot of emphasis on physical appearance. Don't believe it? Just watch some of the weight loss and skin care infomercials that air on an hourly basis.

Most of us would tell others that it's what's "inside" that counts. This is just a pleasantry, of course. Our God says the same thing—but He *means* it.

There's nothing wrong with taking care of yourself or trying to stay fit. But never forget that your heavenly Father is far more interested in the condition of your inner man than He is with how you look.

EVENING: LOVE'S HONEST WORK / *Let us not love with word or with tongue, but in deed and truth.* 1 John 3:18 NASB / One of the few direct commands Jesus gave His followers was to love others (John 13:34–35). But this love—the kind that Jesus showed when He gave up divine privilege to be whipped, beaten, and painfully executed—isn't for wimps. It demands a burning drive to seek someone else's best and highest good.

Even if your love is imperfect, the occasional wrong but honest note always beats the "clanging cymbal" of a life lived without it (1 Corinthians 13:1 NASB).

MORNING: GOD'S PURPOSE FOR LIFE'S TRIALS / *Consider it pure joy, my brothers and sisters, whenever you face trials of many kinds, because you know that the testing of your faith produces perseverance.* James 1:2–3 NIV / Albert Einstein once said, "Adversity introduces a man to himself." When life gets difficult, we see where we really are in our walk with our heavenly Father.

God never promised His people an easy ride. In fact, the Bible clearly teaches that trials and suffering will befall every believer. If you don't believe that, just take a look at the lives (and violent deaths) of the very men Jesus chose to take His message of salvation to the world.

Neither patience nor perseverance happens overnight. Instead, God uses trials and storms to strengthen you and mold you into the man He intends you to be.

So when the going gets tough. . .rejoice!

EVENING: CURB APPEAL / *The Lord says, "I will guide you along the best pathway for your life. I will advise you and watch over you."* Psalm 32:8 NLT / We need curbs. They guide water to drains, give shape to the streets, act as a boundary when we park, and keep us from driving where we shouldn't.

When everyone acknowledges these curbs, traffic flows smoothly. Imagine the chaos if everyone suddenly decided to cut across someone's lawn!

Likewise, we all have our own set of internal curbs—fundamental boundaries like refusing to touch a hot stove. God has also given us moral curbs in the Bible. When we refuse to live within them, we only cause chaos and ruin.

MORNING: SHOW YOUR LOVE / *Love. . .does not seek its own.* 1 Corinthians 13:4–5 NKJV / Western culture has fallen into the trap of so many decaying cultures before it: we incessantly chase our own desires at the expense of others. But 1 Corinthians 13 tells us that love does not seek its own. Instead, the indwelling of the Holy Spirit changes our perspective from self to others.

You may have ordered flowers for your wife or girlfriend. But are you in tune with her enough to know what she really wants?

Is she interested in working in theater? Take her to a play. Does she want to mentor young women at church? Step in and relieve her of some of her duties at home.

Don't just say you love her; *show* her.

EVENING: STARTING AND FINISHING WELL / *Whoever walks in integrity walks securely.* Proverbs 10:9 NIV / The Bible is filled with stories of men who either started out with zeal for God but ended poorly (like King Saul) or struggled at the beginning and ended well (like Peter).

Daniel fit neither category: he started *and* ended well.

Born during an era of moral bankruptcy and taken captive by a strange culture as a teenager, Daniel somehow managed to wholeheartedly attach himself to the God of his people. He, along with his godly friends, even stood up to his captors by requesting food that God had permitted him to eat.

Daniel's life was a textbook example of godly integrity, drawing the attention—and trust—of three separate kings.

If you've found yourself drifting from God, today can be your new beginning—a chance to get back in the race. How strong is your desire to finish well for God?

MORNING: CHARACTER THAT MATTERS: HUMILITY / *Be completely humble and gentle; be patient, bearing with one another in love. Make every effort to keep the unity of the Spirit through the bond of peace.* Ephesians 4:2–3 NIV / Over a century ago, the British passenger liner *Titanic*—whose builders had hailed as "unsinkable"—struck an iceberg in the North Atlantic and sank. Arrogance had led to recklessness, and recklessness had led to tragedy.

It's better to live with humility than to be humiliated!

Humility doesn't mean thinking less of ourselves than we should—it means recognizing that we all have strengths and weaknesses. Knowing this will cause us to become gentle, patient, tolerant, and peaceful toward others. Humility brings unity to our churches, our families, and all our relationships.

It takes a truly humble man to avoid the shipwreck of arrogance and pride.

EVENING: A WORLD OUT OF WHACK / *The vine is dried up and the fig tree is withered; the pomegranate, the palm and the apple tree—all the trees of the field—are dried up. Surely the people's joy is withered away.* Joel 1:12 NIV / Tough times in our personal lives are hard enough. But often the whole world seems out of whack. When the national economy is teetering or terrorists are snarling threats or wars are flaring up around the world, "people's joy is withered away" in the words of Joel.

Nobody enjoys hard times, but as a Christian, you can trust they have a purpose. In Joel's time, the drought and famine and weeping were intended to bring sinful people back to God. Your own hardships may have the same purpose. Or maybe God is just building your trust-muscles. No matter what, you can be sure that "in all things God works for the good of those who love him, who have been called according to his purpose" (Romans 8:28 NIV).

DAY 47

MORNING: A TIME OF FAILURE / *"It's time to change your ways! Turn to face God so he can wipe away your sins [and] pour out showers of blessing to refresh you."* Acts 3:19 MSG / Men despise failure: we don't want to admit mistakes, and we even hate asking for directions.

Perhaps this is why men, when they are caught in sin, tend to spiral out of control. After trying (and failing) to fix things on their own, blaming others, and holding the sin inside, we may decide it's no longer worth the effort and begin spiraling into behaviors we never dreamed possible.

Failure should bring us face to feet with Jesus. There's no shame in this—in fact, God promises to heal and purify us if we do (1 John 1:9).

God is perfectly aware of our failure, yet He chooses to love us anyway. Only in Him can restoration be found.

EVENING: WISDOM'S SOURCE / *If any of you lacks wisdom, you should ask God, who gives generously to all without finding fault, and it will be given to you.* James 1:5 NIV / Too often, we think we can become wise only by living through difficulties and learning a lesson afterward. While that's a great source of common sense—and part of the reason why older folks offer so much good advice—true wisdom from God offers *uncommon* sense, inspired instructions from the Creator Himself.

So don't let age fool you. Wisdom is available to all, and godly wisdom surpasses the earthly wisdom of anyone you know.

The Bible contains hundreds of pages filled with what God can teach about how to be wise. Maybe those young people who are "wise beyond their years" have simply been spending time learning wisdom from its original source.

MORNING: HARDWIRED FOR SUCCESS? / *Earn a reputation for living well in God's eyes and the eyes of the people.* Proverbs 3:4 MSG / Men seem to be hardwired to crave success. Some, for instance, will fight for their marriages (as they should), but only to prove themselves as successful.

However, when failure strikes, some men shift direction. They start embracing failure as an old, inevitable friend. Viewing themselves as mistake-prone, they rush to make bad choices, dismiss their wives and children, and bounce from job to job.

God longs for authentic, transparent warriors. He longs for us to stop wearing masks and believing that we can control our destiny if we just try hard enough.

Our greatest success is to be forgiven by God. Let's focus our efforts on knowing and pleasing Him—then, as we put our attention on what He thinks, the opinions of others won't matter so much.

EVENING: THERE WILL BE A FUTURE / *"I know the plans I have for you,"* says the LORD. *"They are plans for good and not for disaster, to give you a future and a hope."* Jeremiah 29:11 NLT / There are no problems God cannot solve, no future that can't be adapted to His plan. Yet in difficult times we struggle, misunderstand, and blame God.

However, what we don't see—but God does—is that there *is* an ending that proves His faithfulness. We just haven't gotten there yet.

We're familiar with the beginning of our story, and we're living the present. But the future? That's the part only God understands. Hold on. Trust your loving Creator's promise that His plan is perfect and for your good, even when nothing seems further from the truth.

MORNING: ALL THINGS NEW / *Anyone who belongs to Christ has become a new person. The old life is gone; a new life has begun!* 2 Corinthians 5:17 NLT / A relationship with Jesus invites us to do things we never thought we could. Somehow, impossible reactions become possible. Forgiveness overcomes grudges, love triumphs over hate, and grace prevails over revenge.

God's covenant with us, in which we get everything and He doesn't seem to get much, should change our perception, attitude, and thoughts toward others. We should live not to hoard time or resources but instead to help others. By remembering what it's like outside a partnership with God, we should strive to help others discover the new covenant for themselves.

We come to Jesus just as we are, but we should never stay the way we came.

EVENING: WHEN YOU'VE MISSED THE BLESSING / *"God bless you and keep you, God smile on you and gift you."* Numbers 6:24–25 MSG / We each carry invisible tattoos that people gave us when we were small: *last to be picked, slow, stupid, worthless.*

On bad days, we'll believe these labels, no matter if they're true or not. Our future isn't defined by our five-year-old selves, but we'll act the part.

If no one's ever spoken a blessing into your life, consider this: before you were born, God knew your name, fit you together in your mother's womb, and called you a masterpiece (Psalm 139:13–16). He wants you on His team, so He created you for something only you can do. He even sent His Son, Jesus, so that you could be a part of His family.

Don't pay attention to what others may have called you; pay attention to God's call in your life.

MORNING: SAVED ONLY BY GRACE / *Christ Jesus came into the world to save sinners, of whom I am chief.* 1 Timothy 1:15 NKJV / Paul wasn't just acting humbly when he declared that he was the worst of sinners. He never forgot that he had once arrested, tortured, and called for the deaths of numerous Christians.

Why did God choose such a violent sinner to be one of His leading apostles? Paul explained that God wanted to show, by Paul's example, that no man is so vile that God can't redeem him (1 Timothy 1:16).

Once you've been serving the Lord for a few years, you might forget what a bad state you were in. You might even begin to think you're quite righteous and can make it on your own.

If that happens, remind yourself that it's by grace you are saved, not by your own goodness (Ephesians 2:8–9).

EVENING: KIND TO THE UNGRATEFUL / *Love ye your enemies. . .and your reward shall be great, and ye shall be the children of the Highest: for he is kind unto the unthankful and to the evil.* Luke 6:35 KJV / Jesus' command to love our enemies is disturbing to many Christians. It just seems too unrealistic. However, Jesus said that loving your enemies is sure proof that you are a child of God.

Why? Because God is loving and patient by nature. And as His child, you're to emulate your Father and show this same love and kindness.

Jesus doesn't expect you to be naive or deny that certain people are evil; rather, He asks you to "overcome evil with good" (Romans 12:21 KJV). And yes, He knows this is a difficult thing to ask. That's why He promises great rewards for obeying Him.

MORNING: PUT OUT FIRES BEFORE THEY START / *He that covereth his sins shall not prosper: but whoso confesseth and forsaketh them shall have mercy.* Proverbs 28:13 KJV / Tragedy struck a Rhode Island nightclub in 2003, when pyrotechnics from a rock concert touched off a fire that killed one hundred people. The band Great White had insisted in their contract that a certain type of fireworks be used, but the club's safety standards weren't up to the task. People died as a result.

Sin works like that, a hidden livewire behind the walls of your life. It progresses like a burning fuse: desire tempts you then drags you away to do its bidding. Once it has conceived, it gives birth to sin, which grows up and gives birth to death (James 1:13–15).

Whatever temptation beckons you—whether women, status, or wealth—root it out at the point of contact.

EVENING: PROTECTED IN GOD'S SHADOW / *He who dwells in the secret place of the Most High shall abide under the shadow of the Almighty.* Psalm 91:1 NKJV / Much of the Negev in southern Israel is one vast, scorching desert. Travelers take shelter behind great rocks during windstorms and rest in their shadows during the hottest part of the day.

Likewise, God is a "shelter from the wind and a refuge from the storm. . .and the shadow of a great rock in a thirsty land" (Isaiah 32:2 NIV). How can you find rest when life's blistering winds are howling? By staying close to God and dwelling under His mighty shadow.

Because you're a Christian, Jesus lives in your heart. Therefore, you must also live continually in Him, seeking Him in prayer and staying close to Him through obedience.

MORNING: LAUGHTER AND WELLNESS / *A cheerful heart is good medicine, but a crushed spirit dries up the bones.* Proverbs 17:22 NIV / Many doctors affirm the truth of this scripture: people who laugh will begin to enjoy improved health.

Laughter benefits one's physical and emotional well-being. It can help prevent heart disease, relax the entire person, relieve stress, strengthen the body's immune system, and even alleviate pain.

Life is often serious business, sometimes to the detriment of our health. And if you have a crushed spirit, your health will definitely suffer.

It will do you a world of good to rent a comedy movie and spend a couple of hours laughing. It will lighten your mood and give you a more hopeful attitude.

"For the happy heart, life is a continual feast" (Proverbs 15:15 NLT). Enjoy God's gift of laughter as much as you can!

EVENING: AVOID DRIFTING AWAY / *We must pay the most careful attention. . .to what we have heard, so that we do not drift away.* Hebrews 2:1 NIV / Most people who abandon their faith in God don't make a sudden, deliberate decision to do so. Rather, they slowly drift away, gradually losing interest in prayer, Bible study, and Christian fellowship.

First, they become nearsighted. Eventually, they completely lose all spiritual sight. They often still go through the outward motions of being a Christian, but their heart has departed. They question the basic beliefs of the faith and believe it's irrelevant to the modern world.

How can you avoid this happening to you? First, follow the advice in Hebrews 3:7–8 (NIV): "Today, if you hear his voice, do not harden your hearts." Next, pray for God to renew your relationship with Him. Finally, determine to truly live your faith.

MORNING: MEDITATE ON GOD / *Be still, and know that I am God.* Psalm 46:10 KJV / There's a time to earnestly pray for what you need and a time to praise God for providing all your needs. But there is also a time to meditate, to think deeply on who God is and what He's done for you. When you do, God will reward you with a deeper knowledge of His nature and His love.

Some Christians shy away from meditation, thinking Eastern religions have a monopoly on it. However, the Bible spoke of meditation thousands of years ago.

So when you read the Bible, don't simply hurry through it. Pause at a verse and think deeply on its meaning. Paul said, "Meditate on these things; give yourself entirely to them" (1 Timothy 4:15 NKJV).

EVENING: BETTER DAYS AHEAD / *"You will surely forget your trouble, recalling it only as waters gone by."* Job 11:16 NIV / Sometimes, you're made to pass through a valley of family issues, financial crises, or health problems. At the time, survival seems uncertain. It looks like you'll crash.

Yet, difficult as it may be to believe it, you'll be laughing again and will forget your troubles soon enough. As David said, God's "anger lasts only a moment, but his favor lasts a lifetime; weeping may stay for the night, but rejoicing comes in the morning" (Psalm 30:5 NIV). When passing through tests it's vital to remember that God's favor lasts your entire lifetime; His discipline, by contrast, is usually brief.

Yes, God does allow suffering, but it's only purpose is to bring about good in your life. "The LORD comforts his people and will have compassion on his afflicted ones" (Isaiah 49:13 NIV).

MORNING: CONFIDENT IN CHRIST / *In him and through faith in him we may approach God with freedom and confidence.* Ephesians 3:12 NIV / Often, when men pray to God about a pressing need, a sense of sinfulness rises up to discourage them. The thoughts frequently come in waves: *You're unworthy. God won't answer your prayers. You might as well stop praying.*

This is the voice of Satan, your enemy. His name means "accuser" in Hebrew, and he doesn't just accuse you—he accuses all believers (Revelation 12:10).

If you've given your heart to Christ, you are an heir of His eternal kingdom. "Let us therefore come boldly to the throne of grace" (Hebrews 4:16 NKJV).

The devil may try to condemn you, but don't listen to that lie! Your sins are forgiven in Christ. You can come to God's throne with your prayer requests, boldly and with confidence.

EVENING: GOD CARES ENOUGH TO ACT / *Anyone who wants to approach God must believe both that he exists and that he cares enough to respond to those who seek him.* Hebrews 11:6 MSG / Many men believe that God exists and sent His Son to die for their sins, yet their disappointment over seemingly unanswered prayers has led them to believe that God rarely involves Himself with people today.

Small wonder that they end up thinking that they can manage without God's help—they believe that they have to!

It's true that God expects you to work hard and use your mind to solve problems, but God is still very active in the world. He still helps the helpless.

Yes, He cares. And yes, He responds to those who earnestly seek Him. But you have to *continually* seek Him—giving up is never an option.

DAY 55

MORNING: CAST YOUR CARES ON GOD / *Cast your cares on the* Lord *and he will sustain you.* Psalm 55:22 NIV / Some people will read this morning's verse and protest, "So when huge problems come, I simply hand them to God and He takes care of everything? I *wish*!" But let's look at this verse in context.

Having faced conspiracies, battles, and the stinging betrayal of friends, David confessed, "The terrors of death have fallen on me. Fear and trembling have beset me" (verses 4–5).

David had to plan, strategize, and defend against his enemies' attacks. But through it all, he continually cast his fears upon God until he finally received an answer.

Yes, you can simply hand small problems over to God; however, when huge problems assail you, you may have to cast your cares on Him desperately and repeatedly.

And He will answer.

EVENING: HEAVY BURDENS / *"This is the word of the* Lord *to Zerubbabel: 'Not by might nor by power, but by my Spirit,' says the* Lord *Almighty."* Zechariah 4:6 NIV / At times, most everyone gets overwhelmed. The task is too big, the burden too heavy.

Zerubbabel was leader of the exiled Jews who returned to Jerusalem some five hundred years before Jesus was born. He laid the foundation for a temple to replace the one destroyed by the Babylonian army decades earlier. Apparently, Zerubbabel felt a bit stressed by the job, because God told the prophet Zechariah to pass along the message of today's scripture.

Though that was a specific promise to a specific man at a specific time, there's a principle in it for all of us: It is only by God's power that we accomplish anything. Jesus reminded us that we are simply branches connected to Him as the life-giving vine (John 15:5).

DAY 56

MORNING: COMMITMENTS THAT MATTER: GOD'S PEOPLE
/ *Do nothing out of selfish ambition or vain conceit. Rather, in humility value others above yourselves, not looking to your own interests but each of you to the interests of the others.* Philippians 2:3–4 NIV / To leave a godly legacy, we must commit not only to God and our family but to the people of God, His church. That's not always easy. All too often, pain and conflict erupt in the church—but that doesn't mean we should walk away from God's people.

Today's verses challenge us to act selflessly, value others, and do what's best for others. Even those who hurt us are worthy of our forgiveness. It's God's church, and they are God's people.

We are all guilty of asking, "What can the church do for me?" But the more important question is "What can *I* do for *you*?"

EVENING: NERVOUS, NERVOUS, NERVOUS / *For what I received I passed on to you as of first importance: that Christ died for our sins according to the Scriptures, that he was buried, that he was raised on the third day according to the Scriptures.* 1 Corinthians 15:3–4 NIV / We are God's ambassadors. This means that people will hold God to whatever we say about Him. And if what we tell people about God is wrong, He will hold us accountable too.

Who on earth can handle that kind of responsibility? The answer is. . . nobody. That's why the stories God asks us to tell are so breathtakingly simple!

Plus, we have the Holy Spirit to back us up and His Word to tell us *four times* what Jesus did to save us.

This isn't metaphysics. It isn't some convoluted quest for enlightenment. So why would we be nervous?

MORNING: SUCCEEDING IN THE LORD'S EYES / *When Solomon had finished the temple of the Lord. . .the Lord appeared to him.* 2 Chronicles 7:11–12 NIV / When a man of God serves the Lord with fervor and zeal then later walks away from God, the damage extends to thousands of people and is felt for years to come.

In biblical history, only a small number of men ever talked directly with the Lord. Yet King Solomon did *twice.* Sounds like Solomon was God's man, right?

Well, if Solomon was wholeheartedly devoted to God early on, he clearly became halfhearted—and eventually no-hearted—as the years rolled on.

No one is exempt from spiritual failure—that's why we must guard our walk with God with everything we have. It's the only way to succeed in the Lord's eyes.

EVENING: NOTHING / *For we know that our old self was crucified with him so that the body ruled by sin might be done away with. . .because anyone who has died has been set free from sin.* Romans 6:6–7 NIV / It is the inescapable paradox of Christianity: to have everything, we must become nothing.

In C. S. Lewis' book *The Screwtape Letters*, the titular demon trains his student, Wormwood, how to tempt his target. When Wormwood tries to tempt his young Christian subject with the big things—lying, theft, adultery, giving up his faith—Screwtape criticizes him: Don't try to get him to deny his faith; just get him to spend a little too much attention on himself.

What an effective strategy! When we stop concentrating on the Lord, our own petty concerns start stealing the spotlight.

The only way to be free is to sink our nothing into His everything.

MORNING: SPIRITUAL DEPENDENCY / *I am reminded of your sincere faith, which first lived in your grandmother Lois and in your mother Eunice and, I am persuaded, now lives in you also.* 2 Timothy 1:5 NIV / Spiritual dependency can have tragic consequences.

Too often, Christian men let other spiritual people become their compass, but they never bring themselves to make that spirituality a part of themselves. Once the compass is gone, the dependent Christian has no pole to point to. So he just spins.

Such was not the case with Timothy. The spiritual maturity that lived in his mother, his grandmother, and Paul himself now lived in the young man himself.

Do you have a mentor? If so, are you walking in his footsteps, or is he taking all the steps for you? A source of encouragement is always great to have, but every man must learn to start taking his own steps before it's too late.

EVENING: A LITTLE PLATO / *"Because you have rejected the word of the Lord, he has rejected you as king."* 1 Samuel 15:23 NIV / The ancient Greek philosopher Plato gave what is known as the "Allegory of the Ship." The allegory is simple: There is a struggle over who is going to be captain of a ship. Who is likely to win? Someone who is good at running a ship, or the one with the most strength?

You know the answer.

Similarly, politicians who want power the most are usually the worst public servants—yet they're the ones who generally win.

We have to be very discerning with who we follow. We should look for leaders—in all areas of life—who have a history of effective service. With people like that at the helm, our ship is more likely to remain steady.

MORNING: JOSEPH AND POTIPHAR / *When [Potiphar] heard the story his wife told him. . .he burned with anger.* Genesis 39:19 NIV / When Potiphar's wife falsely accused Joseph of trying to seduce her, notice that Potiphar didn't become angry *at Joseph*—he just became angry. If he were furious at Joseph—a mere foreign slave—his option would've been clear: kill him.

But Potiphar didn't. He probably knew his wife was lying. But how could he side with a slave against his wife? Consequently, he treated Joseph about as well as he could, sending him to a prison for the privileged.

Joseph was forgotten for two years—but not by God. Soon, Joseph began his rise from the ashes to vice president of Egypt.

Because Joseph refused to sin, God looked down with favor upon him—something He's willing to do to us as long as we follow Joseph's example.

EVENING: DARKNESS ON THE OFFENSE / *"If then the light within you is darkness, how great is that darkness!"* Matthew 6:23 NIV / People have been looking for the middle ground between darkness and light for generations. They call it "agnosticism" or "humanism" or any number of other names. But Jesus was right when He said darkness is not the absence of something. It's an offensive, spreading, radiating force.

There's no such thing as a "neutral" act. When Jesus spoke of the "light" that is in us being "darkness," He meant darkness can radiate from us just as light would. A self-centered man who only seeks God's miracles for himself; young men who don't care about their own souls; people thinking they're just "passing time"—all these become springboards for Satan's attacks.

Neutrality? Ridiculous! We're all on the offensive with something.

MORNING: FAITH WHEN IT REALLY COUNTS / *"Do not rebel against the Lord. And do not be afraid of the people of the land, because we will devour them. Their protection is gone, but the Lord is with us. Do not be afraid of them."* Numbers 14:9 NIV / Worn down with four decades of desert wanderings and facing the monumental task of taking the promised land before them, Joshua and Caleb courageously urged their people to believe in God's presence, blessing, and encouragement.

Their faith in God was a gritty, all-encompassing kind of faith. Why? Because their lives depended on it. In order to lead Israel into God's promise, Joshua would have to feel God's presence on a second-by-second basis and step out in faith, trusting that God would come through.

God rewarded Joshua's determined faith. He'll do the same for us as well.

EVENING: COMMITMENTS THAT MATTER: FUTURE / *I consider that our present sufferings are not worth comparing with the glory that will be revealed in us.* Romans 8:18 NIV / This is a world of cause and effect. What we choose today will inevitably matter tomorrow. Sometimes, the most "trivial" decisions have the greatest impact. But here's the catch: it's impossible to predict those impacts before they arrive. All we can do is guess. So how do we live with an eye on the future?

First, don't let your past determine your present. What's done is done—but it doesn't have to repeat itself. Second, act ethically, not expediently. Make wise long-term decisions, not easy short-term ones. Third, ask yourself, "Do I want this choice to be a chapter of my life that my children or grandchildren can read?"

Finally, trust God, not your circumstances. Remember that He alone controls the future.

MORNING: CONDUCT THAT MATTERS: APOLOGIZE / *Godly sorrow brings repentance that leads to salvation and leaves no regret, but worldly sorrow brings death.* 2 Corinthians 7:10 NIV / In the movie *Love Story*, a dying young woman says to her lover, "Love means never having to say you're sorry."

Nothing could be further from the truth! Nothing damages relationships more than a prideful refusal to take responsibility for our actions and apologize to those we injured. That refusal denies both sides of the forgiveness and healing we need.

Repentance lies at the core of our faith. It's a way to apologize to God for the harm we've done, thus opening the door to His grace. All who choose this path are welcomed. Those who refuse it lock themselves away from God's love and care.

When we apologize, we also set an example, helping mend broken relationships as we grow in grace and humility.

EVENING: GIDEON: GOD'S STRENGTH, OUR WEAKNESS / *When the angel of the LORD appeared to Gideon, he said, "The LORD is with you, mighty warrior."* Judges 6:12 NIV / As Gideon was working in secret so that his grain wouldn't be stolen by the regular raids of the Midianite troops, God sent His angel to him. Isn't it strange that the angel would call Gideon a "mighty warrior"? As far as we know, Gideon hadn't done anything to demonstrate courage. But deep down, every man is who God says he is.

Perhaps you're discouraged by a poor performance review at work. Perhaps you've recently gone through an unwanted divorce. Perhaps you're facing your retirement, convinced that your most productive years are behind you.

Be encouraged today! Gideon was an ordinary man, but God used him to deliver His people. Remember: you are who *God* says you are.

MORNING: WHAT HAPPENS TO THE BAD GUYS? / *"All who see you will flee from you and say, 'Nineveh is in ruins—who will mourn for her?' Where can I find anyone to comfort you?"* Nahum 3:7 NIV / If you want to live as a Christian in this world, you will suffer. That's the word from Jesus Himself (John 16:33). But God will avenge the trouble others pour on you.

The Old Testament prophets warned Israel's enemies that they faced God's wrath for their misbehavior. Once in a while, those enemies repented, as Nineveh did under Jonah's preaching. But as you can see in Nahum's prophecy, the Ninevites were back under God's curse. Anyone who rejects His mercy will pay His very steep price.

Don't let the bad guys get you down. You will be vindicated, when God punishes your enemies. . .or possibly makes them your brothers.

EVENING: SAMSON'S LAST BATTLE / *Then Samson prayed to the LORD, "Sovereign LORD, remember me. Please, God, strengthen me just once more."* Judges 16:28 NIV / Judges 13–16 details the life of Samson—a great, but deeply flawed, hero—and his twenty-year reign as judge over Israel.

This evening's passage leads us to Samson's final stand, during which he had the opportunity to strike a major blow against God's enemies. After hearing Samson's prayer of reliance, God used him to destroy the enemy's temple, killing thousands.

Throughout the book of Judges, we read that the "Spirit of the LORD" (note the capital S) was who gave Samson his power. This same Spirit empowers us today. Strength, courage, and honor—all of it comes from the Holy Spirit living within us as believers in Christ.

How will you move out in faith today?

MORNING: UNPLUG AND RECONNECT / *Come close to God, and God will come close to you.* James 4:8 NLT / We exist in a wireless yet constantly logged-on society. Many drivers pay more attention to social media than traffic. Conversations in restaurants have devolved into meme- and video-sharing—no one looks up until it's time for the check.

Unplugging is almost as rare as living off the grid. It almost seems barbaric. However, those who practice it know the reward—improving their human connection with loved ones—is worth the stigma.

Why not take a break from your newsfeed notifications and comments from strangers? In doing so, you'll find more time to give to those who are most important in your life.

When you unplug, you might also discover the God who's available for real-time conversation—to listen to your status updates and offer perfect answers to your deepest concerns.

EVENING: WHAT'S YOUR SLING? / *"The Lord who rescued me from the paw of the lion and the paw of the bear will rescue me from the hand of this Philistine."* 1 Samuel 17:37 NIV / When David heard about Goliath's arrogance in the face of God's people, he knew he couldn't stand by. Even King Saul saw the fire in David's eyes, so he gave him his blessing.

As this boy approached Goliath with a sling, God's Spirit encouraged him with an eagerness to prove God powerful in the face of His enemies. David relied wholeheartedly on God to fight for him—and to win.

This kind of practical faith is the hallmark of the man of God. How has God equipped you to face your own circumstances? What's the sling in your hand, and what are the stones in your pouch?

MORNING: AN UNUSUAL CANVAS / *"Everything is possible with God."* Mark 10:27 NLT / Paul Smith was born in the 1920s. While other children attended school, he lived with cerebral palsy. However, inside his diseased body lived an artist.

In the mid-1930s, Paul discovered a typewriter in his neighbor's trash. After meticulously repositioning the paper, Paul began creating art that resembled traditional charcoal drawings.

Friend Jim Mitch said Paul "developed a distinct, beautiful way of creating art. . . . Paul's technique required that the entire picture must be planned before he started."

God has given you something only you can do. Are you trusting Him to help you? Yes, it will be hard. Yes, you will have setbacks. It's true, you may not know how you can reach the finish line, but when determination meets God's provision, the result is always possibility.

EVENING: A PROMISE OF LEGACY / *"Your house and your kingdom will endure forever before me; your throne will be established forever."* 2 Samuel 7:16 NIV / In our quest to find God's encouragement in scripture, we'll find no declaration better than the one spoken in this evening's verse to David by Nathan, God's prophet.

This verse echoes God's lavish promises to Adam, Noah, and Abraham—each of which were global in scale and given by a generous God to His faithful followers.

Today, we stand in this line of promise along with Adam, Noah, Abram, and David. We have the promise of Jesus, the fulfillment of all of the other promises God made in the Bible combined.

Eternal promises given by a grace-filled God to His unworthy followers—amazing!

DAY 65

MORNING: THE WIND OF GOD / *"In this godless world you will continue to experience difficulties. But take heart! I've conquered the world."* John 16:33 MSG / Researchers suspect that a change in ions on windy days contributes to irritability. Most agree that wind does, in fact, change the way people feel—and that change is usually negative.

Similarly, difficult situations in our lives often make us irritable. But those difficult situations give us access to resources we may not have at any other time. God never promised trouble-free days. But He did promise His presence, love, and provision.

Like power accessed through a windmill, we gain strength when we face adversity, letting it bring us closer to the source of our spiritual strength.

So let the wind blow. God is closer than you think.

EVENING: WISDOM FOR THE ASKING / *God gave Solomon wisdom and very great insight, and a breadth of understanding as measureless as the sand on the seashore.* 1 Kings 4:29 NIV / God loved Solomon. Shortly after Solomon assumed the throne, God appeared to him with an enticing proposition: "Ask for whatever you want me to give you" (1 Kings 3:5 NIV).

So what did King Solomon ask for? *Wisdom.*

Pleased with this request, God delivered with astounding generosity.

Wouldn't it be amazing to have access to such wisdom? The truth is, you do. Jesus told His disciples (and us) in John 14:26 (NIV), "The Holy Spirit. . .will teach you all things."

When we're looking for wisdom, we need look no further than God's Word. Then sincerely pray for the Spirit's direction and guidance. Solomon's wisdom was legendary; with the Spirit's help, yours can be as well.

MORNING: PANIC WITHOUT PROOF / *Open your mouth and taste, open your eyes and see—how good GOD is.* Psalm 34:8 MSG / In fall 2014, some Americans were overwhelmed by the news that the entire country was to be inundated with unprecedented snow depths. Only seasoned survivalists would make it to spring.

Within a news cycle or two, the truth was revealed: the website, according to its own *About Us* page, was a "satirical and entertainment website."

However, few people opened that tab. Most simply panicked.

God always wants us to test our sources. First John 4:1 (MSG) says, "Carefully weigh and examine what people tell you. Not everyone who talks about God comes from God."

Every idea should be measured by what God has already told us.

EVENING: A PEOPLE FOR HIMSELF / *"For the sake of his great name the LORD will not reject his people, because the LORD was pleased to make you his own."* 1 Samuel 12:22 NIV / Since Adam and Eve departed from His will, God has been on a mission: to gather back to Himself a people of His own. The apostle Paul described it to the Greek philosophers like this: "From one man he made all the nations. . .and he marked out their appointed times in history and the boundaries of their lands. God did this so that they would seek him. . .and find him" (Acts 17:26–27 NIV).

God is so persistent in having a people for Himself that He sacrificed His only begotten Son to make His desire a reality. Ultimately, a people belonging to God will be like Him, eager to do good works and bring others into His family.

DAY 67

MORNING: USING GOD'S APP / *I am not ashamed of the gospel, because it is the power of God that brings salvation to everyone who believes.* Romans 1:16 NIV / Cell phones consume our lives, buzzing and blipping to alert us of incoming messages, calendar events, and phone calls.

"Communication is important," we tell ourselves. But sometimes in our online world, we don't even act like we do in real life. We pretend and think no one really pays attention.

God, however, is the master of communication. His life app allows you to use your voice, your life, and your generosity to share His love with real people.

Effective communication with God allows more effective communication with those who need to access His status updates. We can share them face-to-face. . .and directly from His book.

EVENING: FROM THE MESS, VALUE / *Where no oxen are, the trough is clean; but much increase comes by the strength of an ox.* Proverbs 14:4 NKJV / Oxen are messy creatures. But there's no way to take advantage of their strength without having to watch where you step.

Other things in life can be quite messy too. In the business world, for instance, people don't always do what you expect, customers demand more than you can provide, and every week you have to clean up whatever hit the fan. Marriage, for all its delights, can generate piles of conflict, financial issues, and inconvenience. And having kids may be (literally and figuratively) the messiest choice of all.

But for those who persevere, the rewards are well worth it.

Nothing of value comes without work, consequences, and risk. God wants us to work at whatever He's put into our lives, not fearing the consequences but focusing instead on creating something of value.

MORNING: GOD'S SPENDING LIMIT? / *"For all the animals of the forest are mine, and I own the cattle on a thousand hills."* Psalm 50:10 NLT / Accountants are experts at keeping track of expenses. They make sure every payment is noted.

God's economy, however, is a bit different. He's a lavish God who makes sunsets, forests, stars, and oceans for us to enjoy. He owns everything, so He can use anything to do the most amazing things. God doesn't even get upset at the cost it takes to rescue people. He just keeps relentlessly pursuing with incredible compassion.

God never has to worry about running out of resources. He just keeps loving real people with real compassion leading to real change. And when He asks you to share what you have, it's so that you'll share the joy He felt when He gave His all for you.

EVENING: LISTENING: A DANGEROUS ACTIVITY / *When Herod heard John, he was greatly puzzled; yet he liked to listen to him.* Mark 6:20 NIV / John the Baptist was one of the greatest prophets in Israel's history, preaching "in the spirit and power of Elijah" (Luke 1:17 NIV). Influential people flocked to hear him.

John didn't pull punches for anyone—not even for Herod the tetrarch. When he publicly rebuked Herod for adultery, his message landed John in prison and ultimately cost him his life.

Herod made the worst mistake possible—he treated the good news like entertainment. Jesus bluntly said, "There is a judge for the one who rejects me and does not accept my words; the very words I have spoken will condemn them at the last day" (John 12:48 NIV).

Listening to God is dangerous business if we don't intend to apply what we hear.

DAY 69

MORNING: OVERTHINKING AND UNDER-PRAYING / *Do not be anxious about anything, but in every situation. . .present your requests to God.* Philippians 4:6 NIV / The Bible is full of stories of very intelligent men. Joseph was described as discerning and wise (Genesis 41:39); Daniel and his three companions had "knowledge and understanding of all kinds of literature and learning" (Daniel 1:17 NIV); and God granted Solomon "a breadth of understanding as measureless as the sand on the seashore" (1 Kings 4:29 NIV). But the real strength of these men came from their willingness to meet God in prayer.

Prayer does not replace knowledge, wisdom, or discernment—it transcends it. It invites God, who delights in trading His peace for our anxiety, to participate in our lives.

Therefore, let us always ask for wisdom (James 1:5), remembering that we exercise the highest wisdom by coming to God in prayer.

EVENING: SEEING OURSELVES RIGHTLY / *For he knows how we are formed, he remembers that we are dust.* Psalm 103:14 NIV / As our Creator, God knows that we were made from the dust of the earth (Genesis 2:7) and are a mere "mist that appears for a little while and then vanishes" (James 4:14 NIV). Even when we don't, God knows our time is short and our power limited.

Thankfully, God doesn't look on our frailty with contempt. Instead, our vulnerability moves Him with a Father's compassion.

God doesn't want His children to have a false sense of strength and thus miss His blessings. While we may spend our time making great plans, God spends His time making great sons.

Let's ask Him to open our eyes to our own limitations, not disdaining what we see but allowing it to cause us to lean on Him.

MORNING: INSECURE MUCH? / *There is no fear in love. But perfect love drives out fear.* 1 John 4:18 NIV / When thinking about asking a girl out on a date, some guys either hesitate or skip out entirely. We may not want to admit it, but many guys have a crippling fear of rejection. It may be easier to think of what might have been instead of facing the possibility that she might say no.

Every guy faces insecurity. Even the most masculine among us can sometimes wonder if he really understands what it means to be a man. We feel like pretenders, and no place seems safe to admit our insecurity.

God's love, however, offers acceptance, invites trust, and is always the safest place to share our darkest secrets.

Real men accept God's love and engage life—fearlessly.

EVENING: THE GOSPEL'S COMPETITION / *"But the worries of this life, the deceitfulness of wealth and the desires for other things come in and choke the word, making it unfruitful."* Mark 4:19 NIV / Receiving the Word sown by Christ is just the beginning; His goal is to have it grow and become fruitful. But the world is always pulling against us.

Getting the right job, finding a wife, buying a house, raising kids, and planning for retirement can be blessings from God, but they can also engross us to the point that we grow cold in following Christ. Likewise, the pursuit of a comfortable life and the desire for influence, entertainment, or political power may cause us to lose sight of the race we were designed for.

A seed that sprouts is a good start, but fruitfulness is the goal. We need to be alert to the weeds that choke the fruit God wants to produce in our lives.

DAY 71

MORNING: PRAY FOR THAT PEACE / *"I am leaving you with a gift—peace of mind and heart. And the peace I give is a gift the world cannot give. So don't be troubled or afraid."* John 14:27 NLT / Adam and Eve, the first man and woman, disobeyed God's singular request, "Don't eat from this tree." It was sin that caused Cain to kill Abel. It was this sin that led to wars.

But a world without war is not the peace God offers; rather, His peace comes from the assurance that He's faithful and in control.

Peace is a heart issue. Wars can be waged on every continent, yet God's people can still have a peace that can't be explained. This peace can quiet individual hearts, provide reassurance, and encourage individuals to send their fear into exile.

Pray for *that* peace.

EVENING: THE LIKENESS OF GOD / *But God disciplines us for our good, in order that we may share in his holiness.* Hebrews 12:10 NIV / Holiness is God's nature and His fondest hope for His children. But the concept of holiness is often mired with misconceptions: *Holiness is boring, holiness is too hard to attain, holiness means becoming "too religious,"* and so on.

Holiness, however, is actually freedom. Nothing about it is boring or restrictive. Of course, when we deny our new nature in Christ and value things that God says are worthless, then holiness will most certainly seem burdensome. That's because, even for believers, "the mind governed by the flesh is hostile to God" (Romans 8:7 NIV). On the other hand, "the mind governed by the Spirit is life and peace" (Romans 8:6 NIV).

Holiness is our birthright, and God is committed to seeing it in us.

MORNING: THINGS WE THINK / *You will keep in perfect peace all who trust in you, all whose thoughts are fixed on you!* Isaiah 26:3 NLT / The things we think often astonish, embarrass, and torture us. We think about things we know are off-limits, and without our permission, the thoughts return.

When we spend time meditating on God's Word, however, good decisions start showing up in our lives. Hebrews 12:2–3 gives some great advice on redirecting your brain toward God's plan: "Keep your eyes on Jesus, who both began and finished this race we're in. Study how he did it. . . . When you find yourselves flagging in your faith, go over that. . .long litany of hostility he plowed through. That will shoot adrenaline into your souls!" (MSG).

Grow your thought life in God's direction. A full benefits plan awaits.

EVENING: THE TRUE BATTLE / *What causes fights and quarrels among you? Don't they come from your desires that battle within you?* James 4:1 NIV / The inner life of a man is the real life of a man. Our hearts will determine everything we do and say—from them come our value systems. That's why we are warned, "Above all else, guard your heart, for everything you do flows from it" (Proverbs 4:23 NIV).

When we experience conflict with others—especially sincere believers—we may be allowing the inner turmoil of our own hearts to express itself in those relationships. Other people may not be "the problem." We may be engaging in the wrong battle. The real battle is saying no to our own desires and humbling ourselves to serve.

MORNING: NO SECONDHAND STORY / *Do your best to win God's approval as a worker who doesn't need to be ashamed and who teaches only the true message.* 2 Timothy 2:15 CEV / There are two key parts to Christian ministry. The first is to love God enough to serve those He loves. The second is to know enough of God's message that we're not ashamed when someone asks us why we're helping.

We don't assume or guess when it comes to answering questions about our faith. We hold on to God's hand and dig deep in His Word, watching our spiritual muscles grow as we discover what God said in the Bible.

Study and serve. Learn and give. Memorize and share God's love. He will approve this plan—every time.

EVENING: WHOLEHEARTEDLY HIS / *[Amaziah] did what was right in the eyes of the LORD, but not wholeheartedly.* 2 Chronicles 25:2 NIV / Religion may ask, "Are you in or are you out?" But God asks, "How far in are you?" His interest is in an active, real relationship.

Everything God has done in history is so that His people can be "really in." Following the rules is never enough for a father. Character and heart matter more. And in Christ, we are given a whole heart to be His (Jeremiah 24:7).

No man ever impressed his wife, his boss, his commanding officer, his dad, or anyone else with a halfhearted effort. So why should we expect God—who "did not spare his own Son, but gave him up for us all" (Romans 8:32 NIV)—to be any different?

We certainly won't resemble our Father by holding back in doing His will.

MORNING: NOTHING ESCAPES HIS ATTENTION / *"For all that is secret will eventually be brought into the open."* Luke 8:17 NLT / If you ever take a hot air balloon ride, one of the first things you'll notice is how quiet it can be. Because there's no engine, the only noise is the occasional blast of the propane burner above you.

Equally remarkable are the clear sounds from the earth below. You can hear dogs barking, the excitement of children when they notice you, and the calls of people who think you can't hear them.

In a way, this is a bit like God's relationship with us. He sees, hears, and knows all about us, even when we think He's not paying attention.

But this means He also sees us break His law. Thankfully, however, He watches not as a judge but as one who's eager to offer forgiveness.

EVENING: YOUR WILL BE DONE / *He was near Jerusalem and the people thought that the kingdom of God was going to appear at once.* Luke 19:11 NIV / Sometimes, we start loving our expectations of God's will so much that we stop watching to see where His will actually takes us.

Jesus' disciples, angry at the Samaritans for not receiving Jesus, asked Him, "Lord, do You want us to command fire to come down from heaven and consume them?" (Luke 9:54 NKJV).

Talk about being on the wrong page! Clearly, they hadn't been paying attention to Jesus' teaching.

We can avoid the disciples' worldly mindset by applying Paul's sound advice: "Do not be conformed to this world, but be transformed by the renewing of your mind, that you may prove what is that good and acceptable and perfect will of God" (Romans 12:2 NKJV).

MORNING: TEACHING OBEDIENCE / *"Therefore go and make disciples of all nations, baptizing them in the name of the Father and of the Son and of the Holy Spirit, and teaching them to obey everything I have commanded you."* Matthew 28:19–20 NIV / In a study of nearly three thousand American Protestant churchgoers, only 42 percent said they intentionally spend time with other believers to help them grow in their faith. The remaining 58 percent have a truncated view of the Great Commission.

One leader observed, "Rather than teaching everything [Jesus] taught us, which would change the culture, we're just going after 'fire insurance.'"

You probably know men at work, school, or church who are baby Christians. If you haven't already, invite one of them to get together. Find out what he's struggling with and offer to disciple him by walking him through the scriptures.

EVENING: UNSTOPPABLE / *"I will put enmity between you and the woman, and between your seed and her Seed; He shall bruise your head, and you shall bruise His heel."* Genesis 3:15 NKJV / Nothing is beyond God's control. Immediately after Adam and Eve's fall, God announced His prophetic plan to redeem His people.

Satan's whole plan is predicated on disrupting God's redemptive plan. He's tried time and time again—Cain's murder of Abel, Pharaoh's and Herod's infanticide, and even the crucifixion of Jesus. With the latter, Satan thought he had finally won—but "the one who rules in heaven laughs. . . . For the Lord declares, 'I have placed my chosen king on the throne'" (Psalm 2:4, 6 NLT).

God doesn't promise you a pleasant life, but He does insure that, through Jesus Christ, you'll one day receive the best He has to offer.

MORNING: ARE YOU LIKE DAVID? / *A psalm of David. When he fled from his son Absalom.* Title of Psalm 3 NIV / Why was David a man after God's own heart? Perhaps because David's every heartbeat pulsed in rhythm with God's own. And no matter what happened to David, God was the first to hear about it.

David called out to the Lord for mercy when his reputation was attacked (Psalm 4:1–2), pleaded for compassion when he was weak and troubled (Psalm 6:1–3, 6), praised God for the marvels of stars and humanity (Psalm 8:3–4), and even questioned the Lord when he felt like God was far away (Psalm 10:1–6).

David's heart lay open before God in anguish, grief, joy, and exaltation. Don't be afraid to share your own emotions, no matter how painful they might be, with the Lord.

EVENING: ST. PATRICK'S DAY / *How beautiful on the mountains are the feet of those who bring good news, who proclaim peace, who bring good tidings, who proclaim salvation.* Isaiah 52:7 NIV / St. Patrick's Day began as a Catholic feast day to honor the life of the man who brought Christianity to Ireland in the AD 400s. These days, however, the holiday is widely known for its parades, festivals, the wearing of green, the display of shamrocks. . . and the drinking of alcohol.

Almost forgotten amongst the partying is the figure at the holiday's center: an outstanding missionary who was simply following Jesus' command: "Go ye into all the world, and preach the gospel to every creature" (Mark 16:15 KJV).

There is still a great deal of missionary work to be done in the world—often right in your own neighborhood. Ask God to help you bring eternal hope to whomever you see today.

MORNING: VISIBLE AND ONGOING REPENTANCE / *"Bear fruit in keeping with repentance. And do not presume to say to yourselves, 'We have Abraham as our father,' for I tell you, God is able from these stones to raise up children for Abraham."* Matthew 3:8–9 ESV / John the Baptist wanted his listeners, the religious leaders of the day, to know that their past faithfulness did not guarantee God's blessings in the future. God was more concerned with the condition of their hearts in the present.

The religious leaders' false belief is still an easy trap to fall into. Have you repented of your failures? Are you willing to change how you live? If you choose to live in obedience to God, the visible fruit of that choice will be a changed life, not just a title or a position within a group.

EVENING: LIFE'S POP QUIZZES / *I treasure your word above all else; it keeps me from sinning against you.* Psalm 119:11 CEV / Here's some good news: life is an open book test! But there's some bad news too: the only book you need is often overlooked.

Somehow, we've come to believe that we don't have to be an expert in anything. Why? We can make new discoveries online in a matter of seconds—and then forget them immediately, choosing instead to store up unimportant information.

God has always wanted us to know what He thinks about important issues. But even though we have access to His Word, we often stand back, guess, or complain when life's pop quizzes show up.

The Bible isn't an optional textbook or a bookshelf ornament—it's a treasure for consultation.

MORNING: FORETASTES OF HEAVEN / *"The blind receive sight, the lame walk, those who have leprosy are cleansed, the deaf hear, the dead are raised, and the good news is proclaimed to the poor."* Luke 7:22 NIV / Two thousand years ago, Jesus' earthly ministry gave His followers amazing glimpses of eternity. But make no mistake: these heavenly foretastes are also ours to experience today.

As followers of Christ, our sins—past, present, and future—are already all forgiven, yet we experience His grace anew each time we confess our sins. Immediately afterward, we should slow down and savor that specific experience of being forgiven. If we do, we enjoy a delicious foretaste of heaven.

So right now, slow down and savor each specific foretaste experience this side of eternity. Each one is Jesus Christ's rich and valuable gift to you.

EVENING: SPIRITUAL PROSPERITY / *Better is the poor who walks in his integrity than one who is perverse in his lips, and is a fool.* Proverbs 19:1 NKJV / The man who walks in his integrity is satisfied and unashamed at the end of the day. He's done an honest day's work and treated people well, and he comes home to a pleasant meal. He's put forth his best effort, and tomorrow is another day.

The crooked man, however, is foolish. He speaks lies, cuts corners, and mistreats people to get ahead. His conscience bothers him occasionally, but he rationalizes it away. He hides his sin and falls asleep scheming about tomorrow.

The Hebrew word for *integrity* in this evening's verse can be translated as *prosperity*. So the poor man who tends to spiritual matters is actually more prosperous than the man who schemes to get ahead. Which life are you cultivating?

DAY 79

MORNING: HEARING THE BEATITUDES AS A COMMONER / *Arriving at a quiet place, he sat down and taught his climbing companions. This is what he said: "You're blessed when you're at the end of your rope. With less of you there is more of God and his rule."* Matthew 5:2–3 MSG / To a person living in Jesus' day, the Beatitudes would have sounded like a fairy tale. *I can enter the realm of God's kingdom? God will grant my wish if I talk with Him?*

But these seemingly outlandish statements are true. Even better, God will adopt you as one of His children, showering you with rewards as you face persecution. You will be honored the same as the great prophets of old. Like them, you are now the salt of the earth and the light of the world.

So be courageous and shine the light and praise God as your Father in heaven.

EVENING: TRUST, NOT CERTAINTY / *In peace I will lie down and sleep, for you alone, O LORD, will keep me safe.* Psalm 4:8 NLT / Even as a committed follower of Christ, it's tempting to turn to worldly success for comfort. When Satan tempted Jesus in the wilderness, he fired off the big three: material needs, physical comfort, and financial success.

Jesus' response gave the template for resisting this temptation: "Away with you, Satan! For it is written, 'You shall worship the LORD your God, and Him only you shall serve' " (Matthew 4:10 NKJV). You must trust God more than your own ability to provide. When you're set apart for God, He will answer when you call on Him (Psalm 4:3).

Faith is a matter of trust, not certainty—and you can rest assured in what the Bible tells you about God.

MORNING: A TIME TO UNITE / *In Christ's family there can be no division into Jew and non-Jew, slave and free, male and female. Among us you are all equal. That is, we are all in a common relationship with Jesus Christ.* Galatians 3:28 MSG / Of all the people on earth, Christians should be the one group with the most interest in eliminating racial discrimination. Yet every generation of believers has struggled to embrace this truth: God does not discriminate based on skin color.

We must remember that Jesus' sacrifice was for *all* mankind. He preached both to the Jews and to the "half-breed" Samaritans. He didn't add a list of exceptions, and neither should we.

All Christians—whatever their background—are part of God's beautiful and ever-expanding family.

EVENING: NEVER TOO LATE / *Is anything too hard or too wonderful for the Lord?* Genesis 18:14 AMPC / When Abram recalled God's promise that a nation would spring from his body, he was ninety-nine. His wife, Sarai, was ten years younger. Hadn't they done what God asked? Where was the promised child? Wasn't it too late?

It must have felt that way. But when three divine strangers dropped by, everything changed. The promise became more specific. A boy named Isaac would arrive in a year. And when Sarah laughed in disbelief, one of the heaven-sent guests said, "Is anything too hard or wonderful for the Lord?"

The answer was a resounding *no*! Several months later, the laughter of a child erased all doubt.

When you grow tired of the wait, remind yourself that God has always been faithful—and that nothing is too hard for Him.

DAY 81

MORNING: THE BEST TIME TO PRAY / *Listen to my voice in the morning, Lord. Each morning I bring my requests to you and wait expectantly.* Psalm 5:3 NLT / There technically isn't a "best" time to pray. Yet the writers of scripture mention one time far more than any other: the morning.

Consider how each day begins. At dawn, the air is silent. Soon, televisions start chattering, cars fill the roads, smartphones buzz, and calendars fill up. Before long, you're bouncing from one task to another with an endless list of things to do. The mayhem only ends when you crash on your bed at the end of the day.

It's no accident that the psalmist sought God in the quiet morning hours. At that moment, nothing else mattered except his attention to God.

Take some time this morning to wait patiently on a loving and present God.

EVENING: WRITE ON HEARTS / *Proclaim the Message with intensity; keep on your watch. Challenge, warn, and urge your people. Don't ever quit. Just keep it simple.* 2 Timothy 4:2 MSG / The process of writing the Bible required painstaking accuracy, long hours, and antiquated writing utensils made of bird feathers. The ballpoint pen wouldn't arrive until the 1880s.

Yet from the first sentence penned in God's Word, there was a deliberate purpose behind every stroke.

If God had waited on technology to improve, how many generations would have never heard of the life, love, and forgiveness God provides?

But since we have such technology today, God wants us to use it to share His love. Use a pen, computer, video, stage presentation, poem, painting, or any other creative means to write His message on hearts—no one will ever benefit if we're reluctant to share.

MORNING: JESUS CHRIST: FULLY HUMAN / *For this reason he had to be made like them, fully human in every way.* Hebrews 2:17 NIV / According to pollsters, people have many misconceptions about the Bible, God, and Jesus Christ.

One common mistake is failing to understand that Jesus Christ is eternal. Many speak as if He'd been created at the point of conception in the virgin Mary's womb. But as God's Son, Jesus has existed for all of eternity past. There is no point at which He didn't exist. His conception was simply the moment He became *human.*

And just as Jesus existed as God from eternity past, He will continue to exist as fully God and fully human for all eternity, thus serving as living proof of His love for us.

Your God knows exactly how you feel, because He's worn the same humanity on the same earth.

EVENING: PRESERVED FOR THE KINGDOM / *The Lord preserves those who are true to him.* Psalm 31:23 NIV / In this evening's verse, King David explains the benefit of faithfulness to the Lord: He preserves us.

But how? Don't bad things happen to faithful believers all the time?

While God may intervene in your troubles, that's not what the psalmist is referring to. He's actually speaking of the eternal.

In his *Exposition of the Entire Bible,* Bible commentator John Gill observes, "He preserves them in a way of special grace; he keeps them. . . from the evil of sin. . .so as not to be drawn off from Christ and his ways. . . and these are preserved safe to the kingdom and glory of Christ."

Spend some time this evening thanking God for preserving you. And then set your mind on being faithful to Him.

MORNING: PUT FAITH FIRST / *"But seek first his kingdom and his righteousness, and all these things will be given to you as well."* Matthew 6:33 NIV / Following Christ means trusting Him to keep this promise. You understand that He will because of who He is and all He has done for you, but when it comes down to brass tacks—unpaid debt, piles of bills, unemployment, sickness—part of you wonders, *I know He can, but will He?*

Even Abram found this difficult. He had God's promise of blessing—of guidance, presence, descendants, and land—and yet he fled the promised land and lied about his wife out of fear and uncertainty. As a result, the Philistine Abimelech chastised him for his dishonesty and lack of integrity.

Small faith fails to put God's priorities first. . .but a little faith gets you back on track.

EVENING: ARE YOU LIKE SARAH? / *The LORD kept his word and did for Sarah exactly what he had promised.* Genesis 21:1 NLT / It isn't always easy to believe God's promises.

For years, Sarah had heard about God's promises to Abraham and his descendants. Tired of waiting, Sarah tried to hurry along the process by seeking a surrogate son. But all she got was more sorrow, distress, and pain.

As each year passed, Sarah perhaps felt less and less a part of God's plan. No wonder Sarah scoffed when she heard the angels predict her coming pregnancy—even Abraham had laughed at the thought.

As the baby grew within Sarah, Sarah's faith grew as well. Part of Sarah still couldn't grasp what a marvelous thing God had done, but when her baby—the promised son of Abraham—was finally born, laughter of disbelief transformed into laughter of delight.

MORNING: DOES PRAYER REALLY WORK? / *"So if you sinful people know how to give good gifts to your children, how much more will your heavenly Father give good gifts to those who ask him."* Matthew 7:11 NLT / Parents care deeply for their children, but that doesn't necessarily mean they give their kids everything they ask for. Sometimes, the answer is "no" or maybe even "wait."

Although it's not a comprehensive image of prayer, Jesus used this analogy to convey to His listeners God's concern for His people and prayer's more complex dynamics. Since God only wants to give you good things, He sometimes doesn't give you what think you need. After all, how could you possibly know what's best for you in the long run?

Hopefully, this (admittedly oversimplified) explanation will encourage you to pray with greater hope and expectation.

EVENING: AWE AND WONDER / *They traded the true God for a fake god, and worshiped the god they made instead of the God who made them.* Romans 1:25 MSG / Men are made to worship, and we will—but it's often directed toward the wrong things.

When left with a sense of awe and wonder, we can quickly turn away from God and toward whatever inspired the wonder. Perhaps a visit to the mountains finds us thinking more about nature than the God who made it. Maybe watching sports causes us to be in awe of the player instead of the God who gave the skill. Indeed, anything—cars, jobs, entertainment, comfort, even sex—can replace God in our lives with something that's powerless to rescue, forgive, or transform.

Faith is critical in worship. We must always remind ourselves that God is the ultimate source of awe and wonder in everything we see.

MORNING: WHO IS KING OF YOUR LIFE? / *Jesus and his companions went to the town of Capernaum. When the Sabbath day came, he went into the synagogue and began to teach.* Mark 1:21 NLT / After recruiting His first disciples, Jesus took them to the synagogue in the city of Capernaum, where—for a brief moment—an unseen spiritual war became visible. When a demon-possessed man tried to tell Jesus what to do, He immediatly rebuked the evil spirit and told *him* what to do. To everyone's astonishment, the demon had to obey what Jesus said.

Everyone has to obey Jesus. Some may shake and scream. Some may try to tell Jesus what to do. But in the end, everyone will obey. The question isn't, "Is Jesus the Lord of all?" The question is, "Have you acknowledged that fact in your own life?"

EVENING: OPEN YOUR HOME / *God has given each of you a gift. . . . Use them well to serve one another.* 1 Peter 4:10 NLT / When Peter penned these words, the destruction of the Jewish temple and nation were at hand. With persecution imminent, Peter wanted believers to keep loving one another, opening their homes, and serving others using the spiritual gifts God had given them (verses 7–10).

Are you concerned that the end of the American church—and nation—may be at hand? Do you frequently get caught up in bitter political exchanges? Listen to Peter's advice. Open your home to fellow believers. Pray, study, laugh, and weep with them. Serve them using your spiritual gifts.

If you aren't sure about your spiritual gifting, ask a leader at church to help you identify it. And then start exercising it. By doing so, you'll make a greater impact for the kingdom of God.

MORNING: FAMILY MANAGERS / *If anyone does not know how to manage his own family, how can he take care of God's church?* 1 Timothy 3:5 NIV / When Paul spelled out the qualifications for a bishop (or deacon) to Timothy, he included the requirement that a bishop must be able to manage his own family.

To Paul, this office wasn't a calling—it was an aspiration. Persecution and death hung around every corner—especially for leaders. Yet the Holy Spirit still inspired young converts to shepherd other believers.

As a man, if you don't desire to lovingly lead your family in devotions, prayer, spiritual discussions, and guidance, then something is wrong. Paul's guidelines for a bishop should be the call for every Christian man, no matter what his position.

How are you shepherding your family today?

EVENING: FIRST THINGS FIRST / *"First things first. Your business is life, not death. Follow me. Pursue life."* Matthew 8:22 MSG / Part of being a responsible adult is making plans and following through on commitments. But how many times do you bring God into those plans?

Trusting God includes trusting His timing. Life is busy, and with work and family appointments and church activities, it's easy to reach a level of unrealistic spiritual expectation—that just because you're doing the best you can, God's schedule will fit into yours.

Are you willing to let God interrupt your plans? Part of being His son means being willing to slow down, ask Him for perspective, and trust that His interruptions are for your ultimate benefit.

Stay focused on God, not the tyranny of urgency.

MORNING: DON'T BE LIKE REBEKAH / *"Now, my son, listen to me. Do exactly as I tell you."* Genesis 27:8 NLT / Just as God gave Sarah the promise that she would have a son, so He gave a promise to Rebekah. This time, God promised that her youngest son would not only father a nation but rule over his brother. However, as the day approached for Isaac to bless his sons, Rebekah became desperate and fell into the same trap that Sarah had.

To ensure the right outcome, Rebekah used deceit in an attempt to gain what God had promised. She believed God, but not enough to wait for Him to overcome what looked impossible.

Even if God doesn't meet our expectations, we should always rest assured that His promises will come true. There's no need to "help" Him.

EVENING: A PROMISED SON / *"Don't lay a hand on that boy! Don't touch him! Now I know how fearlessly you fear God; you didn't hesitate to place your son, your dear son, on the altar for me."* Genesis 22:12 MSG / God put Abraham's faith to a test most couldn't imagine facing—He asked him to offer his son as a sacrifice.

Abraham had learned that God could be trusted even when he didn't understand, so this aging father walked with Isaac to Mount Moriah, built an altar, and prepared for the unthinkable. But just before Abraham reached the point of no return, he heard the welcome words, "Don't lay a hand on that boy!"

Similarly, Jesus was God's promised Son, destined to become the rescuer of mankind. But unlike Abraham, Jesus' sacrifice went all the way.

Because Jesus bore the brunt of mankind's worst affliction, Christians have citizenship in a forever home. Thank God!

DAY 88

MORNING: WILL GOD NOTICE WHAT'S WRONG? / *Why does the wicked man revile God? . . . You, God, see the trouble of the afflicted; you consider their grief and take it in hand. . . . You are the helper of the fatherless.* Psalm 10:13–14 NIV / Of the many reasons people sin, one is surely the belief that God isn't watching and won't call anyone to account for his conduct. Yet this morning's psalm can assure you that God *will* hold the wicked to account for their actions. He will also take notice of those who are suffering affliction and loss.

God sees those who suffer and those who don't have advocates. This should serve as a reminder for you to notice them as well. If God helps the fatherless, God's people surely should do the same.

EVENING: INTERRUPTIONS ENCOURAGED / *So whenever we are in need, we should come bravely before the throne of our merciful God. There we will be treated with undeserved grace, and we will find help.* Hebrews 4:16 CEV / Try to think of someone—anyone—who likes being interrupted. Can't think of any? Well that's not surprising.

When you were in school, the teacher would invite students to ask questions, but never during a test or quiz. Your parents may have been patient, but they probably didn't tolerate you butting into their phone calls and important conversations.

God, however, never objects to interruptions. In fact, God tells us to be brave when we come to Him, expect grace we don't deserve, and find the help we need.

Relationships begin with conversation, so interrupt God whenever you need to. You'll find a closeness that you can never obtain by doing things on your own.

MORNING: SHOW GRACE / *Be gentle with one another, sensitive. Forgive one another as quickly and thoroughly as God in Christ forgave you.* Ephesians 4:32 MSG / To her, he's just the nice man that helps her. To him, it's heartbreaking to see the woman he fell in love with so long ago view him as *the helper*.

The care she requires falls almost entirely on his shoulders. Not fair? Absolutely. Not fun? Who would think such a thing? But every time her recollections sparkle or a comment makes her laugh, he is reminded of the importance of his commitment.

Over five million American men and women suffer from Alzheimer's disease—that's five million overlooked, misunderstood families struggling to understand the incomprehensible.

And this is only one disease out of many.

Today, choose to show God's grace, love, and compassion to everyone you meet. You never know who might need it the most.

EVENING: GRACE UNDER FIRE / *"Do not worry about how or what you should speak. For. . .it is not you who speak, but the Spirit of your Father who speaks in you."* Matthew 10:19–20 NKJV / Well, you went and did it. You took a leap of faith and talked about your faith in a public forum. You listened first, trying to understand other people's situations and thoughts, and you did your best to present the gospel clearly and with compassion.

No matter how it went, know that God's grace is with you when you're under fire. Look past the emotions of the moment and know that He cares—both about you and the people you spoke with.

Whether you feel peaceful or uneasy, rest in this: you have been faithful to what God called you to do, and that's a success.

MORNING: ACCURATE WEIGHTS / *The Lord detests the use of dishonest scales, but he delights in accurate weights.* Proverbs 11:1 NLT / Imagine going to the supermarket and purchasing two pounds of roast beef. You watch the butcher put the meat on the scale, you see that it's two pounds, and you thank him. But when the person after you places the same order, the butcher switches the measuring device and places much more meat on the (clearly unjust) scales for the same price you paid.

Just as you'd be understandably upset over such a thing, the Lord also detests such business practices. He is just; therefore, He's on the side of those who are treated unjustly.

As you head to your workplace today, consider all your business practices. Are they all fair and just?

EVENING: CHOOSING GOD'S WORD ANEW / *You, Lord, will keep the needy safe and will protect us forever from the wicked.* Psalm 12:7 NIV / When David began his psalm with this lament, "Help, Lord, for no one is faithful anymore; those who are loyal have vanished from the human race" (verse 1 NIV), he felt pretty hopeless.

Matters don't improve in the next few verses, in which David further describes these hypocrites and evildoers and asks the Lord to silence them. Thankfully, the Lord assures David that He will arise and act. In deep gratitude, David affirms the absolute trustworthiness of the Lord's words. What a contrast between the deceitful, doomed men and God's perfect, everlasting Word!

How have things looked to you in recent days? Hopeless? Or hope-filled? Or somewhere in between? Like David, you can tell the Lord how you feel and ask Him to rise up and act.

MORNING: A TIME TO PREPARE / *Jacob said to Laban, "Send me on my way so I can go back to my own homeland."* Genesis 30:25 NIV / Many years had passed since Jacob had begun working for Laban so that he could marry Rachel. He was more than a little eager to leave. His father-in-law, however, was making it as hard as possible to do so, repeatedly and unfairly changing his wages.

But Jacob's time in the divine waiting room was almost over. And no matter how unfair the labor talks became, God found a way to bless Jacob.

All waiting will eventually come to an end. You'll discover an open door, and God will lead you through. Waiting is not stopping—it's simply preparing for God's next step for you.

Whatever you're waiting for, endurance will ensure that difficulties will seem small when the answer arrives.

EVENING: GOD TREASURES HIS PEOPLE / *"Not a single sparrow can fall to the ground without your Father knowing it. And the very hairs on your head are all numbered."* Matthew 10:29–30 NLT / It's impossible to count how many birds fly overhead each day. You have more important responsibilities, after all! Even if a bird dies, that's hardly your concern. Life must go on.

To describe God's love and concern for you, Jesus adopted an expansive image of God's deep love and concern for all of creation. Just as the Father knows when a single bird falls to the ground, He also knows the smallest details about you and your well-being.

This truth can give you an unshakable confidence in God's deep love for you. There's no such thing as God being too busy to notice you—He knows exactly what you need in each moment.

MORNING: THE SAMARITAN WOMAN'S FAITH / *Then, leaving her water jar, the woman went back to the town and said to the people, "Come, see a man who told me everything I ever did. Could this be the Messiah?"* John 4:28–29 NIV / When the Samaritan woman came to the well, she met a man who promised to fill her with living water that would never run dry. A minute or two later, Jesus told her something He hadn't told anyone else: He was the Messiah.

Instead of running back to the safety of her sin, this hurting woman grabbed hold of Jesus' invitation to come into a love relationship with the Father. A minute later, she forgot all about her empty water jug in her excitement to run back to town and tell others.

What clear evidence that the water of eternal life was already welling up within her!

EVENING: REMEMBERING THEIR CHAINS / *I, Paul, write this greeting in my own hand. Remember my chains. Grace be with you.* Colossians 4:18 NIV / In April 2014, Boko Haram—an Islamic extremist group—abducted 276 girls in Nigeria, compelling them to convert to Islam and forcing many into marriage. To this day, roughly one hundred girls remain missing.

Kristin Wright, advocacy director of Open Doors (an organization that serves persecuted Christians worldwide), observed that the girls' fathers saw "the persecution they are facing as. . .a natural part of. . .walking in the footsteps of Jesus."

This very moment, persecuted believers need you to remember their chains, just as Paul said in this evening's verse. Always keep your less fortunate brothers and sisters in your prayers.

MORNING: ABSOLUTE COMMITMENT / *"He who does not take his cross and follow after Me is not worthy of Me."* Matthew 10:38 NKJV / You've heard people say they have a "cross to bear." They're usually referring to some burden they must endure—a hard relationship, chronic disease, or addiction. But Jesus' call in this morning's verse really means only one thing: killing your plans and desires and letting God replace them with His.

This is especially difficult for those who think they're doing God a favor by receiving Christ. If they had anything to offer God, would the cross have been necessary?

In Christ, you're reborn spiritually, but you'll bear the burdens of the flesh for as long as you walk this earth. However, God can redeem these hardships, turning them into bridges to others' pain.

It's not easy to love people the way Jesus loves you, but it's worth it.

EVENING: FORGOTTEN, BUT NOT FORGOTTEN / *The chief butler did not remember Joseph, but forgot him.* Genesis 40:23 NKJV / Joseph came to Egypt as a slave. Then, falsely accused of misconduct, he was placed in prison. None of this was fair. This wasn't where Joseph wanted to be. Yet God was with him, and it wasn't long before this prisoner ran the prison: "The keeper of the prison did not look into anything that was under Joseph's authority, because the LORD was with him" (Genesis 39:23 NKJV).

God never promised you a life free of trouble, but He promised to be with you. He never said today would be perfect, but He said you can live in joy daily because He never leaves or forsakes you. He never said everything would go according to your plans, but He did say that when you love Him, He can transform bad things into something good.

DAY 94

MORNING: HAVING DINNER WITH GOD / *God, who gets invited to dinner at your place? How do we get on your guest list?* Psalm 15:1 MSG / Each year, the king or queen of England invites thirty thousand men and women to four summer afternoon garden parties.

Sorry, you can't request an invitation by writing to Buckingham Palace. Instead, guests are nominated by a network of leaders from Britain's major institutions.

What does it take to have dinner with God? First, you need to be a citizen of His kingdom. Second, you need to love the Lord with all your heart, soul, strength, and mind. Third, you need to know that Jesus counts you among His friends.

Thankfully, Jesus already is knocking on the door of your heart (Revelation 3:20). He's waiting for you to swing the door open, embrace Him, and invite Him in.

So what are you waiting for?

EVENING: HOW BADLY DO YOU WANT GOD'S BLESSING? / *Then he said, "Let me go, for the day has broken." But Jacob said, "I will not let you go unless you bless me."* Genesis 32:26 ESV / It may be odd to think that Jacob actually wrestled with God and even demanded a blessing. But whether or not Jacob actually knew whom he was wrestling against, there is no doubt that he considered his opponent holy and righteous enough to bestow a blessing.

What are you willing to endure for the sake of a blessing? For most of us, it's safe to rule out an all-night wrestling match—but are you willing to wait on God, struggle through your doubts, and ask someone else to pray for you?

If you hope to stand firm in your faith, take some time to seek a blessing from someone else.

DAY 95

MORNING: A PLACE TO SIT / *Seeing the multitudes, He went up on a mountain, and when He was seated His disciples came to Him. Then He opened His mouth and taught them.* Matthew 5:1–2 NKJV / When we think of the Sermon on the Mount, we picture Jesus (as Hollywood has coached us) reciting the Beatitudes to the multitudes gathered atop a mountain. But scripture says He walked *away* from the crowd and taught His closest followers.

Men too often long for the spotlight. We want to hear the applause and the "amen." But Jesus looks for faithfulness in little things (Luke 16:10), calling us to teach and care for our own households first and foremost (Matthew 24:45; Ephesians 6:4; 1 Timothy 5:8).

Today, take time to step away from the crowds and sit with the few in your life who matter most.

EVENING: HOPE / *Now the God of hope fill you with all joy and peace in believing, that ye may abound in hope, through the power of the Holy Ghost.* Romans 15:13 KJV / All the unbelievers in your life are lacking one thing: eternal hope. Some find earthly hope in work, wealth, or even family. Others have false hope in their good deeds. But none of them have real assurance or peace about their standing before a holy God.

In Romans 15, Paul explains that Christ is the great hope for Jews and Gentiles alike. Jesus is the long-awaited Messiah. Believing in Him brings joy and peace right now, but it also settles eternity in the heart of the believer.

Sometimes, even Christians fall into despair. Even Jesus, God's Son, felt sorrow on occasion. But beyond the tears and grief is the great hope of heaven.

What a glorious expectation!

MORNING: DEVOTED WORDS / *Pharaoh asked them, "Can we find anyone like this man, one in whom is the spirit of God?"* Genesis 41:38 NIV / Pharaoh recognized that Joseph had something most men didn't—the *Ruach Elohim*, or Spirit of God.

The Holy Spirit indwells every believer at salvation, but most don't fully grasp who He is or what He does. He's the third person of the God-head, present at creation and salvation. He empowers leaders, convicts unbelievers, and guides and intercedes for believers.

Joseph's heart reflected the work of God's Spirit in and around him. Similarly, if what's stored in your heart is good, good things will come out. If not, bad things will (Matthew 12:34). When God's words fill your heart, His love and wisdom follow, and people will recognize the overflow and glorify God.

Is God's Spirit evident in your words?

EVENING: THANKFUL FOR GOD'S GENTLENESS / *You have given me the shield of your salvation, and your right hand supported me, and your gentleness made me great.* Psalm 18:35 ESV / How would you describe Jesus? Biblically, you could say He's the Messiah, the King of kings, the Son of God, and so on.

Theologically, you could talk about Jesus as the second member of the Trinity, coequal with God the Father and God the Holy Spirit and infinite in His sovereignty, holiness, and love.

More importantly, how did Jesus describe Himself? The answer is found in a single verse, Matthew 11:29. Here, Jesus says He is gentle and humble in heart.

For that, you can give much thanks. You don't want the full power of God, who created everything by merely speaking the word, to land on you! As King David wrote, His gentleness makes *you* great.

MORNING: THE REUNION / *[Joseph] presented himself to [his father] and fell on his neck and wept on his neck a good while. Israel said to Joseph, "Now let me die, since I have seen your face and know that you are still alive."* Genesis 46:29–30 ESV / Many stories, as their plots unfold, slowly reveal shocking details about certain characters. Maybe the reason we love such stories is because they're so relatable: all of us have skeletons in our closets too.

Joseph's family certainly did. His brothers had to live with the memory of selling Joseph into slavery, and his father believed for many years that Joseph was dead.

God, however, has always told His family to confess sin. This means agreeing that God's laws are better than your own judgments, making things right with whomever you've wronged, and accepting God's forgiveness.

For Joseph's family, unflinching honesty led to an epic reunion.

EVENING: YOUR WORDS WILL LAST / *"I tell you this, you must give an account on judgment day for every idle word you speak. The words you say will either acquit you or condemn you."* Matthew 12:36–37 NLT / Jesus often heard His followers say troubling and irresponsible things, from James and John asking Jesus to call down thunder on people to Peter trying to persuade Jesus to avoid the cross. Jesus wanted His listeners to know that God was listening.

Your words have power to give life, encouragement, and freedom. But they also have the power to condemn, discourage, and bind. Basic everyday statements can have eternal consequences. The stakes are high, so you can't afford to speak thoughtlessly.

It is far better to carefully weigh your words today than to worry about how you'll give an account for them before God.

MORNING: REORIENTATION / *Let everyone see that you are considerate in all you do. Remember, the Lord is coming soon.* Philippians 4:5 NLT / At first glance, Paul's instructions here are surprising. Aren't Christians supposed to avoid calling attention to themselves? (Matthew 6:3, 6).

But a closer look reveals no contradiction. Jesus was talking about giving and praying in secret to avoid self-glorification. Paul, on the other hand, wanted believers to live out loud for God's glory because Jesus is coming back soon. Having that sense of urgency reorients the way a man lives and keeps him from becoming self-centered.

If you knew Jesus was coming back today, you'd probably make sure each action you took glorified Him. You'd empty yourself of selfishness and seek the good of those around you.

Wouldn't that be a refreshing way to live? Prayerfully commit yourself to such a vision today.

EVENING: GOOD FOR THE SOUL / *How can I know all the sins lurking in my heart? Cleanse me from these hidden faults. . . . Then I will be free of guilt and innocent of great sin.* Psalm 19:12–13 NLT / Confession is typically something you save for when you really mess up. Even though you know you're a sinner who needs a Savior, what man wants to be reminded of his mistakes all the time?

That's why the gospel is such good news—God doesn't want to recall your sins either. Confession goes beyond the moment of salvation; as part of your sanctification, it becomes a daily habit like taking a shower each morning. Sometimes, confession is difficult. But it's the only way to bring healing to yourself and others.

Trust that God has good things ahead and prepare your heart to receive and appreciate them.

MORNING: ARE YOU LIKE MOSES? / *Moses and Aaron went and spoke to Pharaoh. They told him, "This is what the LORD, the God of Israel, says: Let my people go."* Exodus 5:1 NLT / What did Moses feel when he re-entered the palaces of Egypt after a forty-year absence? Those halls had once been his home—he practically owned them. But none of the splendors of Egypt could ever capture his heart or eye again (Hebrews 3:5). Now, he approached the new Pharaoh as a stranger with a wild demand: "Release the Israelites to go and worship their God."

Like Moses, you live in an era of spectacular culture and extravagant resources that actively seek your attention. But all your attention and affection must belong to the Lord God. As you openly identify with Him, you will find that no cost is too great in order to gain God's friendship.

EVENING: A NEW BAPTISM / *John answered them all, "I baptize you with water. But one who is more powerful than I will come, the straps of whose sandals I am not worthy to untie."* Luke 3:16 NIV / John the Baptist, blood relative of the Savior, never claimed to be the Messiah; he merely came to prepare the way for Jesus.

John was certainly an odd sight—living in the desert, eating a strange diet, and passionately urging people to repent from their evil ways and change their hearts. But he was a harbinger of a new era; his appearance signaled a new age, and his message still resonates with those who hope in Jesus for their salvation and live empowered by the Spirit.

John came to point others toward Jesus. Does your life point your family, friends, neighbors, and coworkers toward Him as well?

MORNING: WHAT KEEPS YOU FROM GOD? / *"The Kingdom of Heaven is like a treasure that a man discovered hidden in a field. In his excitement, he hid it again and sold everything he owned to get enough money to buy the field."* Matthew 13:44 NLT / Jesus' audience likely had limited resources, so this parable would have resonated deeply with them. They knew selling all of one's possessions for a treasure could leave a man destitute, yet Jesus taught that the reward would prove to be much more valuable.

Jesus is asking you to consider your commitments and priorities today. Is there anything—a jam-packed schedule, professional priorities, a leisure activity, or possessions—keeping you from pursuing God and His priorities?

If so, remember: your security in His kingdom is the only unshakable thing you can count on. That's why it's worth giving up everything to obtain it.

EVENING: BLUE-COLLAR CELEBRATION / *And there were shepherds. . .keeping watch over their flocks at night. . . . The angel said to them, "Do not be afraid. I bring you good news. . . . Today in the town of David a Savior has been born to you."* Luke 2:8, 10 NIV / Who was the first group to understand that the Messiah had come? A group of hardworking shepherds, tired after a long day of finding suitable food for their sheep. It doesn't get more blue-collar than that.

The men who heard the angels sing that night never imagined they'd take part in the culmination of history, the news that the Jewish people had been waiting for centuries to hear.

God doesn't always entrust kings or politicians with His good news. He often uses unexpected people, such as the hardworking shepherds (or *you*?) to fulfill His purposes.

MORNING: GLOWING IN THE DARK / *When Aaron and all the Israelites saw Moses, his face was radiant.* Exodus 34:30 NIV / In one of the Bible's strangest moments, Moses returned from the presence of the Lord glowing!

The apostle Paul used this moment to illustrate the observable transformation believers experience in the presence of God: "And we all, who with unveiled faces contemplate the Lord's glory, are being transformed into his image with ever-increasing glory" (2 Corinthians 3:18 NIV).

However, Paul also wrote, Moses "put a veil over his face to prevent the Israelites from seeing the end of what was passing away" (2 Corinthians 3:13 NIV). When our true spiritual vitality starts waning, our religious lives can function like that veil and hide the truth. If that happens, all it takes is another visit into God's presence to renew our vitality once more.

EVENING: ANGEL'S SONG / *In a loud voice they were saying: "Worthy is the Lamb, who was slain, to receive power and wealth and wisdom and strength and honor and glory and praise!"* Revelation 5:12 NIV / When Jesus was born, the people of Israel were waiting for a powerful earthly Messiah to save them from earthly rulers. They were expecting the Lion of Judah. Instead, they got the Lamb of God.

Jesus came in humility, and His revolution differed from what the Israelites expected. When they decided that their hope in Jesus was misplaced, they had Him crucified. But that was God's plan all along!

Peace on earth wasn't possible before Jesus took the punishment for our sins on the cross. Only after He was slain could He be both the Lion and the Lamb, worthy of all our praise. Today, sing praises with the angels—because Jesus made a way for peace.

MORNING: CONFESSION / *If we confess our sins, he is faithful and just and will forgive us our sins and purify us from all unrighteousness.* 1 John 1:9 NIV / In *Scientific American* magazine, psychologist James W. Pennebaker writes that the act of confession, whether religious or through expressive writing, is linked to less stress, better sleep, and improved cardiovascular function.

But health benefits aren't the best part of confession—God's forgiveness is. Only forgiveness can restore our broken relationship with Him.

Confession doesn't give God any new information. Rather, it allows us to take responsibility for our actions. God won't necessarily remove the consequences of our sins, but He will take away the barrier between us and Him.

Are unconfessed sins holding you back from a right relationship with God? Confess, be forgiven, and start living the life God intended for you.

EVENING: THE RICH YOUNG RULER'S MISTAKE / *Jesus looked at them intently and said, "Humanly speaking, it is impossible. But with God everything is possible."* Matthew 19:26 NLT / When the rich young man came to Jesus, he sincerely thought he wanted eternal life—and he asked Jesus what he could do to get it. Jesus genuinely loved the man, so much so that He pinpointed the one obstacle that had to be removed first.

This particular man, like many other wealthy people, wanted to do something to gain eternal life. Alongside his impeccable character qualifications, his résumé listed all his favorite charities. The man had indeed obeyed the everyday commands Jesus listed—but not the greatest command of all. He didn't love the Lord his God with all his heart and soul and strength.

Unlike the rich young man, you can make the right choice. Is there anything you should let go of, something that's keeping you from enjoying God's very best?

MORNING: TRUSTING GOD'S JUDGMENTS / *"Yes, Lord God Almighty, true and just are your judgments."* Revelation 16:7 NIV / Western society tends to be very democratic in its thinking—sometimes overly so. For example, when public opinion polls show a certain position, people tend to assume that position is absolute truth.

But a preponderance of people believing something doesn't always make it true. The crowd can be wrong, and sometimes in overwhelming numbers. God, however, doesn't hold "opinions"—He bases His judgments on a perfect knowledge of what is right and just. The apostle Paul stated it well when he wrote, "Let God be true, and every human being a liar" (Romans 3:4 NIV).

No man, no matter how well educated, possesses perfect knowledge of all things. But God's judgments are 100 percent true and just, 100 percent of the time.

EVENING: DISQUALIFYING YOURSELF / *Then the Lord said to him, "Who has made man's mouth? . . . Is it not I, the Lord? Now therefore go, and I will be with your mouth and teach you what you shall speak."* Exodus 4:11–12 ESV / Moses had plenty of persuasive reasons to disqualify himself from the work God set before him. Having spent a large portion of his life isolated as a shepherd, he didn't feel qualified to speak to the ruler of Egypt. The Lord, however, promised to guide Moses.

Do you have ready-made excuses when God calls you to help others? There's no doubt that you may feel unqualified. Yet if God has truly called you to serve, you have everything you need to obey.

God wants you to depend on His Holy Spirit working in your life, not any talent or ability of your own.

MORNING: SUFFERING SERVANT / *He poured out his life unto death, and was numbered with the transgressors. For he bore the sin of many, and made intercession for the transgressors.* Isaiah 53:12 NIV / This morning's passage portrays Jesus as an attorney, pleading our case before God, the righteous Judge.

What do you see when you hear the word *transgressors*? Criminals? Prostitutes? Drug addicts? Maybe, but we should also think of ourselves in this context.

As the sinless Son of God, Jesus could have condemned us when we were lost in our sins. But, like a lawyer passionately pleading before a judge on our behalf, Jesus continues to make intercession before God. He knows we're guilty, yet He fights for us every single day. Why? Because He's already taken our death sentence.

Now we can live in freedom every single day.

EVENING: SPEAKING JOYFULLY / *He put a new song in my mouth, a hymn of praise to our God.* Psalm 40:3 NIV / Christians have more reason than anyone to be joyful—after all, Jesus has promised us abundant life on earth and an eternity in paradise.

Sadly, too many Christian men play the part of Gloomy Gus. You might even be thinking of one now. Is that guy fun to be around? Are you?

The Bible is filled with examples of men who, instead of groaning about their terrible situations focused on what God was accomplishing through them. The result? The joy of the Lord so filled them that everyone they encountered could see it.

Never forget that no matter what life throws your way, you can be joyful in the Lord—so much so that it overflows in every word you speak.

MORNING: MIRRORS / *Anyone who listens to the word but does not do what it says is like someone who looks at his face in a mirror and. . .goes away and immediately forgets what he looks like.* James 1:23–24 NIV / Imagine this: you're at the office, in front of the restroom mirror, preparing to give an important presentation to your boss.

While washing your hands, you notice that your fly is down, your shirt is buttoned incorrectly, and a glob of toothpaste has dried on your chin. You chuckle and walk straight into the meeting.

That's a poor use of a mirror.

The Word of God is a spiritual mirror exposing the areas of our lives that need attention. So when we read the Bible and don't change the way we live, something's wrong.

Don't just look in the mirror of God's Word—start doing something about it!

EVENING: GOD'S BOUNDARIES OF BLESSING / *"I am the* Lord *your God, who brought you out of the land of Egypt, out of the house of bondage. You shall have no other gods before Me."* Exodus 20:2–3 NKJV / Today, people often view the Ten Commandments as God's idealistic but impossible demands for the Jewish people of long ago. If only we could see the commandments as God's boundaries of blessing.

Each of God's "big ten" protects you from serious harm and loss. Invest tens of thousands of dollars worshipping false gods? Bad idea. Work long hours seven days a week to get ahead? Another bad idea. Take a neighbor to court on false charges and commit perjury? *Super* bad idea.

After nearly thirty-five hundred years, the Ten Commandments are still relevant. May we never tire of enjoying what God meant for our good.

MORNING: A MIGHTY, AFFECTIONATE GOD / *"The Lord your God is with you, the Mighty Warrior who saves. He will take great delight in you; in his love he will no longer rebuke you, but will rejoice over you with singing."* Zephaniah 3:17 NIV / Young kids have a way of almost deifying their fathers. In their minds, Dad is strong enough to move mountains—at least fix their bicycle chain. And they really hit the jackpot if their he-man daddy also regularly speaks words of love and affection.

Sadly, not all fathers are like the one above. But there is one perfect Father who embodies everything His child could ever need or want. God is infinitely strong and mighty yet tender and affectionate in His love. And when you feel unworthy of that kind of love, let this morning's verse be your source of assurance.

EVENING: LETTING GO OF SHAME / *Remember, Lord, your great mercy and love, for they are from of old. Do not remember the sins of my youth and my rebellious ways.* Psalm 25:6–7 NIV / The psalms are filled with confessions of guilt, but the good news is that shame never has the last word. The authors always returned to God's mercy, patience, and forgiveness as their source of hope. Even the failures of the past didn't disqualify them from God's love.

Perhaps you carry shame over a personal failure that left another person wounded. Even if you see this mistake for what it is, it can take on an oversized role in your identity. Do your failures really define who you are?

God's mercy and forgiveness are so much larger than your shame. When you confess your sins, you can find comfort and freedom in His love.

MORNING: THE FIERY FURNACE / *He said, "Look! I see four men walking around in the fire, unbound and unharmed, and the fourth looks like a son of the gods."* Daniel 3:25 NIV / Daniel and his friends were captives in a foreign land. Their past was gone, their present was difficult, and their future not their own. Loyalty to a pagan king was demanded of them, yet they remained loyal to God.

Nebuchadnezzar didn't believe it when they boasted of God's power to rescue—but when he looked into the fire, he was forced to change his opinion.

If you believe in the saving power of Jesus, you know what it's like to be delivered from an eternity in the fire. Do unbelievers see your life and understand this truth? Can they see your faithfulness to Jesus, who stands beside you in the midst of whatever trials you face?

EVENING: GUARDING YOUR REPUTATION / *A good name is more desirable than great riches; to be esteemed is better than silver or gold.* Proverbs 22:1 NIV / Benjamin Franklin once stated, "It takes many good deeds to build a good reputation, and only one bad one to lose it." Clearly, Franklin understood the value of a good name.

Recent history has seen many highly esteemed men ruin their lives with just one misdeed. And once destroyed, a reputation is exceedingly difficult, sometimes impossible, to reestablish.

You may never make headlines with one big error, but your reputation still matters. News reporters may not be watching, but your family, coworkers, business associates, partners in ministry, and unsaved friends certainly are.

Few things in life are worth guarding more than your personal reputation. So make sure your conduct always reflects who—and whose—you are.

MORNING: DESERTION / *We are not of those who shrink back and are destroyed, but of those who have faith and preserve their souls.* Hebrews 10:39 ESV / During World War II, the US military tried nearly three thousand army personnel for desertion. Of those, forty-nine were convicted and sentenced to death, but only one man—Pvt. Eddie Slovik—was actually executed.

Slovik had been drafted and sent to France, where the fight against the Nazis was hottest. After seeing war up close, Slovik decided that a court-martial was preferable to dying on the battlefield, so he decided to desert.

Though he was repeatedly encouraged to retake his post and avoid punishment, Slovik was committed. He never believed he would be sentenced to death.

In the Christian fight against sin, you are on the front lines. You may know the consequences for deserting are high, but one man—Jesus Christ—has already been executed for them. Would you desert Him now?

EVENING: DON'T BE LIKE THE SADDUCEES / *That same day Jesus was approached by some Sadducees—religious leaders who say there is no resurrection from the dead.* Matthew 22:23 NLT / Talk about a bunch of rich fools. The high priest and his fellow Sadducees acted like Jewish aristocrats. They ruled the temple and ran the Lord right out the door. They denied some of the most basic teachings of scripture—life after death, heaven, hell, angels, demons, miracles—to the point of casting doubt on God Himself. No wonder Jesus harshly rebuked them (Matthew 22:29).

Like the Sadducees, we may be tempted to doubt the supernatural details of God's Word. Yet if God is God, nothing is impossible! Unlike the Sadducees, stand in awe of the Lord, gladly acknowledge His mighty power, and heed His every word.

MORNING: JOYFULLY MERCIFUL / *Who is a God like You, pardoning iniquity and passing over the transgression of the remnant of His heritage? He does not retain His anger forever, because He delights in mercy.* Micah 7:18 NKJV / If you've ever spent time in the company of a perpetually angry man, you know he's no joy to be around. He hangs on to wrongs done against him as if they were his life preserver.

God can get angry too. But unlike the angry man just described, God enjoys letting go of His anger and offering mercy.

That's an important part of God's character to remember when (not if) you mess up and sin against Him. When you approach Him seeking forgiveness, you can trust Him to joyfully show you mercy.

EVENING: UNSHAKABLE—INCOMPARABLE / *The Lord will give strength unto his people; the Lord will bless his people with peace.* Psalm 29:11 KJV / *Unshakable.* If this word could describe anyone, it would be God. He doesn't need to rely on anyone or anything to exist without doubt, fear, and anxiety.

From His place of unshakable glory, God offers His family peace, strength, and blessing. A weak and disturbable god could not do that. He wouldn't be at peace, so he couldn't offer peace. His strength would be in question, so few would attempt to rely on it. His blessings would be meaningless.

If you want to live an unshakable life, you must connect with an unshakable God. You will need to trust in a powerful God who loves you and has a future for you. Only then can you live fearlessly, unmoved by circumstances that challenge your willingness to stand strong.

DAY 110

MORNING: SACRIFICIAL SYSTEM / *"Sacrifice a bull each day as a sin offering to make atonement. Purify the altar by making atonement for it, and anoint it to consecrate it. For seven days make atonement for the altar and consecrate it."* Exodus 29:36–37 NIV / The word *atonement* appears three times in this morning's passage. The dictionary definition for the root word is "to make amends or reparation."

The people of Israel were called to atone for their sins on a daily basis. As they brought their sacrifices to the tabernacle and saw the blood splashed on the altar, the reality of their sins hit home.

Now that Jesus has become the perfect, once-for-all sacrifice for our sins, our responsibility is to turn to Him daily in gratitude, giving our lives in service to Him and proclaiming His hopeful message to others.

EVENING: CAUTION: THINKING AHEAD / *You'll do best by filling your minds and meditating on things true, noble, reputable, authentic, compelling, gracious—the best, not the worst.* Philippians 4:8 MSG / A famous children's song says, "Be careful, little mind, what you think."

Whenever we think about off-limit things for too long, evil always results. When bad ideas gain a foothold, it takes us places we never thought we could go. Apparently, this song for children applies just as much to men.

Allowing bits and pieces of bad ideas to simmer in our mental Crock-Pot creates a stew that leaves us unfocused and confused. And in those vulnerable moments, our greatest adversary, the devil, will try with all his might to tempt us into a life that God has warned us against.

God knows that our toughest battles start in the mind. Consciously tending to our thinking, therefore, can keep our decisions honorable.

DAY 111

MORNING: VITAL CONFLICT / *For the time will come when people will not put up with sound doctrine. Instead, to suit their own desires, they will gather around them a great number of teachers to say what their itching ears want to hear.* 2 Timothy 4:3 NIV / We don't like being told we're wrong. But in our walk with Christ, such conflict is vital to success.

One of the factors that led to the bankruptcy of Lehman Brothers bank, the fourth-largest investment bank in the United States, was its habit of firing employees who voiced dissent.

Likewise, if you surround yourself only with those who tell you just what you want to hear, your relationship with Christ will suffer. If you haven't been offended at church recently, ask yourself if you're listening to sound doctrine.

If not, it's time to get your itchy ears checked and find some teachers who will give you the truth.

EVENING: STOP DREAMING ABOUT EASY STREET / *Many re the afflictions of the righteous, but the LORD delivers him out of them all.* Psalm 34:19 ESV / God and His principles haven't changed over time. Neither have life's difficulties. David's heart-wrenching psalms apply just as well to you.

The great paradox of life is that suffering and humility are necessary steps to God's best in your life. This is a very unpopular and countercultural message, however. We'd much rather enjoy a nice, comfortable lifestyle perpetually free of pain and suffering. But reality rarely complies.

God hardly ever speaks in David's psalms, but His fingerprints are everywhere. They help us see that God is behind the scenes, at work within the narrative of our lives.

In the meantime, stop dreaming about Easy Street.

MORNING: THE PERIL OF GREED / *The greedy stir up conflict, but those who trust in the LORD will prosper.* Proverbs 28:25 NIV / *The greedy stir up conflict.* This statement shouldn't surprise anyone. Think of those men whose "white collar" crimes resulted in billions of dollars in losses to those they defrauded. . .and also landed them in prison.

This morning's verse contrasts two different heart attitudes: greed and trust in God. It's not a stretch, then, to infer from this verse these two attitudes can't dwell within the same heart. If you trust in God, there's no place in your heart for greed.

Do you want to guard your heart against the sin of greed? Then devote yourself to trusting in God to care and provide for you.

EVENING: A FUTURE WITH GOD / *I am trusting you, O LORD, saying, "You are my God!" My future is in your hands.* Psalm 31:14–15 NLT / Being unshakable, immovable, and steadfast comes from trusting in what God says about your future. If you really understand that a future with God exists beyond your life on earth, then it's easier to trust Him with the temporary existence you're living now.

Your future should never stay in your hands. You aren't in a contest to be the most self-reliant. You are in God's hands because He holds you there. He offers protection, comfort, and closeness.

In God's hands, you get to see Him work in your life and in the lives of others. You get to hear others—and yourself—praise Him for bringing about miraculous outcomes.

Go to sleep tonight saying, "I trust You. You are my God. My future is in Your hands."

MORNING: A LAUGHABLE PROMISE / *The Lord appeared to Abraham near the great trees of Mamre while he was sitting at the entrance to his tent in the heat of the day.* Genesis 18:1 NIV / The promise that the Lord made to Abraham in this story is one that made its hearers laugh—first Sarah, Abraham's wife (verses 12–15), and then the billions of people who have since heard this story. *A hundred-year-old man and his ninety-year-old wife having a child? Rubbish!*

But God's promise came true, adding yet another proof of His ability to use ordinary, unqualified people to accomplish His extraordinary tasks. If God can use two senior citizens to move His plan of redemption forward, think of how He can use you today to expand His kingdom!

Think big, pray hard, and move forward.

EVENING: REASON TO REJOICE / *We can rejoice, too, when we run into problems and trials, for we know that they help us develop endurance.* Romans 5:3 NLT / Sometimes, you'll see bad news coming. But more often than not, it'll ambush you, a single shot in the dark: *downsizing, accident, cancer.* Soon, you're wrestling with the *whys* and the *what nexts* beginning to find out what you're made of.

If you've habitually sown to the flesh, a blend of bitterness and hopelessness will gush out, and you'll let God know how He's disappointed you.

But if you've habitually sown to the Spirit, you'll fall to your knees and find God waiting to comfort and strengthen you. Suddenly, this evening's verse will no longer seem like mere holy-sounding advice—you'll see the truth behind it.

God uses trials to produce endurance, building character and producing hope. When hope spills over, you have reason to rejoice: God is with you.

MORNING: GOD'S WILL FOR YOUR LIFE / *Be thankful in all circumstances, for this is God's will for you who belong to Christ Jesus.* 1 Thessalonians 5:18 NLT / "What are you going to be when you grow up?"

It's a common question for small children. But when those children grow up and graduate high school, the question becomes more serious and urgent: "What is God's will for my life?"

The Bible doesn't specifically say which job you should have or what your spouse's name will be. But it may be comforting to know that God does have a perfect plan that your own indecisiveness cannot thwart. If you belong to Christ, it doesn't matter if you're rich or poor, married or single, a street sweeper or a rocket scientist—you are God's child, and that's enough.

Be thankful.

EVENING: THE LAMP SHADE OF NEGATIVITY / *Do all things without grumbling or disputing, that you may be. . .without blemish in the midst of a crooked and twisted generation, among whom you shine as lights in the world.* Philippians 2:14–15 ESV / Robert Sapolsky, professor of neurology and neuroendocrinology at Stanford University's School of Medicine, found that exposure to negativity for more than thirty minutes can lead to increased levels of cortisol, which can harm brain function and increase cell death. So negative people literally hurt your brain.

When believers engage in the kind of grumbling and fighting that is common in the world, people naturally tune out whatever positive message they are trying to convey.

In order to be an effective light in the darkness, you must take off the lampshade of negativity. Don't let God's people become known for squabbling. Aspire to show God to others through love.

MORNING: PUT WHAT GOD GIVES YOU TO GOOD USE / *"To one he gave five bags of gold, to another two bags, and to another one bag, each according to his ability."* Matthew 25:15 NIV / Throughout the wisdom literature of the Old Testament, "gold" refers to the tremendous value of God's words and wisdom, and His commands and instructions.

In this morning's verse, Jesus speaks of three men of differing abilities. Two of the men wisely used the bags of gold entrusted to them. In turn, their master rewarded both men the same way. The third man fearfully hid his bag of gold and had nothing to show; therefore, he faced his master's worst judgment.

God is not impressed when you give your resources back to Him—they're His anyway. Instead, He wants you to use your resources—your heart, soul, time, attention, talents, resources, and wealth—for His glory.

EVENING: HUMBLE BEGINNINGS / *"The Lord took me as I followed the flock, and the Lord said to me, 'Go, prophesy to My people Israel.'"* Amos 7:15 NKJV / Humanly speaking, Amos doesn't look like the kind of man God would send to preach to Israel. He was a simple shepherd when he was called. Yet God used Amos in powerful ways.

God doesn't need the highly educated or the credentialed to accomplish His purposes. (Just look at Moses, Joseph, and most of the apostles!) On the contrary, He uses those who are humble, willing, and courageous enough to say, "I'm here and available, Lord. Use me!"

If you feel unworthy or unprepared, it may just be that God has you right where He wants you. Your part in that equation is to respond, "I'm willing. Use me as You will."

MORNING: SHOUT IT OUT / *Shout for joy in the Lord, O you righteous! Praise befits the upright.* Psalm 33:1 ESV / When was the last time you shouted out of excitement? If you're like most men, your answer probably pertains to sports.

Perhaps you cheered when your team scored and booed when the opponent responded in kind. Maybe you're wearing a team jersey right now, ready at any moment to discuss the latest game. You want people to know and appreciate your team. . .maybe even to become fans themselves.

Of course, you see where this is going.

When you are unwavering in your thoughts about God, you have the freedom to shout for joy. Other people might hear it, and that's good! They need to know Jesus. Who better to share Him than you? What better time than now?

EVENING: JESUS THE CREATOR / *In the beginning was the Word, and the Word was with God, and the Word was God. . . . Through him all things were made; without him nothing was made that has been made. In him was life, and that life was the light of all mankind.* John 1:1, 3–4 NIV / Here, the apostle John mirrors Genesis 1, but adds information: Jesus was the creative force behind everything that we see, taste, touch, hear, and smell—including our very own eyes, tongues, hands, ears and noses. The very Creator of the universe, as part of His plan to redeem the creation that had fallen into sin and rebellion against Him (Genesis 3), literally put on skin so that He could advance His plan to save the human race.

For those of us living in a complex, lightning-fast, and sometimes frustrating world, this truly is good news!

MORNING: PROTECTING THE YOUNG / *"But if you cause one of these little ones who trusts in me to fall into sin, it would be better for you to have a large millstone tied around your neck and be drowned in the depths of the sea."* Matthew 18:6 NLT / Ancient Jewish men feared drowning above all else. So what could possibly be scarier than having a hundred-pound milstone tied around your neck and getting tossed to the bottom of the sea? Jesus, however, warned that such a fate would be preferable than the one that's coming to anyone who deliberately harms a child—physically, psychologically, socially, sexually, or spiritually.

We must make every effort to protect, nurture, and build up the faith of children. By doing so, we build up and protect our own hearts.

It's a dangerous world out there. Be on guard.

EVENING: COMMITMENTS THAT MATTER: GOD / *Now all has been heard; here is the conclusion of the matter: Fear God and keep his commandments, for this is the duty of all mankind.* Ecclesiastes 12:13 NIV / Some commitments matter more than others. If you can't keep a commitment to have coffee with a friend, it's no big deal. But your commitment to your wife or kids? That's a different story.

The most fundamental commitment any Christian man must make is to God. It must be non-negotiable. No matter what challenges, failures, or successes may come, our commitment to God should be the one anchor that holds.

Sadly, plenty of men have given this up. Most likely, they began wavering in a moment of temptation. As they gradually loosened their grip, they brought suffering and left a woeful legacy. Pray today for the strength to maintain your commitment. . .God will be happy to answer.

MORNING: INDEPENDENCE VS. FREEDOM / *So I say, walk by the Spirit, and you will not gratify the desires of the flesh.* Galatians 5:16 NIV / Take a minute and think of all the advertising slogans that appeal to your selfishness. *Have it your way. Just do it. Obey your thirst.* You can probably think of others.

Oswald Chambers once wrote, "Whenever God touches sin it is independence that is touched, and that awakens resentment in the human heart. Independence must be blasted clean out, there must be no such thing left, only freedom, which is very different. Freedom is the ability not to insist on my rights, but to see that God gets His."

When you listen to your natural desires, you trade your freedom for something less than God's goodness. So tune out the ads that appeal to your selfishness, and start listening to the God who knows what is best for you.

EVENING: LEVITICUS: A SHADOW OF THE SAVIOR / *The LORD called Moses and spoke to him from the tent of meeting, saying, "Speak to the people of Israel."* Leviticus 1:1–2 ESV / Unlike the first two books of Moses, Leviticus contains only a handful of narrative accounts. It's primarily a handbook the Israelites used to answer one tough question: "Since the Lord is so holy, what must I do to worship Him properly?"

Throughout the book of Leviticus, we see that sacrifices played a very important role in Old Testament worship, illustrating humanity's need for God's cleansing and forgiveness. Within these rituals lie clear foreshadowing of the saving work of the promised Savior.

Praise God that we don't have to worship God in these shadows anymore—our Savior has come, and He's taken our sins once and for all!

MORNING: PREPARED FOR A PURPOSE / *In the hearts of all that are wise hearted I have put wisdom.* Exodus 31:6 KJV / After God told Moses what needed to be done to construct and maintain His tabernacle, He chose men to manage the artistic design, metalwork, and other details.

This morning's verse indicates that God made these men wise. It also suggests that before these men knew they were chosen, God had given them wisdom for the work they would do.

It's reasonable to conclude that God sometimes uses the lessons you've learned to help you do what He needs you to do—but He can also call you first and equip you on the job. God isn't limited in the ways He works.

Today, let God unfold your purpose. Then add it to your story and share it with others.

EVENING: DISCIPLINE FROM A LOVING FATHER / *"As many as I love, I rebuke and chasten. Therefore be zealous and repent."* Revelation 3:19 NKJV / A lot of things go into being a good father, and one of them is discipline. The Bible goes so far as to say that a father who doesn't correct his children doesn't actually love them as he should (Proverbs 13:24).

God is more than a good Father; He's a *perfect* Father. He's perfect in His holiness and love, and that's why He disciplines every man He calls His son.

When God's hand of discipline is upon you—and it can be unpleasant when it happens—you can be grateful, for it reminds you to trust in God and His intense love for you. It also encourages you to zealously examine your attitudes and actions to make sure they're pleasing to Him.

MORNING: LOVING CHILDREN LIKE JESUS / *From infancy you have known the Holy Scriptures, which are able to make you wise for salvation through faith in Christ Jesus.* 2 Timothy 3:15 NIV / During His three and a half years of ministry, Jesus talked with children, something only parents and grandparents usually did in that culture. He also commended the faith of little children, who in that culture were sometimes considered unable to embrace religious faith. Even more, Jesus blessed children and fed them. And He used a little boy's sack lunch to feed the multitudes.

Jesus healed boys and girls who were demon possessed, cured those who were sick and dying, and even resurrected a twelve-year-old girl and an older boy from death.

In His preaching and teaching, Jesus valued children as a strategic, essential part of His kingdom in heaven and on earth.

Are there any children in your life who could use your positive influence?

EVENING: THE BIGGER PICTURE / *Do you despise the riches of His goodness, forbearance, and longsuffering, not knowing that the goodness of God leads you to repentance*? Romans 2:4 NKJV / Why is patience a virtue? Sometimes, people just need to be corrected—like your kids when they're headed for the wall socket with a fork. Sitting back and being "patient" isn't going to help anyone.

In such situations, quick action is needed. But here's the rub: how will you do it?

Think of all the times Jesus' disciples—Peter, James, and John especially—messed up. While Jesus did correct His followers' failures, He was gentle, courteous, and polite. He saw a bigger picture—their overarching needs rather than their momentary misdeeds. Patience, then, seems to be made up of other virtues—love, mercy, and humility among them.

Consider God's patience when others test yours.

MORNING: ACT LIKE MEN / *Be watchful, stand firm in the faith, act like men, be strong. Let all that you do be done in love.* 1 Corinthians 16:13–14 ESV / The Greek word *andrizomai* is used only once in the New Testament. In 1 Corinthians 16:13, it is translated as the imperative statement, "Act like men."

The apostle Paul wasn't encouraging the believers of Corinth to act macho, cheer on their favorite sports team, or belch loudly. Rather, the word *andrizomai* is something a commanding officer might say to his soldiers: *Be courageous!*

In this life, we must watch out for invisible enemies, stand firm in our Savior's grace, and remain strong against temptations. We must act like men, courageously loving others when it feels more natural to fight.

Today, arm yourself with the Savior's love and show the world what it really means to act like a man.

***

EVENING: LOVING THE UNLOVABLE / *"If You are willing, You can make me clean."* Mark 1:40 NKJV / In ancient Israel, you could be wealthy and well married with a house full of children and yet. . .if you became leprous, you instantly and permanently lost it all. Eventually, you became a disfigured and hideous exile, the walking dead.

Matthew, Mark, and Luke, however, all record the story of a leprous man who ran up to Jesus, fell on his face, and humbly yet desperately begged Jesus to heal him. The disciples cringed, but Jesus wasn't afraid of lepers.

Jesus touched the man, healing his disease. Then He sent the man ahead to testify to the priests and Levites: "Look, I've been healed. I can enter the temple again and offer my sacrifices with joy and singing. I'm with my family again!"

Never doubt God's love for the unlovable.

MORNING: REAL RICHES / *Better is the poor who walks in his integrity than one perverse in his ways, though he be rich.* Proverbs 28:6 NKJV / Far too often in our culture, the measure of a man is stated in terms of what he earns or what he possesses. Those with the biggest bank accounts or the best "toys" are the ones many see as the most admirable.

Your Father in heaven, however, applies no such measure to men. He sees men's hearts and is concerned above all that your thoughts and behavior reflect the standards He's given in His written Word.

Whether you're rich or poor by worldly standards, God calls you to make your thoughts and actions align with your verbal profession of faith. The man who does that, whether he's filthy rich or dirt poor, is wealthy indeed.

EVENING: STRUGGLE VS. VICTORY / *Let me hear you say, "I will give you victory!"* Psalm 35:3 NLT / David was being pursued by people who didn't have his best interests in mind. He was certain he would be destroyed if he didn't receive help. He wanted to be unshakable, but he felt shaken and alone.

You've been there, right?

Even the shaken, however, can be transformed when they understand that little things mean big things in the hands of a good God. It's okay to pray, "God, I'm asking You to declare victory in my struggle." God fully understands the struggles you're going through, and He has a specific way to deal with each one of them, to eliminate your unsettled feelings.

Worry will always leave you shaken, and anxiety will leave you with unanswered questions. But being unshakable means trusting God's ability to answer in a way that satisfies your deepest longings.

MORNING: WANTING GOD'S BEST FOR YOU / *All the best from our God and Christ be yours!* 2 Timothy 1:2 MSG / What does it mean to want and receive God's best for you? First, it means discarding inadequate, ignoble thoughts of God. David Needham writes, "I am convinced that the answers to every problem and issue of life. . .are resolved through a correct understanding of God."

Second, it means shedding your intense desire for temporal pursuits. George MacDonald observed, "God finds it hard to give, because He would give the best, and man will not take it."

Third, it means desiring His will over your own. C. S. Lewis commented, "There are two kinds of people: those who say to God, 'Thy will be done,' and those to whom God says, 'All right, then, have it your way.'"

What are you pursing today? Is it God's best?

EVENING: PLUG INTO THE POWER / *When I am afraid, I put my trust in you.* Psalm 56:3 NIV / The big choices you make—the woman you marry, the job you take, the place you live—should be guided by your trust in and understanding of God. The main mark of a son of God, however, is his battle against sin (Romans 8:13).

Fear is a red flag that alerts you to oncoming danger. But if your sin doesn't scare you as much as those big decisions you face, you're poised on a precipice.

When you confess your sins to God, however, you're plugging into hopeful expectation. The results will be initially painful but ultimately empowering.

This ruthless approach to being more like Jesus is what conquers fear and confirms you as His son.

MORNING: BE HOLY IN ALL YOU DO / *"You are to be holy to me because I, the LORD, am holy."* Leviticus 20:26 NIV / Sometimes, the Bible says something so important that it's repeated. This morning's verse, for instance, is the fifth time the Lord makes this statement in ten chapters of Leviticus (see also 11:44, 11:45, 19:2, and 20:7).

Some may be tempted to think, *Holiness is impossible. Besides, the Lord understands my struggles.* Really? Listen to the apostle Peter's emphatic words: "Just as he who called you is holy, so be holy in all you do. . . . Live out your time as foreigners here in reverent fear" (1 Peter 1:15, 17 NIV).

Holiness is a definite hallmark of a Christian. It doesn't mean you'll never sin, but it does mean you keep short accounts with God, focusing on heaven and forsaking your old life.

It means you seek God's "Well done!"

EVENING: REDEEMING THE PAST / *"So I will restore to you the years that the swarming locust has eaten, the crawling locust, the consuming locust, and the chewing locust."* Joel 2:25 NKJV / Regret is a terrible feeling. It causes a man to look at his mistakes and think, *If I could only go back in time. I'd make much better decisions.*

Nearly every man has done things he's not proud of—things he knows God would not approve of if he did them in the present. But the past is just that—the past. There's nothing you can do to change it. But when you bring your past to the Lord, He has a way of redeeming even your worst mistakes and using them to build something good.

MORNING: UNNERVED AND HUMBLED / *[Jesus] came to the disciples and found them sleeping. And he said to Peter, "So, could you not watch with me one hour? Watch and pray that you may not enter into temptation. The spirit indeed is willing, but the flesh is weak."* Matthew 26:40–41 ESV / Every man has endured some personal shaking that left him unnerved, embarrassed, and humbled.

It's good to know, however, that such experiences are mirrored in the Bible. For every story of a man being bold, there's a beginning defined by timidity. For every instance of unwavering determination, there's a period of indecision.

There's no condemnation here, just an encouraging voice inviting you to leave indecision behind and make the decision to follow.

The disciples weren't always unshaken. They just learned to follow Jesus, who stands firm forever.

EVENING: REMEMBERING WHY WE NEED GOD / *It cost God plenty to get you out of that dead-end, empty-headed life you grew up in. He paid with Christ's sacred blood.* 1 Peter 1:18–19 MSG / Scores of times the Bible speaks of an empty life. Christians throughout the centuries have echoed its words.

In *Confessions*, Saint Augustine wrote: "Our hearts are restless until they rest in You." And although Blaise Pascal didn't exactly coin the phrase "God-shaped vacuum," he talked extensively of the idea.

C. S. Lewis wrote a great deal about this concept as well. In *Mere Christianity*, he said, "If I find in myself a desire for something which nothing in this world can satisfy, the most probable explanation is that I was made for another world."

What is the longing of your heart? Ask God to fill it—with Himself—so that you can enjoy life abundantly (John 10:10).

DAY 126

MORNING: STRONG AND SILENT / *Don't make rash promises, and don't be hasty in bringing matters before God. After all, God is in heaven, and you are here on earth. So let your words be few.* Ecclesiastes 5:2 NLT / Sometimes, being a man of few words is the best route to take.

When you're trying to resolve difficult problems, remember that you're a limited mortal. It's impossible for you to know *all* the relevant bits of information.

God, on the other hand, "inhabits eternity" and dwells "in the high and holy place" (Isaiah 57:15 NKJV). He can see all the puzzle pieces from His lofty vantage point. So don't waste time trying to persuade Him to go with your plan—it might be doomed from the start.

When confusing events swirl around you, don't be hasty in your words or actions; always make sure God is in them first.

EVENING: CARRY ON / *Love bears all things, believes all things, hopes all things, endures all things.* 1 Corinthians 13:7 ESV / Kevan Chandler has good friends and a love of adventure. So when someone offered him the opportunity to backpack across Europe, he was all in. But Kevan didn't carry a backpack. . .he rode in it.

Chandler has spinal muscular atrophy and would normally be confined to a wheelchair—hardly a device fit for long-distance travel. Their adventure, documented in the book *We Carry Kevan*, has not only redefined accessible travel but shined a spotlight on the strength of friendship in the face of adversity.

This love is the kind that *literally* bears all things. Our love for one another should be no less. God calls His people to work toward greater unity, even if it means carrying one another along.

DAY 127

MORNING: RELATING TO OTHERS / *Jesus saw the huge crowd as he stepped from the boat, and he had compassion on them because they were like sheep without a shepherd. So he began teaching them many things.* Mark 6:34 NLT / Jesus knew how draining it could be to meet the spiritual and physical needs of others, but even when He had reached His human limits, He still showed compassion.

Jesus didn't respond to people based on how exhausted He felt. Rather, His compassion was rooted in His ability to identify with their inner struggles.

Do you ever wonder what motivates certain people? Perhaps that angry man you met yesterday is driven by a deep wound from the past. Maybe that guy who struggles to trust anyone was once betrayed by his closest friend.

Ministry can flow out of compassion and the act of relating to the stories of others.

EVENING: LIVING THE CHRISTIAN LIFE / *I have no greater joy than to hear that my children are walking in the truth.* 3 John 4 NIV / In John's deeply personal letter to a man named Gaius, a member of an unnamed church John apparently oversaw, John reveals his greatest joy: hearing that the believers in this church were "walking in the truth."

The phrase speaks of believers who live and think according to the ways that God has revealed to them in the Bible. It means, as the apostle Paul wrote, refusing to "conform to the pattern of this world, but [being] transformed by the renewing of your mind" (Romans 12:2 NIV).

Do you trust God enough to walk daily with Him, in His ways—to allow Him to continually transform you into the man He intends you to be?

DAY 128

MORNING: NO MATCH FOR MY GOD / *For in You, O Lord, do I hope; You will answer, O Lord my God.* Psalm 38:15 AMPC / When you read Psalm 38, verse 15 might seem out of place. David admitted to being foolish and living with wounds. He sinned and struggled with burdens. Friends left him; enemies found him. People were happy to see him flounder. Opposition was his nemesis.

Then a verse of unshakable faith shows up. David declared that God, his Lord, would answer his cry for help. This damaged man knew where to turn. God would make this man king.

This isn't a rags-to-riches story. It's the story of a man who knew his struggles were temporary. Relief would come, and he trusted the God who answers.

Today, join David in saying to your troubles, "You're no match for my God."

EVENING: ENLARGING YOUR VIEW OF GOD / *The LORD is the everlasting God, the Creator of all the earth. He never grows weak or weary. No one can measure the depths of his understanding. He gives power to the weak and strength to the powerless.* Isaiah 40:28–29 NLT / Day by day, your view of God grows either bigger or weaker.

Pastor and author A. W. Tozer wisely points out, "Left to ourselves we tend immediately to reduce God to manageable terms. We want to get Him where we can use Him, or at least know where He is when we need Him. We want a God we can in some measure control."

So who's in control in your life? You? The God in your mind? Or God as He really is?

Over the next few days, meditate on this evening's passage. By doing so, you can keep enlarging your view of God.

DAY 129

MORNING: THE SHIELD OF FAITH / *In addition to all, taking up the shield of faith with which you will be able to extinguish all the flaming arrows of the evil one*. Ephesians 6:16 NASB / In Bible times, archers would cover their arrowheads in pitch and set them aflame to start fires in the opposition's camp. The best thing the other army could do was hold up their shields to protect themselves from the deadly hail. If the arrows thudded into these shields, they went out harmlessly.

The shield of faith is a very important part of your spiritual battle gear. The devil's lies of discouragement and condemnation are flaming arrows that can only be thwarted by faith in God's Word.

Don't become a casualty. Keep your shield of faith in God's love and mercy up so that you can "extinguish all the flaming arrows of the evil one."

EVENING: STRONG TO THE END / *Jesus. . .will keep you strong to the end so that you will be free from all blame on the day when our Lord Jesus Christ returns*. 1 Corinthians 1:7–8 NLT / According to legend, Milo of Croton—a strong Greek man who lived in the sixth century BC—once carried a four-year-old bull around the arena then butchered and ate it. . .all in the same day.

But physical strength, as impressive as it may be, isn't the most important thing in a Christian man's life. In his first letter to the Corinthians, Paul speaks of a strength we can't supply on our own—only God's grace is strong enough to overcome our sin.

By ourselves, we are as powerless as the bull Milo of Croton carried. Thank God that Jesus has worked out our salvation for us.

MORNING: WHERE DO YOU TURN FOR HELP? / *God is our refuge and strength, an ever-present help in trouble. Therefore we will not fear, though the earth give way and the mountains fall into the heart of the sea.* Psalm 46:1–2 NIV / Is there anything that you fear today? The writer of the Psalms provides a picture of a terrifying global cataclysm, yet he reminds us that God remains an ever-present help.

Do you react to troubling situations with fear? Don't worry—that's natural. What matters today is *where* you turn in response. Do you look for comfort, strength, or protection in the many distractions, pleasures, or material items around you? Or do you resolve to trust in the strength of God?

When every other source of protection dissipates, crumbles, or slips away, only God remains.

EVENING: WISDOM FROM AGRICULTURE / *Sow for yourselves righteousness; reap in mercy; break up your fallow ground, for it is time to seek the LORD, till He comes and rains righteousness on you.* Hosea 10:12 NKJV / Hosea's audience would have been familiar with agricultural practices; therefore, his metaphor about how they should prepare themselves to approach God would have resonated deeply.

Today, the average man doesn't know much about agriculture. But Hosea's message is still important. There's not a man of God alive who doesn't have some area of his life in Christ that needs growth. The good news is that God has promised to make that growth happen if you simply prepare your heart to receive what He has for you.

Right now, seek Him in prayer and Bible reading until He shows you what area He wants to grow in you.

MORNING: THAT GUY / *. . .and Judas Iscariot, who betrayed him.* Mark 3:19 NIV / This passage of Mark includes a list of names of men who followed Jesus. At the very end of that list? "Judas Iscariot, who betrayed him."

Judas was *that guy*—the one who did something he would be remembered for, but not in a good way. This disciple not only abandoned Jesus—he betrayed Him. He pretended to follow and then walked away. He encountered love, but he didn't think it was enough.

Judas' story makes it clear that some people will struggle with certainty. They can encounter God the Rock yet trust only their own conclusions, leaving them shaken, uncertain, and weak.

Judas did not endure, persevere, or hold on. He had the proof of three years with Jesus, but that didn't lead him to real, abundant, forever life. Don't be *that* guy.

EVENING: GOD IS GREATER THAN WE CAN IMAGINE / *Oh, how great are God's riches and wisdom and knowledge! How impossible it is for us to understand his decisions and his ways!* Romans 11:33 NLT / What does it mean that God is the Creator and sustainer of the whole universe? It means that He's infinitely bigger than human brains and minds can comprehend.

Of all the truths about God, here's the foundational one: you don't fully know what He's like. The thesis of any discussion about proper theology must be that He is clothed in majesty and mystery.

Walter A. Henrichsen once said, "If you have a big God, you have small problems. If you have a small God, you have big problems."

So no matter how big your struggles are, the question isn't "How big are my problems?" Rather, it's "How big is my God?"

MORNING: LIVING LIKE JESUS / *Those who say they live in God should live their lives as Jesus did.* 1 John 2:6 NLT / What does it mean to "live in God"? The Bible tells us that God sent the Spirit of Christ to live in our hearts (Galatians 4:6), but Jesus also said, "Remain in me, and I will remain in you" (John 15:4 NLT). His Spirit dwells in our hearts, but we in turn must seek to walk so close to Him that we're dwelling in His presence, bathed by His Spirit. This is truly living in God.

May this be true of you. When you read the Bible's commands to serve others, have patience, and love your enemies, may you strive to do exactly that.

Being a true follower of Jesus Christ isn't always easy, but it's what God calls you to do.

EVENING: ENDURANCE THROUGH TRANSFORMATION / *Do not be conformed to this world, but be transformed by the renewal of your mind, that by testing you may discern what is the will of God, what is good and acceptable and perfect.* Romans 12:2 ESV / When a potter makes a jar, the clay must be fire-hardened before it becomes waterproof and useful as a vessel.

In his letter to the Romans, the apostle Paul warns his readers that the world will try to change our identities to fit its mold. If we want to be useful vessels for God, we need to be more than conformed—we must be fundamentally changed by the fire of God's influence. Though this process will be painful, it will make us useful for God's plans.

If you feel like you are in the fire today, thank God for transforming you and making you more suitable for His purposes.

MORNING: TRANSFORMED TO LEAD BY SERVING / *"Whoever wants to be first among you must be the slave of everyone else. For even the Son of Man came not to be served but to serve."* Mark 10:44–45 NLT / What does a great leader look like? The person who draws the attention of others when he walks in the room? The athlete who guides a team to a championship? The CEO who confidently takes charge of a meeting?

In Jesus' eyes, the greatest leader is the one who understands service. Those who sacrifice themselves for others are the ones who understand Jesus' message best.

If you don't aspire to be a leader, that doesn't leave you off the hook—self-sacrifice and service are fundamental aspects of the Christian life.

Today, how might you make sacrifices for others and yield your desires to God?

EVENING: CONFIDENT REQUESTS / *If we ask anything according to his will, he hears us. And if we know that he hears us—whatever we ask—we know that we have what we asked of him.* 1 John 5:14–15 NIV / Jesus once told His followers, "You may ask me for anything in my name, and I will do it" (John 14:14 NIV).

What an amazing promise! However, we mustn't misunderstand: God isn't a heavenly genie, just waiting on people and granting them whatever they wish for. No, you can expect God to do something for you only if that something is in line with His will.

When you know your request is God's will for you, you can approach Him and ask Him for it with confidence, knowing He wants to do it for you.

And how can you know what His will is? By asking Him in prayer, and by searching His written Word.

MORNING: GOD IS NOT INDIFFERENT / *Do you suppose, O man— you who judge those who practice such things and yet do them yourself—that you will escape the judgment of God?* Romans 2:3 ESV / Does God care if you obey His commands? Are there consequences for resisting God's wisdom in your decisions?

The Psalms remind us how unfair life looks sometimes: the evil and disobedient seem to succeed while the righteous struggle, never being rewarded for their obedience.

But Paul offers another perspective: God's patience delays judgment. He's not indifferent to sin; rather, He's offering those living in rebellion a chance to reconsider their ways, repent of their sins, and escape God's wrath.

God will judge each person justly according to his deeds, even those who appear righteous but lead a secret life of rebellion. There may still be some time to delay. . .but not forever.

EVENING: ENCOURAGEMENT FROM ABOVE / *"Yet now be strong, Zerubbabel,'" says the Lord; "'and be strong, Joshua, son of Jehozadak, the high priest; and be strong, all you people of the land,'" says the Lord, "'and work; for I am with you.'"* Haggai 2:4 NKJV / Nearly every father has been faced with a situation in which his son or daughter called to him for help to complete some task. A wise dad knows when to complete the task for his child and when to simply offer words of encouragement.

Similarly, God has arranged His affairs here on earth such that He uses people to accomplish the work He wants done. But when He sends people out, He speaks words of encouragement and promises to be with them.

He'll do the very same for you today.

MORNING: STANDING IN THE WAY / *Not that we are sufficient of ourselves to think of anything as being from ourselves, but our sufficiency is from God.* 2 Corinthians 3:5 NKJV / The problem with self-sufficiency is *self*. This one little word makes the assumption that each individual can find a sense of completeness by simply following his own abilities, decision-making, and strengths.

God made relationship—which is always improved when someone meets the other party's need—a priority for mankind. That's why you'll only be sufficient when you make room for God to begin His good work in you. True wholeness can only be achieved when you accept friendship with the God who knows where you're going and how to get you there.

When you're tired of trying to do life alone only to discover failure, it's time to remove *self* from sufficiency. Wholeness is available. Don't stand in the way.

EVENING: NOTHING TO PROVE / *Don't try to impress others. Be humble, thinking of others as better than yourselves.* Philippians 2:3 NLT / When we feel threatened by others in any way, our natural reaction is to puff ourselves up to appear bigger than them.

It's one thing to strike a defensive posture when physically threatened. It's usually not necessary, however, in a social setting. If you're confident about your identity in Christ, you won't let others' words and actions get to you.

When you have the Spirit of Christ in you, you don't need to be concerned for your self-esteem, but can focus on the needs of others. . . including show-offs.

This is the attitude Jesus was talking about when He said, "Whoever desires to become great among you, let him be your servant" (Matthew 20:26 NKJV).

MORNING: HONEST SELF-APPRAISAL / *If we say that we have no sin, we deceive ourselves, and the truth is not in us. If we confess our sins, He is faithful and just to forgive us our sins and to cleanse us from all unrighteousness.* 1 John 1:8–9 NKJV / There have been numerous movements within Christianity teaching that believers can attain sinless perfection here on earth. The apostle John, the author of this morning's verse, would have to disagree.

But this verse concludes with an amazing promise: If you confess your sin, God will forgive you. This calls for some serious and honest self-appraisal. That's why King David prayed, "Search me, God, and know my heart. . . . See if there is any offensive way in me" (Psalm 139:23–24 NIV).

All sin is a huge deal to God. But His willingness to forgive is even bigger!

EVENING: MOVING AT GOD'S SPEED / *At the command of the Lord the people of Israel set out, and at the command of the Lord they camped.* Numbers 9:18 ESV / Israel recognized that if they ever wanted to venture into the promised land, they had to entrust themselves to God's direction for their lives.

Is it ever hard for you to wait on God's timing? Have you ever felt like rushing ahead without His guidance, provision, or protection? It can be humbling to admit that you don't know what's best for yourself. However, as the story of Israel shows, moving forward without God's transforming presence in your life may result in difficult days ahead.

Perhaps waiting for the Lord looks like seeking the counsel of someone at church or relinquishing your desires for a particular outcome. The delay may be agonizing, but God's presence is worth waiting for.

DAY 137

MORNING: REPENTANCE ISN'T CONVENIENT / *As he reasoned with them about righteousness and self-control and the coming day of judgment, Felix became frightened. "Go away for now," he replied. "When it is more convenient, I'll call for you again."* Acts 24:25 NLT / As Felix, the Roman governor of Judea, listened to Paul, he wrestled with the appeal of the gospel message while also realizing how inconvenient it could become for his career.

But waiting until a convenient time to make a spiritual change is really just another way of saying no. There will never be a convenient time to follow Jesus. He will always disrupt your plans, alter your goals, and cause you to change your values. It won't get any easier to make that first step.

Yet by God's grace, you have the choice today to turn away from your sin, regret, and shame. God's inconvenient mercy is offering you restoration today.

EVENING: THE BIG PICTURE / *God reigns over the nations; God sits upon His holy throne.* Psalm 47:8 AMPC / Warehouse workers for nationwide retail chains don't often think about their company's CEO. They have more immediate concerns—getting their jobs done, trying not to get sick, and making sure they get home on time to take care of their kids. They're caught up in smaller-picture matters.

God's people can be the same way. You might know God rules over everything, but you aren't as concerned with that as you are with keeping your job, feeding your family, and paying your bills. The tendency is to treat God like an immediate supervisor rather than the owner of the whole company.

Don't get lost in your daily grind. Be sure to involve God in *every* aspect of life.

MORNING: GIVING IT TO GOD / *Be of good courage, and let us behave ourselves valiantly for our people, and for the cities of our God: and let the* Lord *do that which is good in his sight.* 1 Chronicles 19:13 KJV / King David sent servants carrying condolences to the king of Ammon, after the death of Hanun's father. Hanun foolishly insulted the servants. Then, assuming that David would be furious, the Ammonites prepared for war. David had no choice but to defend himself.

Have you ever been treated unfairly? Maybe you showed kindness toward someone, only for that person to publicly humiliate you. In such situations, how should you respond?

Joab, David's army commander, offered a valuable answer: "Be of good courage. . .and let the Lord do that which is good in his sight." Joab did his duty, but handed the battle over to God. Trusting in His ultimate resolution is the best thing we can do too.

EVENING: GETTING GOOD NUTRITION / *Bless the* Lord, *O my soul, and forget not all His benefits. . . . Who satisfies your mouth with good things, so that your youth is renewed like the eagle's.* Psalm 103:2, 5 NKJV / Most men know that junk food is harmful. We often read snatches about good nutrition in the media or meet others who preach the values of eating healthy. Yet we often ignore the warnings, assuring ourselves that we will be exempt from blocked arteries and other diseases.

The spiritual life is similar. Scripture says, "Why do you spend money for what is not bread, and your wages for what does not satisfy? Listen carefully to Me, and eat what is good" (Isaiah 55:2 NKJV).

Here's the good news: you're never too far gone to start improving your spiritual diet. When you do, your youth will be renewed like the eagle's.

MORNING: WHEN AN ENEMY FALLS / *Do not gloat when your enemy falls; when they stumble, do not let your heart rejoice, or the Lord will see and disapprove and turn his wrath away from them.* Proverbs 24:17–18 NIV / Have you ever felt at least a small twinge of satisfaction when someone—say a competitor in business or someone who hasn't dealt with you in the way you felt you deserved—fell on difficult times? There's a German word for this feeling: *schadenfreude.*

God, however, doesn't approve of this attitude.

Jesus instructed His followers to pray for their enemies and adversaries, not to rejoice at their downfall (Matthew 5:44). By walking in obedience to this command, you proclaim, "God is bigger than any conflict I have with another person, and I'm going to trust God enough to respond in a way that pleases Him."

EVENING: COULD YOU EVER FAIL? / *"No!" Peter declared emphatically. "Even if I have to die with you, I will never deny you!" And all the others vowed the same.* Mark 14:31 NLT / Peter's profession of faith in this evening's verse didn't guarantee faithfulness once trying circumstances befell him. It's hard to see Peter's denial unfold in the pages of scripture. It may be even more troubling to imagine ourselves making a similar denial.

But we've all denied Jesus in some way or another. Maybe we jumped into our day without any awareness of Him or made decisions that run counter to the values He taught. Denying Jesus doesn't always mean saying, "I don't know You."

But just as Jesus loved and chose Peter, knowing full well that Peter would deny Him, our Lord welcomes us back with open arms and the gift of the Holy Spirit.

MORNING: REPENTANCE BRINGS "MAGICAL" CHANGE / *Many who became believers. . .brought their incantation books and burned them at a public bonfire. The value of the books was several million dollars.* Acts 19:18–19 NLT / The Ephesian people's collection of magic books wasn't in the fantasy section of their library. These books contained spells to gain power, control, wealth, and even favor with false deities. Turning to God in repentance meant a clean break from these practices.

Today may be a good time to consider what *you* rely on. Is it a position, a possession, or a person? Anything you rely on rather than God may be an obstacle that needs to be confessed before Him.

Much like the people of Ephesus, you may want to make a public confession—after all, you're not alone in your struggle, and confessions made with others are more likely to endure.

EVENING: SET APART / *"All the days of his vow of separation, no razor shall touch his head."* Numbers 6:5 ESV / A Nazirite was someone who consecrated himself to the Lord to be used for a special purpose. He couldn't cut his hair, eat any products made from grapes, or touch dead bodies. For Nazirites, long hair was a public display of their dedication to God.

In a similar way, Jesus has reserved you as a believer for a special purpose.

First Peter 1:14–15 (ESV) says, "As obedient children, do not be conformed to the passions of your former ignorance, but as he who called you is holy, you also be holy in all your conduct."

Regardless of your hair length, God is calling you to be holy so that others will see the difference and praise Him for His works.

MORNING: WORKING WITH ALL YOUR HEART / *Whatever you do, work at it with all your heart, as working for the Lord, not for human masters*. Colossians 3:23 NIV / How strange that the all-powerful, omniscient Creator of heaven and earth allows humans to do His will.

The noble man trusts God to work in and through him. He doesn't waste his time longing for an exciting, pleasurable life without God's calling and purpose. A noble man is God-filled, purpose-driven, and busy. His hours and minutes are measured and meaningful.

As Max Lucado wisely observes, "Being busy is not a sin. . . . But being busy in an endless pursuit of things that leave us empty and hollow and broken inside—that cannot be pleasing to God."

Examine the life you've lived over the last month. To what degree have you been a noble man?

EVENING: AN ETERNAL SAFE SPACE / *Only Noah and those who were with him in the ark remained alive. And the waters prevailed on the earth one hundred and fifty days*. Genesis 7:23–24 NKJV / Floodwaters covered every valley and peak in the world. The entire planet was silent, except for a small vestige of human and animal life that floated in an ark.

The ark was designed to protect a remnant from death. It represented hope—a future with family and with the God who rescues.

Today, Jesus is your ark of protection. Go to Him for rescue. But don't be surprised when hardships come. Those brief trials can never compare with the future He's prepared for you.

Just like Noah, you're faced with a choice. Will you cave to the pressure of people who don't understand, or will you trust the rescuer who invites you to an eternal safe space?

MORNING: YOU CAN TRUST GOD'S WORD / *No prophecy of Scripture is of any private interpretation, for prophecy never came by the will of man, but holy men of God spoke as they were moved by the Holy Spirit.* 2 Peter 1:20–21 NKJV / Trying to live a victorious life of faith without reading your Bible is like trying to put together a computer without an instruction manual. Neither will go well.

Every word of the Bible is straight from the mouth of God, who used men as His fountain pens to record what He has to say to every believer who would ever live. The Bible is an amazing book that God went to amazing lengths to give to His people. You can trust it completely, knowing that it came straight from the heart and mind of God.

What a great instruction manual!

EVENING: JESUS IS AHEAD OF YOU / *"Now go and tell his disciples, including Peter, that Jesus is going ahead of you to Galilee."* Mark 16:7 NLT / Although the women were terrified by the sight of an angel at the tomb, they received a message of good news and comfort: Jesus was alive and would be going ahead of them.

For the challenging moments of your life, you may grow fearful and uncertain about the next step. Perhaps you even know what you should do, but following through leaves you weak in the knees.

Imagine for a moment that Jesus is walking in the middle of a road that stretches before you. If you can focus on Him, all the other details of your journey will fall into place. You will find peace and security as you walk in His footsteps.

MORNING: WHAT IF GOD SURPRISES YOU? / *Peter said, "By no means, Lord; for I have never eaten anything that is common or unclean." And the voice came to him again a second time, "What God has made clean, do not call common."* Acts 10:14–15 ESV / When God told him in a dream that Jews and Gentiles were equally important to God, Peter had to quickly rethink his understanding of scripture. Despite not fully understanding God's message, Peter still followed God's command.

Faith doesn't assure us that everything will make sense right away. God may lead you in ways that seem confusing or even contradictory. You may not know what's waiting on the other side. Perhaps God will surprise you. But when you step into uncertainty, your faith will grow and your trust in God will develop.

Are you willing to accept God's judgment?

EVENING: THE HOLE OF SIN / *Behold, I was brought forth in [a state of] iniquity; my mother was sinful who conceived me [and I too am sinful].* Psalm 51:5 AMPC / Have you ever tried to dig half a hole? It can't be done. As soon as you start digging, you have a whole hole, no matter how it's shaped.

There's also no such thing as kind of sinful. As soon as you sin (as everyone does), you are sinful. As Ecclesiastes 7:20 (AMPC) says, "Surely there is not a righteous man upon earth who does good and never sins." Fortunately, God has filled in this "hole" of sin with His own righteousness (Romans 3:22–23).

There's no digging your own way out of sin. You need God's help to fill in the hole. He's willing to give you the righteousness you lack so that you can live sin-free in His grace.

MORNING: JUSTIFICATION BY FAITH ALONE / *As it is written: "The righteous will live by faith."* Romans 1:17 NIV / In the early 1500s, a German monk and professor named Martin Luther was preparing a lecture from the book of Romans when he came to the realization that the original Greek language of Romans 1:17 indicated a faith-based righteousness, not one dependent on works.

This moment changed everything. Luther went on to translate the New Testament into German, giving the common man access to the scriptures and sparking the Reformation.

Even now though, centuries later, we still sometimes try to earn God's approval rather than simply living by faith in the sacrificial work of Jesus Christ on the cross.

Today, let's start a new tradition—living entirely by faith.

EVENING: KNOWING JESUS / *Whatever were gains to me I now consider loss for the sake of Christ.* Philippians 3:7 NIV / Paul was born a Roman citizen, and from reading his epistles, it's clear that he had a wide knowledge of the literature of his day. He quoted the Cretan philosopher Epimenides (Titus 1:12), the Cilician Stoic Aratus (Acts 17:28), and the Greek playwright Menander (1 Corinthians 15:33). But he also knew his native Jewish history and philosophy, as a Pharisee who "studied under Gamaliel and was thoroughly trained in the law" (Acts 22:3 NIV). Even the Roman governor Festus recognized Paul's great learning (Acts 26:24).

When Paul became a Christian, however, he "resolved to know nothing. . .except Jesus Christ" (1 Corinthians 2:2 NIV).

Knowledge is good, but don't forget life's main focus.

MORNING: NO COMPROMISE / *"If we are thrown into the blazing furnace, the God we serve is able to deliver us from it. . . . But even if he does not, we want you to know, Your Majesty, that we will not serve your gods or worship the image of gold you have set up."* Daniel 3:17–18 NIV / Shadrach, Meshach, and Abednego were faced with two agonizing options: either worship King Nebuchadnezzar's gold idol or be tossed into a blazing hot furnace.

However, for these men of God, there really wasn't a choice to make. They weren't going to serve the king's gods. Period. And if that meant dying in a fiery furnace, so be it.

Living in this fallen world means you may be faced with choices between honoring God or compromising your faith. Can you trust God enough to make the right choice?

EVENING: PLANNING FOR THE FUTURE / *So the* LORD *said to Moses, "Take Joshua the son of Nun, a man in whom is the Spirit, and lay your hand on him."* Numbers 27:18 ESV / Part of Moses' calling was to look beyond his own role and into the future. Who would continue to lead Israel after he passed away?

It may be troubling to acknowledge that your own efforts and plans aren't going to last forever. But at a certain point, you will need to ensure that future generations learn something from your faithfulness.

There are ways you can begin to affirm others today, passing along what you've learned about following Jesus and helping them take their role among God's people.

Is there someone you know who needs your affirmation today? Are there ways you can encourage others to pursue God even after you are gone?

MORNING: FREEDOM TO SERVE / *Thus Joseph, who was also called by the apostles Barnabas. . .sold a field that belonged to him and brought the money and laid it at the apostles' feet.* Acts 4:36–37 ESV / This first biblical mention of Barnabas—one of the most important New Testament missionaries—reveals something significant about him: he sold his field to provide for the needs of the poor. Before setting out on his missionary work, he unburdened himself to become a worker in God's harvest.

Is it possible that something you own is keeping you from seeing God's calling? While there's nothing wrong with possessions, the burden of wealth can obscure what God wants to accomplish in your life.

Today, ask God if He wants you to unburden yourself of something you own so that you can better serve Him—and others.

EVENING: MOVE FORWARD / *Peter said to him, "Even if everyone else deserts you, I never will."* Mark 14:29 NLT / Scholars believe Peter was the primary source for Mark's account of Jesus' life and work—the Gospel of Mark. This may surprise you, given how many times Mark paints Peter in a negative light.

When Jesus foretold Peter's denial (Mark 14:27), Peter responded, "Even if everyone else deserts you, I never will." The balance of the chapter, however, tells how he failed.

God knows that His people's best intentions often go awry. But whenever we make bad decisions, we can do what Peter did: own them, then move forward in God's grace.

Peter didn't let his dreadful denial stop him from becoming the rock on which Jesus founded His church. Don't let mistakes stop *you* from being the man God wants you to be.

MORNING: PUTTING ON CHRIST / *Let the Lord Jesus Christ be as near to you as the clothes you wear. Then you won't try to satisfy your selfish desires.* Romans 13:14 CEV / All of us go through spiritually dry seasons in our Christian walk. One day, however, we hear a word from a song, a book, a friend, or a sermon that lifts our spiritual fog. Suddenly, we realize that God was there all along.

Think about your clothes for a minute. You can feel them touching your skin right now, right? You don't have to do anything to make them stick with you. In fact, removing them would take an intentional effort.

Similarly, Jesus never leaves us. The only way we can separate ourselves from Him is by intentionally trying to remove Him from our lives.

Let's never make that mistake.

EVENING: SHINING LIKE THE SUN / *Let them that love him be as the sun when he goeth forth in his might.* Judges 5:31 KJV / This is very appealing imagery, and you're probably glad to envision yourself ardently loving God, proceeding triumphantly through your day.

But there's a price tag for acquiring such strength: you often have to pass through deep, fiery trials. Just as precious metals are purified in a furnace, God often refines us "in the furnace of affliction" (Isaiah 48:10 NKJV).

You may be going through a seemingly endless phase of testing and frustration, and you wonder what good can possibly come of it. Hang on a little longer! God is purifying you. "These trials will show that your faith is genuine. It is being tested as fire tests and purifies gold. . . . It will bring you much praise and glory and honor" (1 Peter 1:7 NLT).

DAY 148

MORNING: KNOW WHO YOU TRUST / *So that your trust may be in the* Lord, *I teach you today, even you.* Proverbs 22:19 NIV / Actors commit to feasting on a script. They start by reading to make sure they understand the story. They keep reading because they want to learn more about their role and what the director expects from them. They read to learn how they think the character will speak the lines. There will come a point when they no longer need the script—they now know their role and have memorized every word.

You can have that same connection to God's Word. Reading the Bible to discover comfort might evolve into reading to discover your place in God's plan. Eventually, what you've read will start affecting how you respond to others, how you pray, and how to step up boldly for truth.

EVENING: WHAT DO YOU DEPEND ON? / *Hear my cry, O God; listen to my prayer. From the ends of the earth I call to you, I call as my heart grows faint; lead me to the rock that is higher than I.* Psalm 61:1–2 NIV / Have you ever doubted whether God is attentive to your needs? This is a common theme in the Psalms, as the writer struggles to reconcile God's power with the troubles that come each day.

What is the psalmist's answer? To call out to God and patiently wait.

Don't stop calling out to God, even if you grow weary and fearful. Even if the promises of scripture don't seem to match your circumstances. You can't stand on your own, but you can assuredly stand on the solid ground of God's promises.

No matter your circumstances, God is still the Rock that you can depend on in your time of need.

MORNING: CHASING FANTASIES / *Those who work their land will have abundant food, but those who chase fantasies have no sense.* Proverbs 12:11 NIV / All of us have land to till each workday. It's our lot that has been assigned to us to provide for our families. For some, it's physical land; for others, it's a schoolroom, delivery truck, or office. While our tasks may feel like drudgery at times, an attitude of diligence and gratitude should spur us on.

When Solomon condemns fantasy chasing in this morning's verse, he's referring to sloth and inactivity—not hardworking entrepreneurs who are busy tilling new ground. Adam Clarke, in his *Commentary on the Bible*, says it this way: "He who, while he should be cultivating his ground, preparing for a future crop, or reaping his harvest, associates with. . .those engaged in any champaign amusements, is void of understanding."

EVENING: RENEWED DAILY / *Therefore we do not lose heart. Though outwardly we are wasting away, yet inwardly we are being renewed day by day.* 2 Corinthians 4:16 NIV / It's easy to become discouraged as the years go by and you start to age and your strength begins to fail. You look at your reflection and wonder who hung a photo of your grandfather where the mirror used to be.

It seems unfair. We mortals are like flowers of the field: we live a few decades, rapidly bloom, then quickly reach old age and wither.

But take heart! Even though you're fading outwardly, within you're growing in glory. God, who remains eternal and awesome throughout all generations, will keep your heart and your faith strong. He is already renewing your spirit, and one day, He will give you a powerful, eternally young body.

MORNING: WORDS THAT RUIN / *By our speech we can ruin the world, turn harmony to chaos, throw mud on a reputation, send the whole world up in smoke and go up in smoke with it, smoke right from the pit of hell.* James 3:6 MSG / First Thessalonians 5:20–21 urges you to test the messages you hear from others. Why? The words you speak and those spoken by others can "ruin the world, turn harmony to chaos, throw mud on a reputation, send the whole world up in smoke and go up in smoke with it."

Words have incredible power. They can hurt or heal, confuse or enlighten, invite trust or instill fear. The only words you can trust completely are the words God placed in the Bible. Be careful about trusting just anything you hear, and be careful about the words you speak to others. Ponder what you say before you speak.

EVENING: REMAIN FAITHFUL WITHIN THE FAMILY / *"Only take care, and keep your soul diligently, lest you forget the things that your eyes have seen. . . . Make them known to your children and your children's children."* Deuteronomy 4:9 ESV / Caring for your soul is critically important for your own salvation—as well as for the future salvation of your children. Daily prayer, scripture reading, and obedience will bear fruit over time, and it will last for generations as your children learn from your example. Each of the times you experience God's provision will encourage your children to remain near to God throughout their lives.

Never underestimate how much a story of God's faithfulness can mean to the people in your family or community. Remembering is a central discipline in scripture, and making space for it will bear fruit for years to come.

DAY 151

MORNING: GOD'S LOVE REMAINS IN YOU / *"I made known to them your name. . .that the love with which you have loved me may be in them, and I in them."* John 17:26 ESV / The love of God the Father that resided in Jesus the Son—and originated in the Trinity's perfect love—is also within you. And as if God's love weren't enough, Jesus Himself promises to remain in you.

God affirmed Jesus as His own beloved Son, and He also sees you as His beloved child. Therefore, when you fail or stumble into sin, you are sheltered by the presence of His Son. There is forgiveness and restoration for you when you repent.

You have been adopted and indwelt by God's love and His Son. Your hope is in the spiritual reality of God dwelling in you.

EVENING: IGNORANCE VS. FORGIVENESS / *The fool says in his heart, "There is no God." They are corrupt, and their ways are vile; there is no one who does good.* Psalm 53:1 NIV / Imagine a classroom in chaos, the students unaware of the teacher watching through the window. That's the picture David paints in Psalm 53.

The next two verses of Psalm 53 (NIV) say, "God looks down from heaven on all mankind to see if there are any who understand, any who seek God. Everyone has turned away, all have become corrupt; there is no one who does good, not even one."

David calls atheists "fools" because they deny God's existence in the face of strong evidence, hoping to avoid sin's repercussions. We as believers, however, know our actions are corrupt and seek forgiveness for sins.

If someone you know denies God's existence, don't act "holier than thou." Show that person that forgiveness is better than willful ignorance.

MORNING: HEALTHY EYES / *"The eye is the lamp of the body. If your eyes are healthy, your whole body will be full of light."* Matthew 6:22 NIV / In commenting about this verse in his *Notes on the Bible*, Albert Barnes says that if a man who is crossing a stream on a log looks steadily across at some immovable object, he will experience little danger. But "if he looks down on the dashing and rolling waters, he will become dizzy, and fall. So Jesus says, in order that the conduct may be right, it is important to fix the affections on heaven."

The healthy eye stays fixed on Jesus and heaven, making it possible to navigate life's difficult waters. The unhealthy eye glances from one object to the next, causing its owner to tread dark paths in a confused search for meaning.

EVENING: FIVE THINGS TO HATE / *To fear the LORD is to hate evil; I hate pride and arrogance, evil behavior and perverse speech.* Proverbs 8:13 NIV / It might surprise you to learn that it's not only kosher to hate certain things, but that—if you love God—it's actually required.

First, if you fear God, you are to hate evil. No surprises there. But you're also to hate pride, arrogance, evil behavior, and evil speech.

Where this can quickly go sour, however, is if you always hate these things in *others*. This can cause you to have a critical and smug attitude. The big question is this: Do you hate these sins when you find them lurking in your own heart? Do you ruthlessly root them out?

Today, pray with the psalmist, "Search me, O God. . .and see if there be any wicked way in me" (Psalm 139:23–24 KJV).

MORNING: MORE THAN A PEP RALLY / *Do not merely listen to the word, and so deceive yourselves. Do what it says.* James 1:22 NIV / You can say you believe something, but without acting on it, you'll end up in self-deception. Likewise, if you say you follow Christ but don't actually do what the Bible says, then those who observe you may feel it's not worth following either.

Church isn't a pep rally. Reading God's Word isn't just spiritual comfort food. And following God isn't simply a matter of well-placed bumper stickers, witness wear, or a list of the top ten Christian phrases.

God probably won't ask you about your collection of spiritual quotes or T-shirts, but He will be interested in whether your trust in His plan led you to obedience.

God's Word changes lives. Changed lives require obedience. Obedience requires action.

EVENING: PARTY WITH PURPOSE / *"There you and your families will feast in the presence of the LORD your God, and you will rejoice in all you have accomplished because the LORD your God has blessed you."* Deuteronomy 12:7 NLT / Have you ever been at a party and wondered, *What in the world am I doing here?* Perhaps the frivolity of the evening's events seemed pointless and left you feeling empty.

In the Old Testament, God invited people to celebrate their accomplishments. Why? Because parties where *He's* the focus are the most meaningful.

When your party's theme involves celebrating all that God has done, the food and festivities suggest a deeper significance. You feel energized instead of exhausted.

Gladness (Psalm 65:12) and astonishment (Luke 8:56) are two intoxicating aspects of your experience when you spend time celebrating what God has done—when you party with a purpose.

MORNING: A VERY SIMPLE COMPROMISE / *Caiaphas, who was high priest that year, said to them, "You know nothing at all. Nor do you understand that it is better for you that one man should die for the people, not that the whole nation should perish."* John 11:49–50 ESV / Insulting the intelligence of the high council, Caiaphas made a simple argument based on math: by killing one man, Jesus, the religious leaders could prevent Him from arousing suspicion from the Roman authorities. The fear of appearing foolish compelled these religious leaders to follow his plan.

One little compromise can lead men to terrible places as one deception builds on the other. Such retreats from truth and honesty rarely make things better.

Even if the math seems simple, beware of sinful compromise—it can undermine even your best intentions.

EVENING: KORAH'S REBELLION / *The earth opened its mouth and swallowed them up, with their households and all the people who belonged to Korah and all their goods.* Numbers 16:32 ESV / Ever get jealous of how God is using someone else? *Why*, you might think, *does that person see himself as superior? After all, I'd do much better if I had the job.*

This was what Korah felt toward Moses. As a Levite, Korah served in the tabernacle. He wasn't a priest, however, so he didn't have the same connection to God. Korah gathered men to his cause and complained.

Korah allowed his jealousy to consume him. As a result, he was consumed by the earth at God's command.

If God has given you a task, do it to the best of your ability. Don't look at how He's using someone else. You are responsible for *you*.

DAY 155

MORNING: ENCOURAGE ONE ANOTHER DAILY / *You must encourage one another each day.* Hebrews 3:13 CEV / Motivational speaker Jim Rohn once said, "You are the average of the five people you spend the most time with." You can find a variation of that sentiment in 1 Corinthians 15:33 (NIV): "Do not be misled: 'Bad company corrupts good character.' "

As Christians, we are called to actively pursue godliness. One way we can do this is by encouraging one another each day. If we don't, sin will fool us, making us easy prey for Satan—much like the lone sheep is easy prey for the hungry wolf.

If you haven't already, find a good, Bible-believing church. Next, seek a kindred spirit or two and figure out the best way to encourage one another on a continual basis—texting, meeting for coffee, prayer meetings, or something similar. Find what works for you, and devise a plan.

EVENING: DON'T GIVE UP / *Let us not be weary in well doing: for in due season we shall reap, if we faint not.* Galatians 6:9 KJV / You've probably heard the old saying, "Well begun is half-done." But you must forget the key word here: *half.* You don't win the prize until you actually cross the finish line.

Whether you're going through a lazy spell, overwhelmed by a new task or responsibility, or worn out by a hard life, it can be easy to become "weary in well doing."

Jesus, however, offers hope and can breathe new life into you. Getting a positive attitude back may take time, and you may have to force yourself to focus on positive, uplifting things to avoid falling back into a negative mental rut. . .but the rewards will be well worth the struggle.

MORNING: TRUST THE TRAINING / *God is educating you; that's why you must never drop out. He's treating you as dear children. This trouble you're in isn't punishment; it's training, the normal experience of children.* Hebrews 12:7 MSG / Soldiers learn to trust their training. They don't always understand the reason for the watching and the waiting. However, there comes a time when all the training pays off.

Following Jesus means not dropping out, even when it feels like you're being punished. You're not. You're being trained much like a parent trains a child.

Trouble delivers education and an opportunity to draw close to the divine educator. God said there would be trouble; however, you've been saved by Jesus, who overcame trouble in this world (John 16:33).

But first, you have to overcome whatever resistance you may have against His plan.

EVENING: A CITY OF REFUGE / *"Then you must set apart three cities of refuge in the land the LORD your God is giving you."* Deuteronomy 19:2 NLT / God knew that for a variety of reasons humans condemn each other far too quickly, so He established cities of refuge. If a man committed a crime by accident, he could flee to one of these cities for protection.

God is all about refuge. In Luke 9, the wronged and misunderstood came to Jesus, who welcomed and fed them. And when the psalm writer wrote, "Praise be to God, who has not rejected my prayer or withheld his love from me!" (Psalm 66:20 NIV), it's clear he found refuge in the same accepting and loving God.

Are you a person of refuge? When wronged and misunderstood family members, neighbors, friends, and coworkers come to you, can they find protection?

MORNING: A SIMPLE TEST OF OBEDIENCE / *Everyone who does evil hates the light. . .for fear that their deeds will be exposed. But whoever lives by the truth comes into the light.* John 3:20–21 NIV / You can know if you are living in confidence or shame before God by doing a little self-examination. If you are willing to stand before God without hiding anything or making excuses, you are living by God's truth and obeying His commands with a clear conscience. However, if your first inclination is to hide from God then you most likely need to confess your sins to God lest you miss out on the intimacy and peace He offers.

Jesus assures you that He will never leave or forsake you. God is working to complete your renewal so that you can see God, yourself, and others clearly and without shame or fear.

EVENING: GOD'S DELIVERANCE / *Deliver me from my enemies, O God; be my fortress against those who are attacking me.* Psalm 59:1 NIV / There was a time when King Saul "sent men to David's house to watch it and to kill him in the morning. But Michal, David's wife. . .let David down through a window, and he fled and escaped. . . . When Saul sent the men to capture David, Michal said, 'He is ill' " (1 Samuel 19:11–12, 14 NIV).

By the time the men searched the home and found the decoy, David was praying and writing psalms miles away.

David knew his life was in danger, but instead of eliminating the threat, David prayed for deliverance. He listened to the life-saving advice of others, but he knew God was his fortress above all else.

When you need deliverance, use common sense and trust the Lord—like David did.

MORNING: JUMP-START YOUR PRAYER LIFE / *When we don't know what to pray for, the Spirit prays for us in ways that cannot be put into words.* Romans 8:26 CEV / In 2007, researchers from the University of Arizona determined that, contrary to popular opinion, men and women speak approximately the same amount of words each day. But while men talked more about technology and sports, women talked more about relationships.

Maybe this explains why so many Christian women are prayer warriors while Christian men are busy talking about theology. Since we struggle to express ourselves in relationships, we struggle to talk to God. We talk *about* Him instead.

But the Spirit is here to help us in our weakness, even going so far as to pray for us when we don't know what to say. Where we fall short, the Spirit takes over. Find comfort and motivation in that truth to jump-start your prayer life.

EVENING: ABSOLUTELY TRUSTWORTHY / *Do not be anxious about anything, but in every situation, by prayer and petition, with thanksgiving, present your requests to God.* Philippians 4:6 NIV / This is the age of super-heroes. They fill comic books, television series, and big-budget movies. Have you ever wondered why they're so popular?

When life seems uncertain, anxiety is inevitably heightened. Super-heroes become substitutes for diminished personal confidence.

But God, who delights in rescuing and caring for His family, has always had a better idea: He wants you to be confident in *Him*. You don't need to wear a cape or have a secret cave full of high-tech gadgets.

Psalm 20:7 (NIV) says, "Some trust in chariots and some in horses, but we trust in the name of the LORD our God."

Find your greatest confidence in the God who has always been *super* trustworthy.

MORNING: HONESTY AND DISHONESTY / *Better to be poor and honest than to be dishonest and a fool.* Proverbs 19:1 NLT / Today's verse links dishonesty and foolishness. It's hard to trust someone who has an open "foolishness account." Those who are poor but trustworthy, however, are in a much better position.

An honest man can sleep well at night, has a greater potential for meaningful friendships, and will be remembered for something more than personal struggles. A dishonest man has to contrive fresh answers for ongoing deceit, never knows when he'll be caught in a lie, and is remembered for his attempts to avoid the truth.

Whether you're poor or rich or somewhere in between doesn't matter; what matters is whether you're honest or foolish.

Which one are you?

EVENING: BRINGING HAPPINESS / *"A newly married man must. . .be free to spend one year at home, bringing happiness to the wife he has married."* Deuteronomy 24:5 NLT / Bringing happiness is a priority for every Christian man, especially those who are married.

Doing so requires the kind of humility Jesus was talking about when He said, "It is the one who is least among you all who is the greatest" (Luke 9:48 NIV). Most people are fine with getting up in the morning and thinking about what might make them happy. What's difficult is getting up and having your first thought be about the happiness of your wife, coworker, family member, or neighbor. Humility helps with that.

When people have no one to bring happiness into their lives, loneliness inevitably results. Today, be the kind of person who sings with the love and humility of the psalmist, "May *they* be happy" (Psalm 68:3 NIV, emphasis added).

MORNING: FREEDOM FROM MONEY'S MASTERY / *"No one can serve two masters. For you will hate one and love the other. . . . You cannot serve God and be enslaved to money."* Luke 16:13 NLT / No matter how counterintuitive it seems, God and money are in competition for the position of master in your life.

Money demands time, planning, and hard work. Money can promise security, solve problems, and lead to comfort and even peace—that is, until you run out of it. That's what makes it a fickle, if not demanding, master.

God, on the other hand, is always present and always cares for your needs. . .as long as you put love for Him and your neighbors first. When you release your cares to God, you are free to love your neighbors without the burden of depending on your own wealth.

EVENING: SIN HAS CONSEQUENCES / *But if you will not do so, behold, you have sinned against the Lord; and be sure your sin will find you out.* Numbers 32:23 AMPC / As they approached Canaan, the Israelite tribes of Reuben and Gad saw that the area outside the promised land was good for livestock and for raising families. Therefore, these tribes came to Moses with an offer: they would lead the Israelites in conquering the land in exchange for the area east of it.

Moses accepted the offer but gave this warning: if they didn't help conquer the promised land, the Lord would know and their sin would find them out.

Whether it's a broken promise or adultery or a lie or simple selfishness, sin always has consequences. Fortunately, Jesus' sacrifice has paid for your sins. Turn from your sin and accept God's grace, and your relationship with Him will be restored.

MORNING: UNSHAKABLE FORTRESS / *For God alone. . .is my rock and my salvation, my fortress.* Psalm 62:1–2 ESV / At one point in the classic film *Raiders of the Lost Ark*, Indiana Jones faces an accomplished swordfighter. The script for the film originally called for Indy to have a long fight with this guy, but the filming process was running behind and the set was incredibly hot. Finally, someone suggested Indy use the gun on his belt to take down the swordsman, and the iconic scene was born.

You may think you have great defenses built up around you. But when it comes to God, your protective measures are as useful as a sword in a gunfight.

Fortunately, God's on your side, and prayer is your key to safety. No matter what troubles you face, your soul is safe with Him.

EVENING: ATTRACTING SINNERS / *"If this man really were a prophet, he would know what kind of woman is touching him!"* Luke 7:39 CEV / Simon, a Pharisee, invited Jesus to dine with him and his friends. But when a sinful woman crashed the party and began washing Jesus' feet by weeping over them, kissing them, and pouring on perfume, Simon began to question Jesus' status as a prophet.

Simon's religious rules didn't allow him to interact with notorious sinners. But the woman wasn't bound by any such rules. She simply saw Jesus for who He was and knew Him to be full of mercy. To Simon's amazement, Jesus praised this woman's actions.

If the unregenerate are repelled by you rather than attracted to Christ who lives in you, you know you've gone wrong somewhere.

Remember: holding to a certain theological bent is of little value if we forget mercy.

MORNING: MY REDEEMER LIVES / *"For I know that my Redeemer lives, and at the last he will stand upon the earth. And after my skin has been thus destroyed, yet in my flesh I shall see God."* Job 19:25–26 ESV / What you believe in your heart is revealed during the most tumultuous times of your life. What have difficult times revealed about your faith? Have you clung to Jesus Christ, believing that He has conquered sin and death? Do your hardships cause you to long for the day when you will see God? Or have your experiences rattled your faith, causing you to doubt God and eternity?

Job didn't have the benefit of knowing Jesus Christ personally. He knew only that God was his Redeemer. You, however, have a personal relationship with the King of kings and Lord of lords.

Why not refresh your commitment to Him and His plan?

EVENING: DON'T FORGET / *Let us not neglect our meeting together, as some people do, but encourage one another.* Hebrews 10:25 NLT / Those who originally read this letter were drawn back to a time when they first heard stories of Jesus' life, death, burial, and resurrection. Some may have met Him personally. But time had passed, and the truth needed a good dusting. The life of Jesus was nearly becoming a ritual in the remembering. The people might have been getting a little *"ho-hum"* about meeting together.

Humans have always been easily distracted. This passage invites you to join in a movement that puts hope in perspective, trusts in the hands of God, and sets encouragement as a prime human motivation.

God will always keep His promises. What better way to celebrate this truth than by meeting with other Christians to proclaim them?

MORNING: UNSELFISH CONVERSATION / *Fools have no interest in understanding; they only want to air their own opinions.* Proverbs 18:2 NLT / Have you ever had a conversation with someone who clearly never heard or understood what you were saying? If so, you know how hard it is to trust people with your opinions or struggles when you know they're only waiting for a moment to share what's on *their* mind—even when it has nothing to do with what they've been talking to you about.

Likewise, you can be sure that if *you* refuse to really listen, other people will either stop talking or quit trying to share anything meaningful with you in the future. They don't like selfish conversation either.

Not everyone can be trusted with knowing what you're going through. Can you be trusted with the words they share with you?

EVENING: WIDE-EYED AWE / *"Gather the people together. . .so they can listen well, so they may learn to live in holy awe before GOD."* Deuteronomy 31:12 MSG / Those who pretend to be the masters of their own fates find the Christian faith scary, even foolhardy. For them, it's more comfortable to explain away apparent mysteries, including the resurrection.

Even those who should have believed in Jesus' miracles found putting their faith in Him difficult. He cautioned them, "Everybody's looking for proof, but you're looking for the wrong kind" (Luke 11:29 MSG).

What kind of proof should they have been looking for? The kind that accepts miracles. The kind of faith that enables people to live in wide-eyed wonder.

The life of wonder is the life characterized by the holy awe that Moses wrote about (Deuteronomy 31:12), and the life the psalmist sang about: "You, God, are awesome in your sanctuary" (Psalm 68:35 NIV).

MORNING: WHAT ARE YOU STORING AWAY? / *"God said to him, 'You fool! This very night your life will be demanded from you.'"* Luke 12:20 NIV / At some point, the rich man's reliance on his material abundance crossed a line, and he became a servant to his wealth and personal security rather than to God. As a result, the man became bankrupt.

How can you avoid the kind of traps that ensnared this rich man consumed with building bigger barns? Perhaps one place to start is to consider your abundance and security as resources to share with others. Your abundant "harvest" can be put to better use blessing others.

You can also watch for ways wealth distracts you from God. Often, the use of money can lead to more diversions and expenses, drawing your attention away from the wealth of God's present love and mercy.

Never let physical wealth replace your spiritual riches.

EVENING: YOUR REFUGE / *The righteous will rejoice in the Lord and take refuge in him.* Psalm 64:10 NIV / No matter how you feel today, God loves you and always will. He is always near enough that you can run to Him whenever you need shelter from life's storms.

The enemy likes to confuse you by saying that God isn't really there for you, that He has left you alone to fend for yourself. But the Bible says otherwise.

Believe that God's love for you doesn't change. Take refuge in Him and stay connected to His Word. In the middle of life's storms, God always stands up for His children and protects them.

So when life is tough and you don't know what to do, rejoice in the Lord—and always remember that you can run to Him, your place of refuge.

MORNING: HEAVENLY CORRECTION / *Our earthly fathers correct us, and we still respect them. Isn't it even better to be given true life by letting our spiritual Father correct us?* Hebrews 12:9 CEV / When you were growing up and faced the possibility of punishment, you probably hid, fretted, begged, and pleaded before finally submitting to your punishment.

But, assuming you had loving parents, you eventually became thankful that your earthly father cared enough to correct you, because it made you the man you are today.

The writer of Hebrews indicates that something much larger is at stake than simply becoming a better person. When we go astray spiritually, our heavenly Father has to step in—eternity in heaven is at stake.

God loves us enough to correct us so that we'll never experience true death. If you're experiencing His correction, rejoice! You're being prepared for heaven by your Creator.

EVENING: LIFE IS SHORT—CHOOSE GOD / *Your life is like the morning fog—it's here a little while, then it's gone.* James 4:14 NLT / At the end of your life you don't get a mulligan, do-over, or a divine reset in an attempt to get it right. You have only one shot to determine your place in eternity.

Life is like grass—here for a season and gone. Life is shorter than you realize, yet long enough that you're sometimes convinced to put off making eternally significant decisions.

You can choose to do things your own way, or you can find out what God wants you to do. You can live as though this life is all there is, or you can discover this life is a small step into forever.

There's no good reason to intentionally separate yourself from God. Life is short, so choose Him.

MORNING: THANK YOU FOR FRIENDS / *You must warn each other every day, while it is still "today," so that none of you will be deceived by sin and hardened against God.* Hebrews 3:13 NLT / The writer of Hebrews laid out a clear battle plan when it came to retaining a strong trust in God: keep your mind from all kinds of deception, and do everything to keep your heart from being hardened. Keep in contact with other Christians who feel comfortable pointing out any red flags in your behavior.

It's easy to get defensive when someone points out your flaws. No man likes to think he's failing. But you're asked to accept such candid observations from other Christians.

Trust is something God requires of you. He wants you to finish your journey well. Christ-following companions can help you stay focused on the finish line.

EVENING: ANSWERS FOR ANXIETY / *"In the future when your descendants ask their parents, 'What do these stones mean?' tell them. . .so that all the peoples of the earth might know that the hand of the LORD is powerful."* Joshua 4:21–22, 24 NIV / Having crossed the Jordan River at flood stage on dry ground, Joshua instructed the people to build a monument of twelve stones as a memorial to the miracle.

That pile of stones continually encouraged God's people to temper their anxieties with trust.

Jesus supported this kind of anxiety reduction. When people prioritized His kingdom, He taught, their other needs were met as well: "For where your treasure is, there your heart will be also" (Luke 12:34 NIV).

Longings of the heart provide the deeper answer for anxiety. Long for money, you'll be stressed. Long for God, you'll be filled.

MORNING: ENDURING SUCCESS / *"Then your reward will be great, and you will be children of the Most High, because he is kind to the ungrateful and wicked. Be merciful, just as your Father is merciful."* Luke 6:35–36 NIV / It's unproductive to head to work without mercy on our minds. Mercy keeps communication climates warm, relationships strong, and productivity high. But despite all the benefits that mercy brings, it's rarely practiced. Why?

Each person expects diligence, kindness, and respect from others—it's in our relational DNA. But mercy requires that you show these behaviors to the very individuals who least extend them.

Just as God shows mercy to "the ungrateful and wicked," our success and happiness depend on our willingness to do the same.

EVENING: GOD'S CONSISTENT LOVE / *Come and see what God has done, his awesome deeds for mankind!* Psalm 66:5 NIV / God doesn't change His mind. He won't tell you He loves you one day and then turn His back on you the next. He wants you to know that His character and love are consistent. He wants you to depend on Him, especially when your life seems to be falling apart and nothing makes sense.

Let His love be your anchor. Only then can you see each day as a gift to be enjoyed with your heavenly Father.

As you study God's Word, let it fill your heart with truth. Let it be your spiritual food that keeps you satisfied all day. Tell God everything that's on your heart—He wants to listen. He loves you and wants you to spend time with Him every day.

MORNING: KNOWING WHEN TO HIDE / *When you see trouble coming, don't be stupid and walk right into it—be smart and hide.* Proverbs 22:3 CEV / Sometimes, situations call for us to stand boldly against injustice or in favor of the oppressed.

Other times, we are called to run and hide. Many translations describe the person in this morning's verse as "prudent." In other words, he is wise—immersed in the scriptures—and able to know when to stand and when to run.

Noah heard God's voice, saw impending trouble, and hid in the ark. Joseph was tempted by Potiphar's wife, and he ran in the opposite direction.

When trouble comes, how does your first instinct compare with the wisdom of scripture? If you haven't fully developed your sense of discernment, consider enlisting a godly friend to help you navigate the situation. It might spare you the biggest mistake of your life.

EVENING: WHITE-WASHED REBELLION / *"I want to see a mighty flood of justice, an endless river of righteous living."* Amos 5:24 NLT / The people of Israel said the right things, sang great songs, and got together to celebrate their national religion. The prophet Amos, however, wasn't impressed. God showed him where the people really stood. He told them in verse 12 (NLT), "I know the vast number of your sins and the depth of your rebellions."

God wasn't interested in their diligent spiritual to-do list—He wanted the hearts of His people to line up with His own. Righteous living and compassion were rarely practiced.

Today, God continues to look for righteousness among His people. He desires to see compassion, not contempt, poured out on behalf of those who need love.

God still desires a people whose outer—and inner—lives line up with His truth.

MORNING: MEANT FOR MORE / *Our people have to learn to be diligent in their work so that all necessities are met (especially among the needy) and they don't end up with nothing to show for their lives.* Titus 3:14 MSG / The life of a Christian man is identified by action, generosity, and trustworthiness. He does the hard things because he knows he's working for God.

Today's verse doesn't promote self-reliance. Rather, it teaches that God has given you a job to help you be productive. Your salary helps provide for your family, but you can also use it to help others who can't work.

You serve a relational God. Therefore, whatever plan God has for your life will also impact others. Money never advances God's objectives when it takes up permanent residence in your bank account.

Use it wisely—for your own needs, and to bless others as well.

EVENING: ON SOLID GROUND / *For the LORD your God will bless you in all your harvest and in all the work of your hands, and your joy will be complete.* Deuteronomy 16:15 NIV / You are God's precious son. He loves you with a love that knows no equal and that will never end.

The enemy will tell you lies about God's love, hoping to make you doubt God's truth. *You're not really as important to God as you think,* the devil might say, *There's no way God can love you like you think He does.*

Nothing, however, is strong enough to pull you away from God's love. Ground your heart in His love for you. Keep your eyes on Him and His goodness—and never forget how much He cares.

When you do, your feet will remain on solid ground.

MORNING: REPLACING OUR CHILDISH WAYS / *When we were children, we thought and reasoned as children do. But when we grew up, we quit our childish ways.* 1 Corinthians 13:11 CEV / A *Christianity Today* article made this observation about the state of men: "Recently, several articles and statistics have shown that. . .men in increasing numbers are seemingly living in a prolonged state of adolescence, sitting back with their buddies and playing video games."

This behavior extends even to our faith. Some of us became Christians at an early age. But once we graduated from high school, got a job, and moved, we quickly fell away. Paul didn't approve of this in his day. He certainly wouldn't approve of it now.

Do you need to put away any childish activities, replacing them with spiritual ones? Doing so will bring spiritual growth that will help you make an impact for the kingdom.

EVENING: JUSTIFYING FAVORITISM? / *If you show favoritism, you sin and are convicted by the law as lawbreakers.* James 2:9 NIV / Favoritism is a plague and can lead to idol worship. By showing favoritism, you may be saying you believe that individuals are more important than God and His commands. Anything placed above God becomes an idol.

Most people rarely consider favoritism a sin, but instead consider ways to justify it. But if God gives a command, you shouldn't redefine His instruction.

God sent His Son for the lost. He didn't exclude people with certain addresses, bank statements, ethnic backgrounds, or a large sum total of personal sins. Any time you shrink the community of God by excluding someone, you tell the world that some people really don't matter.

That message doesn't stand up to God's love letter to all.

MORNING: JUST WALK AWAY / *Stay away from stupid and senseless arguments. These only lead to trouble.* 2 Timothy 2:23 CEV / Pride is easily engaged in stupid and senseless arguments.

In 2013, a fistfight occurred in the parking lot of a Mormon church as a result of "seat saving." The fistfight escalated to the point that one of the men allegedly hit the other one with his vehicle.

Have you ever engaged in a senseless argument in your church, workplace, or home, only to realize several hours later that your anger was a huge waste of time? The apostle Paul knew that such senselessness could get out of hand in a hurry. That's why he advised the young Timothy to avoid such quarrels.

If you are given to such arguments, consider the possible end result before you even begin. Be the bigger man and walk away before it escalates.

EVENING: ENDURING THANKS / *"Blessed is she who has believed that the Lord would fulfill his promises to her!"* Luke 1:45 NIV / When a job doesn't work out, the truck breaks down, or a relationship deteriorates, do you find it difficult to believe that God will fulfill His promises?

During these times, it helps to read passages—like this evening's—because they illuminate the unseen forces at work on earth.

In response to Gabriel's reminder—"For no word from God will ever fail" (Luke 1:37 NIV)—Mary wrote the song recorded in Luke 1:46–55. She committed hours to expressing her thanks because she experienced it so deeply. Maybe this is part of the reason God chose her to mother the Messiah—He appreciates those who will spend time showing their thankfulness.

Will you celebrate God's faithfulness like Mary did?

DAY 172

MORNING: MODELING CONSISTENT SELF-CONTROL / *Tell the older men to have self-control and to be serious and sensible. Their faith, love, and patience must never fail.* Titus 2:2 CEV / The apostle Paul left Titus, one of his charges, behind in Crete to do the difficult work of appointing leaders for the churches in each town (Titus 1:5). Paul gave him instructions about which type of men to choose as leaders, as well as instructing him about the type of people they would be ministering to.

Ordinarily, older men don't need to be told to have self-control, but the older men in Crete were apparently so greedy and lazy that this message was needful.

When young Christian men are unable to look up to older men in the faith, a sense of hopelessness can set in. If older Christian men cannot temper the flesh, what hope does a young man have?

Regardless of your age, self-control is not only possible but required.

EVENING: PRAY ON / *You don't have what you want because you don't ask God for it. And even when you ask, you don't get it because your motives are all wrong—you want only what will give you pleasure.* James 4:2–3 NLT / Many say prayers under pressure. They're not often part of regular conversations with God, and—for many people—may not even be sent with an understanding of who God is or what He wants.

This is the kind of selfish attitude that James addressed: "You want what you don't have, so you scheme and kill to get it" (verse 2 NLT).

Your prayer life always reflects your relationship with God. When you know God wants the best for you, you'll begin to ask for His best because you will *want* His best.

MORNING: WORTHY OF YOUR TRUST / *I know whom I have believed and am persuaded that He is able to keep what I have committed to Him until that Day.* 2 Timothy 1:12 NKJV / Paul had committed his eternal spirit and his earthly suffering to God, and the reason he could do so was because he trusted Him. Paul was convinced that God would reward him for his sacrifices and suffering. Paul trusted God because he knew Him.

Like Paul, you believe in God and trust Him for good reason. Even though it often appears that worldly people are way ahead in the game of life—that you're losing out by playing a clean game and making sacrifices for others—nothing could be further from the truth.

God is on your side, and when His kingdom has come, you'll be way out ahead.

EVENING: GOD IS GOOD / *The land yields its harvest; God, our God, blesses us.* Psalm 67:6 NIV / Think about all the ways God has been good to you. Keep a record of the harvest He has provided for you. Consider this new day an opportunity to rejoice at the goodness the Lord has shown you. Take some time to marvel at the different ways His love has brightened your days.

The devil is lurking around the corner, hoping you won't recognize God's goodness and provisions. He wants you to leave thoughts of God's blessings on the ground as you walk through life untethered to heaven's bounty.

But remember God's mercy—when Jesus saved you, when He made a way from sin's desert to the fertile field of forgiveness. God chose to show you compassion instead of wrath, love instead of fury. Recall just how good God has been—and continues to be—to you.

MORNING: OUR BODIES ARE NOT OUR OWN / *The wife does not have authority over her own body but yields it to her husband. In the same way, the husband does not have authority over his own body but yields it to his wife.* 1 Corinthians 7:4 NIV / Often, men use this morning's verse to point out why a wife shouldn't deny her husband in the marriage bed. "She belongs to us," we say, "not herself!"

However, we rarely consider the second part of the verse. If a man's body belongs to his wife, that means he has no right to pleasure it in any way—fornication, adultery, pornography, and so on—outside of the marriage bed.

This is a countercultural message in a sex-crazed society, but the same power that raised Christ from the dead empowers us.

Surely that's enough to help us obey and embrace the truth of this verse.

EVENING: WISDOM, COUNSEL, AND UNDERSTANDING / *"Is not wisdom found among the aged? Does not long life bring understanding? To God belong wisdom and power; counsel and understanding are his."* Job 12:12–13 NIV / To whom do you listen when you need advice? Is it someone who doesn't have a fully formed picture of life? Or is it someone who's spent time in life's trenches and has lived to gain understanding? There's a reason you might seek the advice of your father or other mature men—their life experiences may help you learn what to avoid and what to pursue.

If you're careful about whom you listen to among your sphere of friends, shouldn't God's voice and the wisdom He's given in His Word take first place as your source of counsel for today's tough choices?

MORNING: KEEP A CLEAR CONSCIENCE / *Cling to your faith in Christ, and keep your conscience clear. For some people have deliberately violated their consciences; as a result, their faith has been shipwrecked.* 1 Timothy 1:19 NLT / John 3:36 (NKJV) says, "He who believes in the Son has everlasting life," so you clearly need faith in Jesus. But if you willfully disobey God then refuse to repent and accept His forgiveness, you violate your conscience. You won't necessarily lose your connection with Christ, but will likely live in defeat, not enjoying the freedom and assurance that's your right in Him.

If you've sinned, repent today, and trust that God will forgive you (1 John 1:9; Proverbs 28:13).

God longs to set you free. He wants to restore your ability to live an overcoming, victorious life by His Spirit.

EVENING: TRUE GREATNESS / *"For it is the one who is least among you all who is the greatest."* Luke 9:48 NIV / When the disciples asked Jesus who was the greatest of their group, His reply showed them the importance of being humble, serving from a heart of love, and knowing that God is in charge.

Your life in Christ is not about trying to be the most important or the greatest. It's about seeing others as more important than yourself. It's about following the example of Jesus, who came to earth not to be served but to serve and to give you His very best. Humility before Jesus will give you all the confidence you need.

This evening, set down whatever pride you might have and embrace humility. When you put Jesus first in every way, He will show you true greatness.

MORNING: A TRUSTWORTHY PLAN / *"When he thunders, the waters in the heavens roar; he makes clouds rise from the ends of the earth. He sends lightning with the rain and brings out the wind from his storehouses."* Jeremiah 51:16 NIV / This morning's verse was intended to illustrate the reliability of God's promised judgments against Babylon. That empire had taken Judah captive, but God had planned it that way. Judah was rebellious, so God used Babylon to help turn their hearts back to Him.

However, because of the atrocities Babylon committed against Israel, God also promised to eventually defend His people from an empire that had gone too far.

Just as God can be trusted with the weather, He can be trusted with nations and current affairs. No detail escapes His attention or catches Him by surprise.

His plan, for the world and for your life, is trustworthy.

EVENING: CROP FAILURE / *All Scripture is inspired by God.* 2 Timothy 3:16 NLT / So, God inspired the writing of scripture, but how extensively? He inspired *every word*.

Why is this important? Well, if only part of the Bible is true, how could you believe any of it? If you're like most, you'll end up picking what seems easiest to believe and follow. You might believe in God's grace, but not His command to obey Him. You'd accept forgiveness while refusing to forgive others.

God never said you could simply accept the "feel god" parts of His Word. In fact, Galatians 6:7 (NLT) plainly says: "Don't be misled—you cannot mock the justice of God. You will always harvest what you plant."

Determine to believe and obey God's Word, starting with His simplest (but hardest) commands—to love others and forgive those who offend you.

MORNING: PEOPLE OF THE PRIESTHOOD / *But to the tribe of Levi, Moses had given no inheritance; the Lord, the God of Israel, is their inheritance, as he promised them.* Joshua 13:33 NIV / Ever thought of yourself as a priest? God does.

God gave property as an inheritance to all of Jacob's descendants, except Levi's sons. These people had the special privilege of inheriting the presence of God Himself.

So do you.

The priest brought sacrifices to God—you bring yourself (Romans 12:1); the priest entered the presence of God once a year—you can enter every day (Luke 13:24); the priest led God's people in proclaiming His mighty acts (Psalm 71:16)—so do you.

Like the Levitical priesthood, you traded possessions for the Lord. When all the people around you inherit temporal things, you inherit an eternal relationship with the Creator.

What better inheritance could you ask for?

EVENING: ENDURING WEALTH / *Jesus called his disciples to him and said, "I tell you the truth, this poor widow has given more than all the others."* Mark 12:43 NLT / Jesus sees what others overlook.

The media notices the generosity of the wealthy. When millions are donated in the name of philanthropy, the reports fill the papers, news programs, and websites. It's easy to celebrate large financial gifts, and it's even easier to overlook the little guys.

But God sees more. When a poor widow offers two small copper coins, Jesus calls His disciples over and points out what others missed—the offering of "everything" (Mark 12:44 NLT).

The same religious leaders who "shamelessly cheat widows out of their property" (Mark 12:40 NLT) should have noticed the extravagant gift this widow made, but they did not.

As you walk through today, will you see the significant in the insignificant?

MORNING: GOD'S PROTECTION / *Summon your power, God; show us your strength, our God, as you have done before.* Psalm 68:28 NIV / God's love and protection are all around you, keeping you safe from the enemy's attacks. Nothing can sneak up and snatch you away from Him.

God's power made the universe, and it also made your heart. His power formed the mountains, and it also sustains your life. God's power is mighty enough to carry you through your current struggles and place you gently down in peaceful places.

The enemy is most effective when he can get you to question God's promises. So in difficult times, recall what God's power looks like. Read your Bible and see how God cared for His servants, even in the most perilous circumstances.

God did that for His people in ages past—and He does it for you today!

EVENING: IN THE PRESENCE OF GREATNESS / *"Show respect to the aged; honor the presence of an elder; fear your God."* Leviticus 19:32 MSG / Years ago, Route 66—a nearly twenty-five-hundred-mile route that many still consider "the Mother Road"—was set aside in favor of faster travel on the Interstate.

Today, Route 66 is the tangible memory of the days of large cars and cross-country adventure when travelers were met with hospitality, full-service gas stations, and drive-in theaters. Some states have even turned portions of it into national historic sites.

God calls us to offer a similar sense of honor to our elders, whose vast supply of wisdom is often overlooked.

Invite them to share their stories, triumphs, and struggles. Younger, more ambitious people may seem to have displaced them, but given enough honor, our elders' legacies can continue to impact others.

MORNING: SPIRITUAL INVESTMENTS / *Godliness actually is a means of great gain when accompanied by contentment.* 1 Timothy 6:6 NASB / Godliness always begins with a willingness to follow God and to line up your decisions with His Word.

Instead of fixating on what you don't own, godly living recommends contentment. The reason is simple. This life is extremely short when compared with the eternal life God has prepared for His children, and some things people invest in have extremely short shelf lives (Matthew 6:19–20).

Chasing things you can never take to heaven is a poor use of time and energy. The three greatest investments you'll ever make in life are relationships with God, family, and friends. *People* are the only investments you have any chance of seeing again in heaven.

EVENING: BECOME A GOD PLEASER / *I am not trying to please people. I want to please God.* Galatians 1:10 CEV / The apostle Paul was indeed a people pleaser at one point in his life. As a persecutor of those who followed Jesus, he pleased men by holding the coats of the haters who stoned Stephen to death (Acts 7:58).

Post-conversion, Paul became a God pleaser, contending for the gospel no matter what men thought. So when he heard that the Galatians were straying from God, he decided to address the matter.

As believers, we are called to love one another as we love ourselves. But when a false gospel is presented, we must speak the truth as lovingly as possible. We cannot afford to be people pleasers when it comes to the good news of Jesus Christ. Souls are at stake.

We are not servants of Christ if we compromise in this area.

MORNING: PUT OFF ANGER, PUT ON CHRIST / *Don't make friends with anyone who has a bad temper.* Proverbs 22:24 CEV / Most of us know that the biblical principle of not befriending bad-tempered people is meant to keep us from becoming just like those people.

But have you ever considered it from the opposite point of view? Are fellow believers avoiding friendship with you because *you* have a bad temper? If so, don't be afraid to ask your pastor, small group leader, or long-time friend for help.

If anybody ever had a right to be angry, it was Jesus. He was betrayed, falsely accused of blasphemy, beaten beyond recognition, and executed in the most painful of ways. But after conquering death, He spoke with His apostles for forty more days about God's kingdom (Acts 1:3)—one that practices love, happiness, peacefulness, patience, kindness, goodness, faithfulness, gentleness, and self-control. Be like Jesus.

EVENING: WHAT GOD REQUIRES / *The goal of this command is love, which comes from a pure heart and a good conscience and a sincere faith.* 1 Timothy 1:5 NIV / Living an authentic Christian faith can be very difficult—you must have the love of God motivating you in everything you do. While loving others can be relatively easy when you're in a good mood, much of the time it goes against your natural instincts.

You really have to believe that Jesus was right about this "love-your-neighbor-as-yourself" thing, and that it's worth it. Of course, the person on the receiving end is convinced that it's a good thing, but when you're on the giving end, it's not always so clear.

Loving others takes a pure heart free of selfish motivation. . .and that takes faith to get you over the hump when the warm emotions dissipate.

MORNING: DESERTERS / *"For a long time now. . .you have not deserted your fellow Israelites but have carried out the mission the Lᴏʀᴅ your God gave you."* Joshua 22:3 ɴɪᴠ / When the younger brother returns to his family in the story of the prodigal son, the older brother, instead of welcoming him, walks away (Luke 15:28).

Have you felt like deserting lately? Maybe deserting your church because of the lack of winsome and strong leaders, maybe a struggling friend because he takes up too much of your time, maybe a relative who makes life unbearable, maybe an employer because he takes credit for your ideas? Are these reasons to walk away?

Semper fidelis, Latin for "always faithful," is a motto of every US Marine. How powerful the testimony of the church is when believers refuse to desert—when they, like every good soldier, rush in while everyone else walks out.

EVENING: CLEANING UP / *"Be generous to the poor, and everything will be clean for you."* Luke 11:41 ɴɪᴠ / After inviting Jesus to his home for dinner, a Pharisee was surprised that Jesus didn't wash before sitting down for the meal. But Jesus knew what He was doing. In fact, He pronounced a handful of "woes" as He explained to the man that his focus was on the wrong things and on the wrong place. Jesus told him that washing the outside is pointless if the inside remains filthy.

To remedy this inward uncleanness, Jesus told the Pharisee to be generous to the poor. To live an unselfish life. To live more like Jesus did.

Think about the ways your life has changed since Jesus "washed" you. This cleansing opened your eyes to see more of God's blessings—and to see how you can bless others.

MORNING: EXPERIENCING GOD, OR THE OTHER WAY AROUND? / *It is God who is at work in you, both to desire and to work for His good pleasure.* Philippians 2:13 NASB / Paul consistently connected knowing God with pleasing Him. He prayed that believers, "may be filled with the knowledge of His will in all spiritual wisdom and understanding, so that you will. . .please Him in all respects. . .increasing in the knowledge of God" (Colossians 1:9–10 NASB).

Our growing understanding of God gives us new experiences of Him, but it also gives God new experiences of us. Just as earthly fathers enjoy seeing their children grow, so does our Father in heaven. And the great news is that He Himself is so committed to this outcome that He actually works in us to ensure that it happens.

If we want to make Him happy, we have nothing holding us back!

EVENING: DEAL WITH IT / *Create in me a pure heart, O God, and renew a steadfast spirit within me.* Psalm 51:10 NIV / The Bible is clear: you must bear with those who struggle with sin (Galatians 6:2). This requires patience, sacrifice, and love.

The only person you're not supposed to give a free pass to, however, is yourself—that's God's job. God wants you to deal with your own sin, and His example is ruthless (Matthew 5:29–30). Some sins (like murder and theft) catch the attention of law enforcement, but other sins (like gossip, envy, and dishonesty) are equally offensive to God.

Wise men understand that we can't deal with our sin alone—it takes God's Holy Spirit to give us a new heart, a steadfast spirit, and a transformed life (Psalm 51:5, 10; Colossians 3).

MORNING: WORKING HIS PURPOSES / *We ought always to thank God for you. . .because your faith is growing more and more, and the love all of you have for one another is increasing.* 2 Thessalonians 1:3 NIV / Jesus warned that often during persecution, "the love of many will grow cold" (Matthew 24:12 NKJV) and believers would betray one another (verse 10).

But this wasn't happening with the Thessalonians, who were suffering intense persecution at the time Paul wrote this letter. Instead, persecution was causing the Christians there to love each other even more!

As bad as it seems, therefore, persecution is actually good for the church. It can take great faith to trust that God is working things for good in such situations, but that's exactly what He's doing (Romans 8:28).

No matter how you might be suffering today, trust God to see you through.

EVENING: JESUS IS ALIVE / *May your salvation, God, protect me.* Psalm 69:29 NIV / The cross holds great worth for you. The Romans intended it to bring death, but God used it to bring salvation. Jesus gave His life so that you could have life eternally.

Once Jesus was placed inside the grave, a massive stone was rolled in front of the opening and guards were ordered to keep watch. The enemy employs a similar tactic in your daily life, throwing one obstacle after another in your path to keep you feeling trapped. He wants all your attention on your problems instead of the empty tomb.

But Jesus is alive! And because He lives, the power of sin and death is broken. Therefore, you can have eternal, unbroken fellowship with God in heaven.

MORNING: SEVEN THOUSAND REASONS / *"I have kept for Myself seven thousand men who have not bowed the knee to Baal."* Romans 11:4 NASB / After the prophet Elijah humiliated 450 priests of Baal in a divine showdown of epic proportions, Queen Jezebel was furious and swore to kill him. He ran away, hid in a cave, and poured out his complaint to God.

What was God's encouragement to Elijah during his spiritual depression? The seven thousand ordinary, anonymous men who had resisted the pressure of their times day after day. Elijah may have been the star of this epic, but God used this remnant of unknown, behind-the-scenes men to encourage him.

Few of us know someone who faces the pressures Elijah did, but we all know someone who feels alone in standing for God. Just remember: all it takes to encourage others is to be one of the seven thousand.

EVENING: FOR EACH NEXT STEP / *Let my cry come before You, Lord; give me understanding according to Your word.* Psalm 119:169 NASB / The Psalms are more than source material for praise songs. They also express human struggle and personal questioning.

God explains in Isaiah 55:10–11 (NLT) that His Word does something remarkable: it lets you know God has heard you and helps you understand what He wants. "The rain and snow. . .water the earth. They cause the grain to grow, producing seed for the farmer and bread for the hungry. It is the same with my word. I send it out, and it always produces fruit."

The Word nourishes and causes you to grow, and it can produce something productive in the soil of receptive hearts. Read it for wisdom, for life, and for each next step.

MORNING: TRUST GOD FOR THE FUTURE / *"For I know the plans I have for you,"* says the Lord. *"They are plans for good and not for disaster, to give you a future and a hope."* Jeremiah 29:11 NLT / Many people focus on the world's problems—sickness, economic crises, war, and weather gone wild—and think it's too late for hope.

If you read only the dismal headlines, it's easy to get a negative mind-set. But in the midst of tragedy, God holds out a promise of hope. . .if you have the faith to receive it (John 16:33).

Jeremiah's message of hope seemed just as counterintuitive to his audience. After all, God was still punishing them for their sins. However, God wanted His people to look beyond the present and trust Him for a wonderful future.

He wants you to do the same.

EVENING: GOD IS FAITHFUL / *The Lord said to me, "Go again, love a woman who is loved by a lover and is committing adultery, just like the love of the Lord for the children of Israel."* Hosea 3:1 NKJV / Some of our toughest challenges don't come from the world. They arise within us.

We are tempted to do wrong. We often fail. And then we struggle to accept the fact that—through Jesus Christ—we are accepted by God. If you have a hard time believing that, reread the whole story of Hosea.

God told His prophet to marry a woman who would cheat on him. Then God had Hosea track her down, buy her back from a slave market, and love her again. It was all a picture of God's love for His own people, the often foolish and sinful Israelites.

If God was that committed to them, don't you think He'll be faithful to those of us who have chosen to follow His Son?

MORNING: SUNLIGHT AND STORM / *Be my rock of safety where I can always hide*. Psalm 71:3 NLT / God is not some faraway entity who won't answer when you call. He loves you and wants you to ask Him to keep you safe. He will answer every time. In fact, He blesses you and protects you even *before* you ask Him.

The enemy wants you to feel alone and isolated, focused on your situation and feelings. He hopes you'll grow weary waiting for God to answer and give up.

But there's hope—and His name is Jesus. He understands everything about you and wants you to find peace and safety in the shadow of His wings as you give Him all your worries and cares.

Whether the sun is shining or the rain is pouring, let Jesus be your constant. He will never let you down!

EVENING: THE PAINFUL TRUTH / *"And you, Capernaum. . .it will be more tolerable for the land of Sodom in the day of judgment, than for you."* Matthew 11:23–24 NASB / While Jesus was certainly gentle and caring, scripture records another side too—a forceful and confrontational side.

Jesus denounced entire towns that refused to repent in the face of many miracles. Sodom, for all its debauchery, would find it more tolerable on the day of judgment than the small fishing village where Jesus called his first disciples, healed Peter's mother-in-law, and marveled at the faith of the Roman Centurion!

Jesus' warning was appropriately blunt, and His message to those who should know better was perfectly clear: "From everyone who has been given much, much will be demanded; and from the one who has been entrusted with much, much more will be asked" (Luke 12:48 NIV).

MORNING: MAKING TIME FOR GOD / *"If they'd have bothered to sit down and meet with me, they'd have preached my Message to my people. They'd have gotten them back on the right track."* Jeremiah 23:22 MSG / The fact that you're making time for God this morning by reading this devotional is wonderful—many men are so busy with their work, marriage, family, leisure time, and hobbies that they give little thought to hearing from God.

As the Word of God sinks down into your heart daily, it increases your knowledge of His ways. Gradually, your thoughts and words come more into line with God's. Soon, you'll find that even the advice you give others will be more helpful.

Don't be like the men who see no need to quietly meditate on God (Psalm 46:10). There are some monstrous waves out there that can sink your ship if you're not drawing strength from Him.

EVENING: INSPIRED VIEWS / *All things have been created through Him and for Him.* Colossians 1:16 NASB / Take a look at the trees, the sky, and the stars. God made it all for you to enjoy, but He also made it for Himself. Sometimes, in the face of nature's grandeur, we forget that everything in nature has its origin in God (Romans 1:25).

As inspired as creation may be, heaven will be far greater. There, the beauty won't lie just in what you see, but in the fact that "'He will wipe every tear from their eyes. There will be no more death or mourning or crying or pain" (Revelation 21:4 NIV).

If you find yourself overwhelmed by the beauty of God's creation, let it remind you that nature is but a reflection of His best future.

MORNING: A RELATIONSHIP WITH GOD / *"There will be more rejoicing in heaven over one sinner who repents than over ninety-nine righteous persons who do not need to repent."* Luke 15:7 NIV / From the very beginning in Eden, God made people to be in relationship with Him. And throughout Jesus' time on earth, He kept relationships with people at the heart of His ministry.

Jesus gave His followers the great commission so that they could know their purpose in life. Leading people to Jesus is often a slow process, because it takes time to build relationships. When people know you really care, they will trust that you have their best interests in mind. Sharing the gospel at that point will be a natural next step.

Let people know that Jesus is your King. Stay connected to Jesus and boldly share His love with a broken world.

EVENING: CURSES TO BLESSINGS / *David replied. . ."If Shimei is cursing me because the Lord has told him to, then who are you to tell him to stop?"* 2 Samuel 16:10 CEV / A willingness to hear from God, even when it comes from someone who hates you, is the truest form of humility. As King David ran for his life from his son Absalom, who had usurped the throne, an embittered old man from Saul's family took the opportunity to ridicule him.

Payback! Shimei cried. He was wrong, of course—David was God's anointed. But David did not even attempt to correct him. Rather, he remained open to the possibility that God was using this moment to speak to him.

When you are rebuked, are you willing to look for God's message even in the words of those who are ignorant and hurtful? God's voice would be worth the effort.

MORNING: NO BARRIER EQUALITY / *There is no longer Jew or Gentile, slave or free, male and female. For you are all one in Christ Jesus.* Galatians 3:28 NLT / Jesus came with a radical and unexpected message: God loves all mankind. He doesn't discriminate against the poor, the sick, or the outcast.

Where women and children were once treated as property, God instructed men, "Love your wives and never treat them harshly" (Colossians 3:19 NLT) and "Do not provoke your children to anger" (Ephesians 6:4 NLT).

Part of Jesus' plan was to equalize humanity. No one was less important to Him than another. He didn't come to save a few—His rescue plan was for *all.*

God doesn't erect barriers when it comes to a relationship with Him. Christian men, therefore, should remove every barrier that prevents others from meeting Jesus.

EVENING: SEND ROOTS DEEP / *You received Christ Jesus the Lord, so continue to live as Christ's people. Sink your roots in him and build on him. Be strengthened by the faith that you were taught.* Colossians 2:6–7 GW / When you accepted Jesus as Lord, His Spirit entered your heart and brought you eternal life. This verse then encourages you to *continue* to live as God's child.

The roots of your faith must become completely intertwined with Jesus, even as a tree's roots reach deep into the rich soil and spread throughout it. Sinking your roots deep will bring constant nourishment and make you unshakable. As 1 Corinthians 15:58 (NKJV) says, "Therefore, my beloved brethren, be steadfast, immovable, always abounding in the work of the Lord."

Build your life on God, sink your roots deep down into His truth—the scriptures—and find your nourishment in Him.

MORNING: NOTHING COMPARES TO JESUS / *I count everything as loss compared to the possession of the priceless privilege (the overwhelming preciousness, the surpassing worth, and supreme advantage) of knowing Christ Jesus my Lord.* Philippians 3:8 AMPC / Who was Jesus? A good man? An enlightened teacher? An anointed miracle-worker?

Yes, but. . .Jesus was far, far more. Before time began, He shared incomparable glory with God His Father in heaven (John 17:5). He is the eternal Word who created everything in the entire universe (John 1:1–3). When John saw Jesus in heaven, he was overcome with awe and fell down at His feet as one dead (Revelation 1:13–17).

To know Jesus is to know Him as God. If you have John's experience even for a moment, you would agree that everything in this world is worth nothing compared to the precious privilege of knowing Jesus.

EVENING: THE RESCUER / *But when the people of Israel cried out to the Lord for help, the Lord raised up a rescuer to save them.* Judges 3:9 NLT / Twice in Judges 3 and several times in the following chapters, God's people succumbed to the following pattern: the people sin, God hands them over to enemies; the people suffer and cry out to God, God sends a rescuer.

In Luke 17, Jesus heard ten lepers cry out "have mercy on us" (verse 13 NIV), so He did. Though He knew that only a sidelined Samaritan would thank Him, the Lord rescued the other nine who cried out to Him. It's just part of who He is.

If you picked up this book because you're in the "suffering" stage, remember—like Old Testament believers and the ten lepers—you have a rescuer!

MORNING: ENDURING EMOTIONS / *So they departed quickly from the tomb with fear and great joy, and ran to tell his disciples.* Matthew 28:8 ESV / Try to imagine the disciples' despair after Jesus died—how could they feel hope when the creator of that hope had died? But it's even harder to imagine the sudden emotional rebirth they experienced at the empty tomb.

Matthew describes their emotions as "fear and great joy." Encountering the supernatural always produces some kind of fear, but this was a delightful kind—one that created an almost uncontainable sense of anticipation.

Through this coming day, look for God in His Word and in your life. Perhaps discovering His supernatural presence will cause you to feel the same emotions those disciples who "took hold of his feet and worshiped him" (Matthew 28:9 ESV).

EVENING: PURE IN HEART / *Surely God is good to Israel, to those who are pure in heart.* Psalm 73:1 NIV / How can you place yourself in a position to receive all God has for you? That's a great question to help you become "pure in heart."

When you commit yourself wholly to the Lord, you can be confident that nothing in the world can defeat you. You'll remain right in the middle of His goodness.

Do a quick inventory of the things that are most important to you. Is Jesus first on that list? If so, your heart is in step with His priorities, and you're in the right place to receive all He has for you.

Stay anchored to God's heart and let His goodness rain over you every day.

MORNING: GODLY REBUKE / *He said to them, "Why are you afraid, you men of little faith?"* Matthew 8:26 NASB / The disciples were an unlikely mix of educated and uneducated, craftsmen and professionals, strong of character and weak. But nothing breaks down barriers like a life-threatening event. When the storm threatened to swamp their boat, the disciples all agreed: wake Jesus up!

He wasn't grumpy for being awakened; He was disappointed in their lack of faith. It's ironic to think that calling on Jesus could bring a rebuke. But in this case, it would have shown more faith for the disciples *not* to have cried out for Jesus' help. After all, He was right there.

The lesson they learned that day is that fear is the most potent form of doubt. Jesus wants us to be free from fear and live like He is truly with us, even in the storm.

EVENING: WAVER NO MORE / *Let us hold fast the confession of our hope without wavering, for He who promised is faithful*. Hebrews 10:23 NKJV / Your opinions can waver about almost anything. You may like a certain restaurant, for instance, but struggle to decide if that's where you really want to eat today.

When it comes to your relationship with God, however, you shouldn't waver. Either God is good or He isn't. If God has proven faithful, then wavering in your opinion of Him doesn't make sense.

God, however, knows that we all struggle with doubt sometimes. Jesus once told a man who came to Him for help that he should believe. The man's reply? "Lord, I believe; help my unbelief!" (Mark 9:24 NKJV).

Today, spend time remembering the faithfulness of God, and discover a harmony between what you've experienced and the God you believe in.

MORNING: KNOWING YOUR SOURCE / *Every good and perfect gift is from above, coming down from the Father of the heavenly lights.* James 1:17 NIV / In a 2016 interview on the ESPN show *E:60*, interviewer Jeremy Schaap asked retiring sports broadcasting legend Vin Scully, "What are the moments that give you the most pride?"

Scully, a man of faith, replied, "Because what has happened to me, I believe. . .it was a gift that was given to me. I can lose that gift as soon as I get out of this chair. . .so there's really no pride."

What a profound application of the wisdom found in this morning's verse!

When the devil whispers in your ear that you should feel pride over something you've done, you do well to simply answer, "It's all a gift from my Father in heaven."

EVENING: FOR GOD'S GLORY / *"This sickness is not unto death, but for the glory of God, that the Son of God may be glorified through it."* John 11:4 NKJV / Lazarus was dead. His body had been in the tomb four days, and the decomposition process was underway. All hope was lost.

But Jesus didn't see it that way. Standing before the tomb, He shouted—"Lazarus, come out!" Soon, a man wrapped in cloths came shuffling forward. Lazarus was alive, and "many of the Jews who. . . had seen the things Jesus did, believed in Him" (verse 45 NKJV).

That's the great takeaway of the story of Lazarus—and of much of the hardship we face. When Jesus works in and through us, He and His Father are glorified. In every frustration and trial and tragedy—if we maintain focus on our Lord—we'll begin to understand how everything combines to fulfill God's master plan.

MORNING: GOD'S WONDERFUL MERCY / *"God, have mercy on me, a sinner."* Luke 18:13 NIV / Jesus told a story about two very different men who went to the temple to pray. One was a local religious leader, and the other was a much-hated tax collector. The religious leader used his prayer to thank God that he wasn't like sinners, while the tax collector confessed that he was a sinner and begged God for mercy. Jesus told His followers that it was the tax collector, not the self-righteous religious leader, who was justified before God.

We as Christians should always approach God with a contrite heart and teachable spirit. Coming to Him this way will put you in a position to receive His wonderful mercy.

EVENING: SPIRITUALLY EFFECTIVE PEOPLE / *Do your best to improve your faith by adding goodness, understanding, self-control, patience, devotion to God, concern for others, and love.* 2 Peter 1:5–7 CEV / To really stand out at something—a sport, job, or hobby—often requires obtaining a set of specific skills.

But in building the kingdom of God, skills are not the main concern. While God gives each of us spiritual gifts that we can use to help others grow (1 Corinthians 12:7), our effectiveness in the kingdom is tied most strongly to our character.

Peter points to seven "qualities" that, if you possess them, will ensure that "no grass will grow under your feet, no day will pass without its reward as you mature in your experience of our Master Jesus" (2 Peter 1:8 MSG).

How many of these qualities do you have?

MORNING: A TRUE PRAYER WARRIOR / *Epaphras. . .is always wrestling in prayer for you, that you may stand firm in all the will of God, mature and fully assured.* Colossians 4:12 NIV / If you've ever watched a real wrestling match, you saw two highly trained, well-conditioned athletes trying to impose their will on each other.

In this morning's verse, the word *wrestling* implies contending passionately and continuously for something. It means coming to God again and again to request that which you're convinced in your heart He wants to do for you.

Can you think of someone you know who could benefit from your prayer? Maybe a pastor who is battling the forces of evil? Or a man who is working to save his marriage? Or perhaps a friend who needs Jesus? If so, learn from Epaphras—don't stop asking until God replies.

EVENING: GOD IS WORKING ON YOU / *There has never been the slightest doubt in my mind that the God who started this great work in you would keep at it and bring it to a flourishing finish on the very day Christ Jesus appears.* Philippians 1:6 MSG / You've seen construction sites that are peppered with signs stating the name of the builder.

The Lord is like that.

God saved you the day you surrendered to Christ, and He stamped your heart with the royal seal of His Holy Spirit (2 Corinthians 1:22; Ephesians 1:13; 4:30). Though you're presently imperfect, God is determined to keep working in you until Christ returns to take you to heaven.

At times, you may become discouraged by your many weaknesses and faults. But rest assured: God started a great work with you, and He'll see it through till it's finished.

MORNING: YOUR KING / *God is my King from long ago; he brings salvation on the earth.* Psalm 74:12 NIV / Long before you were born, God thought about you. He carefully considered all the ways He would make you different from everyone else. There's only one you, and there will never be another.

Make today a time of celebration as you remember everything God has done in your life. He saved you from the chains of darkness. Because of Jesus, your sins are forgiven and you are eternally free to worship and serve Him.

Today is a new chance to reconnect with your King. Rejoice as you see and feel His presence and His never-ending love for you. Reflect on His unfailing love and step out in faith, knowing that the King of kings has you in His hands and will never let you go.

EVENING: FLATTERY WILL GET YOU NOWHERE / *Those who cause dissensions and hindrances contrary to the teaching which you learned. . .are slaves. . .of their own appetites; and by their smooth and flattering speech they deceive the hearts of the unsuspecting.* Romans 16:17–18 NASB / Paul poured out his life to build the church of Christ on a solid foundation. But he knew others would come who worked only for their own interests.

What was their primary weapon? "Smooth and flattering speech." Flattery always comes from an ulterior motive—to manipulate the listener. It always serves the flesh.

To heed Paul's warning about such people, we need to be sure we are not one of the "unsuspecting" who never make the effort to mature spiritually.

Growing in our understanding of Christ is the only way to guard against deception.

MORNING: HANDLING ANGER PROPERLY / *Fools vent their anger, but the wise quietly hold it back.* Proverbs 29:11 NLT / Did you know the Bible never teaches that anger itself is a sin? Godly anger—also known as righteous indignation—can motivate men to act in ways that glorify God and further His kingdom. It moves them to defend the mistreated and stand up for biblical principles that are being violated.

But sinful anger, the kind that moves you to contend for your own selfish desires, can damage relationships, cause unneeded pain to those you love, and hurt your witness for Christ.

So when you feel anger rising up within you, ask if the way you're expressing it will hurt others or displease God. If the answer is yes, quietly hold back. Look for a godlier way to express your emotions.

EVENING: IT'S WORTH TRUSTING GOD / *"What fault did your ancestors find in me, that they strayed so far from me?"* Jeremiah 2:5 NIV / Even after God had brought the Jews' ancestors out of slavery in Egypt, provided for them in a barren desert, and performed miracles to bring them into the promised land, His people *still* turned from Him to worship idols.

Many modern people think they have found fault with God. They say, "He allows innocent children to suffer. Christianity is out of touch with modern liberated worldviews." So they disrespect God and stray in their hearts. Do you sometimes find yourself doing this?

Trust God. His works, however mysterious they may be, are still perfect. Even the worst tragedies will be recycled into a meaningful design.

Believing this takes great trust in God, but He is worthy of your trust.

MORNING: THE GOD WHO FEELS / *He could bear Israel's misery no longer*. Judges 10:16 NIV / Every time God's people experienced the misery that came from following their own hearts, God felt the agony.

Are you like God in your compassion? Do you feel the misery of the people around you?

When a believer strays from the faith and suffers, you can speak with words that communicate your willingness to listen with sympathy.

When people you love share their deepest sorrows, you can openly weep like Jesus.

When a coworker loses a loved one, you can put the date in your calendar and remember to send a card each year on the anniversary.

You can minister to a world full of hurting people when you pattern your life after the God who feels.

EVENING: TAKE DOUBTS AND QUESTIONS TO GOD / *I cry out to God; yes, I shout. Oh, that God would listen to me!* Psalm 77:1 NLT / Asaph, the author of Psalm 77, was an honest, courageous man. Yet even the strongest believers can struggle with serious doubts.

Asaph spent his life serving God. But slowly, the injustices he saw around him began to wear on him. Asaph's faith was shaken. *Why waste my time obeying and serving God*, Asaph wondered, *when others disobey and prosper and live to boast about it?*

Asaph's response was right on target. Stopping to look at the world through God's eyes, he finally understood that the prosperity of the wicked was only temporary.

So what if I don't get all the perks in this life? Asaph realized. *If I have God, I can know true satisfaction and will enjoy great rewards in the life to come.*

MORNING: VITAL CHOICES / *He turns a wilderness into pools of water, and dry land into watersprings.* Psalm 107:35 NKJV / This passage in the Psalms offers two options to all men at all times: death and life. To illustrate this point, the psalmist engages the imagination with real-life scenes.

In Psalm 107:33–34, the psalmist presents fast-motion scenes of ecological disasters, evoking the judgments against Sodom and Gomorrah. But then the psalmist reverses everything, replacing ecological disasters with natural beauty, such as the kind Joshua, Caleb, and the ten other spies found when they explored the promised land.

So what's the difference between "death" and "life"? It comes down to choices: do you humble yourself before the Lord and obey Him, or do you go your own way, blaming God when everything goes wrong and giving up on faith?

The choice is yours—choose wisely!

EVENING: FIRST IMPRESSIONS / *Just then Boaz arrived from Bethlehem and greeted the harvesters, "The Lord be with you!" "The Lord bless you!" they answered.* Ruth 2:4 NIV / When we're first introduced to Boaz in the book of Ruth, he's greeting his workers with a hearty "The Lord be with you!"

These words give you a great first impression, don't they? Right away, you know that Boaz loves God and apparently treats his servants with kindness and compassion. As the story progresses, those first impressions are confirmed.

You have only one chance to make a first impression. What kind of first impression do you make on those you meet? Do they know right away that you're a man who loves God and loves other people—no matter their position in life—and wants to bless them?

That's a first impression any follower of Jesus should want to make.

MORNING: CLAY IN THE MASTER'S HANDS / *But now, O Lord, thou art our father; we are the clay, and thou our potter; and we all are the work of thy hand.* Isaiah 64:8 KJV / You are like clay that God is forming into a vessel of His own design. But for Him to do that, you can't harden your heart. You must be soft and pliable—and God often keeps you that way through tears.

Paul wrote, "If you keep yourself pure, you will be a special utensil for honorable use" (2 Timothy 2:21 NLT). You must allow God to remove any unyielding bits from your life, just as a potter picks hard lumps of clay from his vessel.

Is God shaping your life now? Even when the process is painful, keep yielding to God's loving hands. The end result will be worth it.

EVENING: GIVING OF WHAT YOU HAVE / *"Truly I tell you," he said, "this poor widow has put in more than all the others. . . . She out of her poverty put in all she had to live on."* Luke 21:3–4 NIV / The Bible has a lot to say about giving—giving to God's commission to take the gospel message to the world, giving to individuals in need, and giving with a joyful heart. God has called you to give sacrificially.

Sacrificial giving requires a special kind of faith. It requires a trust that God will provide—especially when times are tight. Without that kind of faith, you'll be stuck hanging on to what you have in order to meet your obligations. With that kind of faith, you give of what little you have, knowing that God will see your sacrifice and meet your needs in ways only He can.

MORNING: ENDURING NEEDS / *He withdrew by boat privately to a solitary place. Hearing of this, the crowds followed him on foot from the towns.* Matthew 14:13 NIV / After John the Baptist's death, Jesus "withdrew" from others. This was His method for dealing with grief.

Nevertheless, Jesus' profound empathy soon interrupted His intent. When a crowd greeted Him as He stepped out of the boat, He didn't follow His culture's grieving process by meeting His own needs. Instead, Jesus had "compassion on them and healed their sick" (verse 14).

Charles H. Spurgeon said, "Carve your name on hearts, not on marble." So the next time you feel sorrowful, step out of your isolation and meet another's needs—it will soften the pain and etch your efforts into eternity.

EVENING: GOD DOESN'T WANT ANY TO PERISH / *Then he said, "Jesus, remember me when you come into your Kingdom."* Luke 23:42 NLT / The young man leaned over the bed, his strong hands surrounding the old man's frail ones. "Do you believe Jesus died for you, Grandpa? Do you want to trust Him to save you?" The old man nodded his head and gave up his lifelong antagonism toward his Creator. "Yes," he whispered.

A criminal hung contorted on a Roman cross, hatred raging in his bursting heart. But suddenly, as he realized the identity of the man hanging beside him, the thief quieted down and offered a humble prayer to Jesus.

Jesus gave the thief his simple request—and more. "Today you will be with me in paradise" (Luke 23:43 NLT).

Augustine once observed, "There is one case of deathbed repentance recorded, that of the penitent thief, that none should despair; and only one that none should presume."

MORNING: FREEDOM'S PURPOSE / *All things are lawful for me, but not all things are profitable. All things are lawful for me, but I will not be mastered by anything.* 1 Corinthians 6:12 NASB / Grace wouldn't be grace if it didn't allow us room to make mistakes without fear of losing our relationship with God.

However, there's always the chance that such wonderful freedom can be misused. Some Corinthian believers, freed from the arduous burden of legalism, were using their new "freedom" as an excuse to indulge in unprofitable things that had replaced God as the focus of their lives. How absurd to think that God's gift of grace would push aside the one who gave it!

No amount of rationalizing should overrule godly common sense (Hebrews 5:14). Today, let's use our freedom to become like God, not to test the limits of His patience.

EVENING: KIND WORDS SPOKEN / *Kind words are like honey— sweet to the soul and healthy for the body.* Proverbs 16:24 NLT / In recent years, leaders in the corporate world have made an interesting discovery: many workers perform better when their boss gives them verbal pats on the back for good work.

People are naturally wired to need affirming, kind words. And while there is certainly a place for correction and discipline, never forget that everyone needs to hear kind words from loved ones and authority figures.

Do you want to see the best in your wife, children, friends, and coworkers? Try speaking kind words to them. Let them know when they're doing well. Tell them you appreciate them. Let them know they're valued. The results might pleasantly surprise you.

MORNING: LET THE SPIRIT WORK / *But the one who plants in response to God, letting God's Spirit do the growth work in him, harvests a crop of real life, eternal life.* Galatians 6:8 MSG / God is the only one who can accomplish anything. That's why Jesus said in John 15:5–6 (MSG), "I am the Vine, you are the branches. When you're joined with me and I with you. . .the harvest is sure to be abundant. Separated, you can't produce a thing. Anyone who separates from me is deadwood."

God has a job for you—to share the life-giving gospel with others. But you can't cause life to spring forth in anyone else if you aren't connected to God yourself. Stay firmly attached to God, allowing Him to work in and through you.

EVENING: REMEMBERING GOD'S AMAZING WORK / *Then I thought, "To this I will appeal: the years when the Most High stretched out his right hand. . . . I will remember your miracles of long ago."* Psalm 77:10–11 NIV / During particularly difficult times, have you ever found solace in recalling better times? If so, then you can probably identify with Asaph.

In the first nine verses of this psalm, Asaph was so miserable that he couldn't eat or sleep. He wondered if he would ever again see God's favor. God, however, gave him a reprieve from his sorrows by reminding him of the days when the Lord worked very clearly in the lives of His people.

There are dangers to "living in the past," but this evening's scripture passage illustrates the assurance and encouragement you can find by remembering those times God has blessed you before.

MORNING: ARE YOU LIKE NICODEMUS? / *There was a Pharisee, a man named Nicodemus who. . .came to Jesus at night and said, "Rabbi, we know that you are a teacher who has come from God. For no one could perform the signs you are doing if God were not with him."* John 3:1–2 NIV / Nicodemus had been trying to get into God's kingdom by way of his Jewish lineage and adherence to human traditions.

"You'll never get there that way," Jesus basically told him. "Time to change direction. You can only get where you want to go by being born again." Nicodemus had no idea what Jesus was talking about, so Jesus patiently explained the way in more detail. It takes belief in God's Son, Jesus said, to obtain eternal life. Only then can the Holy Spirit give someone new birth.

Spoiler alert: Nicodemus believed!

EVENING: JUST DON'T / *"From any tree of the garden you may eat freely; but from the tree of the knowledge of good and evil you shall not eat."* Genesis 2:16–17 NASB / When Adam and Eve ate the forbidden fruit—thus breaking the only rule God had given them—their act of disobedience multiplied into all the sin we see in the world today. No wonder the "don'ts" seem to multiply throughout the Bible. They're just keeping pace with the ways man invents to disregard God.

The Old Testament Law was a gift to set God's people apart and increase their joy, not end it. It was ultimately designed to lead people to Christ (Galatians 3:24).

Now, the things we consider "don'ts" from God do not constitute a law—they provide real freedom and a holy connection with our Lord. Any "don't" from Him means life for us.

MORNING: A GOOD FOUNDATION / *See to it that no one takes you captive through philosophy and empty deception, according to human tradition, according to the elementary spirits of the world, according to Christ.* Colossians 2:8 NASB / The test of every building is in its foundation. No matter how impressive the place looks, if the foundation is faulty, the whole structure is at risk. Sadly, this is also true of our lives if we build our thinking on shifting philosophies. The world offers its perspectives twenty-four hours a day—through every medium imaginable.

But Christ offers truth, reality, and a future that is eternal rather than fleeting. If we build upon His work and His words, we can know that our structure will stand. . .all the way through eternity.

EVENING: GUILT: A USELESS EMOTION / *Where is another God like you. . . ? You will not stay angry with your people forever, because you delight in showing unfailing love.* Micah 7:18 NLT / A big part of the fallen human condition is negative, destructive emotions. One of the worst of them is guilt. Guilt can be an anchor that holds you down and keeps you from living the abundant life Jesus promised those who follow Him.

As a Christian, you needn't dwell on guilt over your mistakes and sins. God didn't save you, forgive you, and set you on a new path in life so that you could spend your days chewing on guilt. Yes, learn from your past and become a better man—but don't ever believe that God is angry over that which He has forgotten (Hebrews 10:17).

MORNING: TRUSTING IN THE MESSIAH / *Who has believed our report? And to whom has the arm of the LORD been revealed?* Isaiah 53:1 NKJV / Jesus' ministry, miracles, and crucifixion were front-page news. As Paul told King Agrippa, "This thing was not done in a corner" (Acts 26:26 NKJV). But sadly, John says, "Despite all the miraculous signs Jesus had done, most of the people still did not believe in him" (John 12:37 NLT). Even astonishing miracles couldn't persuade everyone to trust that Jesus was the Messiah.

What about you? Do you trust Jesus in every area of your life? Do you trust what He says about the need to love your neighbor, forgive family members, or follow His teachings on financial matters? Or do you find yourself picking and choosing?

To "trust" means to put confidence in. Are you confident that Jesus always knows what He's talking about?

EVENING: ENDURING QUESTIONS / *"Are you the Messiah we've been expecting, or should we keep looking for someone else?"* Matthew 11:3 NLT / A common question that Christians ask is "Why doesn't God share more information with us?" John the Baptist certainly felt this confusion. Jesus said that no human being was "greater than John the Baptist" (Matthew 11:11 NLT), but John still wasn't given the inside information he wanted. Sitting in prison, he sent his disciples to ask Jesus if He was the Messiah.

Like John, you serve the Father's purposes on earth. He's using your life to teach the angels who "are eagerly watching these things happen" (1 Peter 1:12 NLT), and He's showing you that your deepest meaning comes from embracing "the evidence of things we cannot see" (Hebrews 11:1 NLT)—a faith that finds its greatest joy somewhere between the questions and the answers.

MORNING: RESTLESS, AND HATING IT / *Why am I restless? I should trust you, Lord. I will praise you again because you help me.* Psalm 42:5 CEV / Have you ever felt restless? You feel like you should do something, but you don't know what. You can't sleep well and you don't know why. You feel like you have a deadline, but you don't know when.

God can send unrest into our lives when we get too comfortable in circumstances He doesn't want for us or in a place where we've stayed too long. *Confusion, apprehension,* and *depression* could be signs of a godly unrest that screams, "Move."

Restlessness can be God's invitation to a new adventure. And if you ignore God's call, the restlessness won't go away until you surrender.

Thank God that we all feel restless at times—it's an incredible opportunity for us to follow His plan.

EVENING: NOT SO FAST / *But Jesus. . .knew all men. . . . He did not need anyone to testify concerning man, for He Himself knew what was in man+.* John 2:24–25 NASB / We all know how different we can be from one day to the next. As an old saying goes, "The only thing constant in life is change."

Jesus knew this better than anyone. Even though He went through physical changes during His life on earth, He was stable in His essential nature and purpose—unlike those who surrounded Him. Fickle crowds would follow Him, one day awed by His miracles and teachings, and the next trying to throw Him off a cliff (Luke 4:29)!

This is why Jesus would not be swayed by popularity. He looked beyond earthly popularity and success to His eternal Father, who never changes. Perfection can't.

MORNING: A PICTURE OF DEPENDABILITY / *As Scripture says, "Anyone who believes in him will never be put to shame."* Romans 10:11 NIV / Do you or someone you know have "trust issues"? Sometimes, those trust issues come as a result of a father who proved himself undependable.

You never have to worry about that with your Father in heaven. He always keeps His promises and is always there for you if you simply call to Him (Matthew 7:9–11).

When you bring your needs to God by faith—seeking salvation or some other vital help—you can trust in Him to generously give you what you ask for. When you place that kind of trust in your heavenly Father, He will never keep you guessing or let you down.

He's always there, even if it seems He's not.

EVENING: DELAYED WRATH / *"For my own name's sake I delay my wrath; for the sake of my praise I hold it back from you, so as not to destroy you completely."* Isaiah 48:9 NIV / God held numerous things against Israel. They invoked His name but didn't walk in righteousness (Isaiah 48:1), and God knew them to be stubborn rebels from birth (48:4, 8). They deserved His wrath, but for His own name's sake, He delayed it.

God is jealous, unwilling to share His glory with anyone else. Does this make you uncomfortable when you think about your own behavior? Just like Israel, you were born a rebel, deserving God's wrath.

But thanks be to God, He paid the price for you in the person of Jesus. You've been set free from the penalty of sin. Now walk in newness of life in a way that honors Him.

MORNING: HUMBLE AND PRODUCTIVE / *"Produce fruit in keeping with repentance. And do not think you can say to yourselves, 'We have Abraham as our father.' I tell you that out of these stones God can raise up children for Abraham."* Matthew 3:8–9 NIV / Dressed in camel's hair and a leather belt, John the Baptist reminded the religious leaders of his day that God doesn't need leaders who took pride in their position as God's children. After all, God could "raise up children" from rocks if He wanted to.

Do you ever descend into this way of thinking? Ever believe you're somehow special because you're a believer? John reminded us that our work is to *produce* fruit in keeping with repentance, not to luxuriate in it! After all, you couldn't produce any fruit without the Spirit working through you.

Stay humble—and stay productive.

EVENING: THE LORD'S JUDGMENTS ARE JUST / *"I can do nothing on my own. As I hear, I judge, and my judgment is just, because I seek. . .the will of him who sent me."* John 5:30 ESV / Since the Garden of Eden, Satan has tried to fool people into believing his first lie—that the Lord is unjust. Don't believe it!

Even Christian men may cringe when they think of God's judgments in scripture—the death and destruction that befell those who defiantly opposed the Lord. God Himself, however, has the first word on these judgments, declaring that He does "righteousness and justice" (Genesis 18:19 ESV).

At the end of history, great multitudes in heaven will have the last word as they proclaim, "Salvation and glory and power belong to our God, for his judgments are true and just" (Revelation 19:1–2 ESV).

MORNING: DOWN TO THE TOP / *The LORD came down on Mount Sinai, to the top of the mountain; and the LORD called Moses to the top of the mountain, and Moses went up.* Exodus 19:20 NASB / Not even Moses—the righteous man who faced Pharaoh, led God's people out of Egypt, and parted the Red Sea—could have reached God's dwelling place, even after he scaled the impressive Mount Sinai. God still had to close the gap by coming down to meet with him.

This story beautifully illustrates man's need to have God fill the space between Himself and us. No amount of human effort will ever connect us to God—only God's effort will bring us face-to-face. Fortunately, we don't need Moses' résumé or to repeat his grueling trip up a mountain; we have perfect access to God through Jesus Christ, who forever closes the gap.

EVENING: MAKING PLANS / *Commit your works to the LORD and your plans will be established.* Proverbs 16:3 NASB / If you've ever been involved in planning for a project or a new direction at work, you know there's one all-important step to take before those plans can become a reality: the boss needs to sign off on it.

The same thing can be said for a Christian who wants to launch out into some kind of new ministry or personal endeavor. In this evening's verse, Solomon says the best kind of planning involves committing your vision to your ultimate boss—God—and allowing Him to give ongoing direction.

Planning is the bedrock of every important thing we do. So, as you make your plans, don't forget to submit them to God for His approval and direction.

MORNING: WHO HAS GOD ENTRUSTED TO YOU? / *It was soon evident that God had entrusted me with the same message to the non-Jews as Peter had been preaching to the Jews.* Galatians 2:7 MSG / When Paul realized that God had entrusted him with reaching the Gentiles, it couldn't have been easy for him. His heart was with the Jews. "If there were any way I could be cursed by the Messiah so they could be blessed by him, I'd do it in a minute," he wrote in Romans 9:3 (MSG). "They're my family. I grew up with them."

Galatians 2:8 (NIV), however, explains Paul's ultimate conclusion: "For God, who was at work in Peter as an apostle to the circumcised, was also at work in me as an apostle to the Gentiles."

Whom has God entrusted to you? If He leads you to reach people who don't look, talk, or think like you, will you obey?

EVENING: CONDITIONAL PROMISES / *"If you return to the Lord with all your hearts, then put away the foreign gods and the Ashtoreths from among you, and prepare your hearts for the Lord, and serve Him only; and He will deliver you from the hand of the Philistines."* 1 Samuel 7:3 NKJV / Any wise father knows some of his promises to his children should be unconditional ("I will always love you!") and some should be conditional ("If you clean your room, you can go to the movies with your friends").

Many of God's promises are conditional, meaning you must do your part before He will do His. This evening's verse is one such promise.

When you read God's promises of blessing in the Bible, make sure you also take special note of what He expects of you before He fulfills them.

MORNING: ENDURING COMPASSION / *"I will strengthen Judah and save Israel: I will restore them because of my compassion. It will be as though I had never rejected them, for I am the LORD their God, who will hear their cries."* Zechariah 10:6 NLT / Jim Elliot once wrote, "Most laws condemn the soul and pronounce sentence. The result of the law of my God is perfect. It condemns but forgives. It restores—*more than abundantly*—what it takes away."

In this morning's verse, Zechariah reminded God's people that after receiving His forgiveness, they would live as though He had never rejected them.

Too often, believers live like their repentance only produces forgiveness rather than restoration. But Jesus' sacrifice not only frees people from the death they deserve, it restores them "more than abundantly." That is the enduring character in God's generous compassion.

EVENING: GOD JUDGES UNJUST "GODS" / *God presides in the great assembly; he renders judgment among the "gods."* Psalm 82:1 NIV / Jesus loved quoting from Psalm 82. Most people, however, are simply puzzled. Why is God talking about "gods"? Isn't the Lord the one and only true God?

First, notice the quotation marks around "gods." The Lord is speaking to those who judge wickedly and unjustly. God is warning earthly rulers, especially religious leaders. Wickedness and injustice can start man to man, but they often occur from the top down.

Unjust "gods" abound today. They purposefully "defend the unjust and show partiality to the wicked" (82:2 NIV), and they've forgotten their God-given mandate to "defend the weak and the fatherless" (82:3 NIV).

These deluded "gods" soon perish, however (82:5–7), while the Most High remains unchanged.

MORNING: OVERFLOWING / *For who is our hope or joy or crown of exaltation? Is it not even you, in the presence of our Lord Jesus at His coming? For you are our glory and joy.* 1 Thessalonians 2:19–20 NASB / Paul's enthusiasm for the Thessalonian believers bursts forth in words, in language usually reserved for God Himself. Imagine! Paul's "hope" and "joy" and "glory" are tied to this small group of people into whom he has poured his life. When Jesus returns, Paul plans on showing them off.

He's displaying the same excited attitude toward the Thessalonians that God has about all of us—pride and joy! God rejoices over us, brags about us, and dotes on us—and the things He's preparing in heaven for His children are beyond imagination (1 Corinthians 2:9).

When we see Him face-to-face, we'll truly understand what an extravagant parent God is.

EVENING: THE IMPORTANCE OF ACCOUNTABILITY / *Confess your sins to each other and pray for each other so that you may be healed.* James 5:16 NLT / Making yourself accountable to others isn't easy most of the time. Most men have some hidden, personal sins they'd rather not reveal even to their best friends.

Today's verse, however, challenges you to come clean with a godly friend. Most men won't be shocked when you do confess—on the contrary, you just might find a brother who is struggling with a similar sin.

Confessing your sins to your brothers allows them to know how to pray for and with you so that you can find lasting freedom. And it helps you to become accountable to those who love you and want you to overcome.

MORNING: SING TO THE LORD / *Sing to the Lord a new song, and His praise from the end of the earth! You who go down to the sea, and all that is in it, the islands and coastal regions and the inhabitants of them [sing a song such as has never been heard in the heathen world]!* Isaiah 42:10 AMPC / In the first nine verses of this chapter, Isaiah heralds the coming Messiah. He calls everyone, from fishermen to island dwellers, to sing a new song—one that had never been heard before in the heathen world—about the Lord's anointed Servant, soon to be revealed.

As Isaiah looked forward in faith, the church looks backward in faith, knowing that the Messiah has already come.

As you go about your normal routines, does the fact that Jesus died for your sins create a new song in your heart?

EVENING: LIFTING UP JESUS / *"And as Moses lifted up the serpent in the wilderness, even so must the Son of Man be lifted up, that whoever believes in Him should not perish but have eternal life."* John 3:14–15 NKJV / In this evening's scripture passage, Jesus likens Himself to the bronze snake Moses had held up in the wilderness so that the people of Israel could be healed of venomous bites (Numbers 21:4–9).

Today, men will turn to just about anything—money, status, alcohol, sex, sports, gambling, or gaming—as a remedy for their loneliness, guilt, and lack of purpose. But as a Christian, you have the one perfect antidote to every trouble—Jesus.

So when desperately needy and hurting people cross your path, God calls you to lift Jesus up, sharing the story of His gift of salvation.

MORNING: ENDURING OBSERVATIONS / *"Look at the nations and watch—and be utterly amazed. For I am going to do something in your days that you would not believe, even if you were told."* Habakkuk 1:5 NIV / Marshall McLuhan's maxim, "the medium is the message," asserts that the media to which we expose ourselves influence how we experience life. The Internet's instant access to any information, for instance, has changed society's degree of patience and contentment.

That's why Habakkuk counseled the people to "look" and "watch" as God used an unlikely nation to accomplish His purposes. God's actions would certainly "amaze" anyone who took the time to observe what He was doing.

Today, spend time—through this devotional book, ministry blogs, and the testimonies of others—looking at what God is doing in the world. Perhaps you'll find yourself so overwhelmed by Him that you can't help but celebrate with Habakkuk "on the heights" (3:19).

EVENING: ARE YOU LIKE KORAH'S SONS? / *A Psalm of the Sons of Korah. How lovely is your dwelling place, O Lord of hosts! My soul longs, yes, faints for the courts of the Lord; my heart and flesh sing for joy to the living God.* Psalm 84:1–2 ESV / Korah's story can be found in Numbers 16 and Numbers 26:9–10. After he rebelled against Moses, Korah and his followers were killed by God's judgment. Numbers 26:11 (ESV), however, adds the interesting note, "But the sons of Korah did not die."

These "sons of Korah" were upright and godly men who went on to become composers, musicians, singers, worship leaders, and prophets—and they're also the ones who authored Psalm 84!

These men serve as exhibit A that an ungodly, rebellious, and wicked father doesn't dictate his son's character or destiny.

MORNING: OPENING YOUR EYES / *For since the creation of the world His invisible attributes, His eternal power and divine nature, have been clearly seen, being understood through what has been made, so that they are without excuse.* Romans 1:20 NASB / Invisibility doesn't mean inaccessibility. Just because something is unseen doesn't mean it can't be known or understood in some meaningful way—for example, the air we breathe.

In the same way, God declares that at least two of His invisible qualities have been "clearly perceived" from the creation itself: His eternal power and His divine nature.

The paradox of seeing the invisible is resolved in creation itself. The fullest revelation of God in Christ is not required for God to hold mankind accountable for their actions—these two qualities He has published across time and space are more than enough.

EVENING: THE PRIVILEGE OF PAIN / *For you have been given not only the privilege of trusting in Christ but also the privilege of suffering for him.* Philippians 1:29 NLT / When the apostle Paul wrote of suffering, he did so with authority. Many times he had suffered beatings, sleeplessness, hunger, thirst, and cold—sometimes narrowly avoiding death—all for the cause of Jesus Christ (2 Corinthians 11:23–28). But instead of complaining, Paul viewed suffering for Christ as a privilege, a means to grow in his faith (Romans 5:3–5).

Few Western Christians have suffered the way Paul did. But whenever suffering does come—through loss, illness, or persecution—you too can see it as a privilege.

True joy is not based on a lack of pain but in knowing God intimately and walking with Him every day.

MORNING: A SECOND CHANCE / *The Lord will save me, and we will sing with stringed instruments all the days of our lives in the temple of the Lord.* Isaiah 38:20 NIV / Hezekiah certainly had reason to celebrate. After he'd fallen ill, the prophet Isaiah told Hezekiah to put his house in order because he was going to die (Isaiah 38:1). The king then cried out to God, and the Lord added fifteen years to his life (Isaiah 38:2–5).

Imagine thinking you're going to die at the age of thirty-nine but learning you would get to live until you are fifty-four. How might you use those final fifteen years differently than your first four decades? Surely *some* of that time would be spent praising the Lord!

Each breath you breathe represents another undeserved moment that God has graciously given you on this earth. How are you using your extra time?

EVENING: OUTWARD APPEARANCES / *But the Lord said to Samuel, "Do not consider his appearance or his height, for I have rejected him. . . . People look at the outward appearance, but the Lord looks at the heart."* 1 Samuel 16:7 NIV / You probably know that good-looking people (men and women alike) have many advantages in this life. It's just an unfortunate side effect of fallen human nature.

But this evening's verse challenges us to see things differently. It teaches that we should never judge or evaluate anyone, including ourselves, based on physical appearance. Rather, we should evaluate our own hearts to make sure we are focused on pleasing God in every area of life.

God doesn't care what men look like or what they've accomplished in this world. He concerns Himself only with what's in our hearts.

MORNING: ENDURANCE IN THE DEPTHS / *"Those who cling to worthless idols turn away from God's love for them."* Jonah 2:8 NIV / On his way down to the depths of the Mediterranean, Jonah made an important discovery: when people love anything more than God, they miss God's love in everything.

Jonah knew God's love would transform the citizens of Nineveh (whom he hated), so when God told him to warn them, he went the opposite direction.

But from the belly of the fish, Jonah learned the suffocating truth that idolatry intensifies isolation—isolation from the love of a God whose everyday interventions make life meaningful.

Today, it's worth taking inventory of your life. Are there any idols that need to be removed? Never turn away from God's love for you.

EVENING: BREAKING "ONLY ONE" COMMAND / "Is not this Bathsheba, the daughter of Eliam, the wife of Uriah the Hittite?" 2 Samuel 11:3 ESV / A man who walks outside the will of God tends to start breaking the Ten Commandments one after the other. Consider the infamous story of King David and Bathsheba.

First, "Thou shalt not kill" (Exodus 20:13 KJV): David plotted the death of a loyal soldier, Uriah the Hittite (2 Samuel 11:15). Second, "Thou shalt not commit adultery" (Exodus 20:14 KJV): David took Bathsheba into his bedroom (2 Samuel 11:4). Third, "Thou shalt not steal" (Exodus 20:15 KJV): David stole a woman from her husband. Fourth, "Thou shalt not bear false witness against thy neighbour" (Exodus 20:16 KJV: David tried to pin Bathsheba's pregnancy on Uriah (2 Samuel 11:13). And fifth, "Thou shalt not covet thy neighbour's wife" (Exodus 20:17 KJV): Coveting set this terrible chain of events into motion (2 Samuel 11:2).

There's no such thing as a "little sin."

DAY 219

MORNING: BOLD LIKE DAD / *...according to his eternal purpose that he accomplished in Christ Jesus our Lord. In him and through faith in him we may approach God with freedom and confidence.* Ephesians 3:11–12 NIV / God is bold in His love, invading history, overturning kingdoms, and even giving His own Son so that we can have a relationship with Him.

Writer Francis Chan has coined a name for this kind of relentless pursuit—"Crazy Love." This kind of love makes no excuses for its audacity.

God wants His children to share in His personality, take on His likeness, and live like Him. He's not looking for reluctance or hesitation in His children—He wants us to cast off everything that hinders us (Hebrews 12:1) and approach Him with freedom and confidence (Ephesians 3:12), knowing He made it possible.

EVENING: LIVING IN THE PAST / *Do not say, "Why were the old days better than these?" For it is not wise to ask such questions.* Ecclesiastes 7:10 NIV / Have you ever gotten together with a group of old friends to catch up and reminisce about your times together many years earlier? Those gatherings can be enjoyable, but they can also be frustrating if they cause you to long for "better times." That's especially true if you feel dissatisfaction with the present. In times like these, you may find yourself feeling ungrateful for what God is doing in your life right now.

There's nothing wrong with reminiscing about great times you've enjoyed in the past. But never let your great memories get in the way of living what God has for you in the here and now.

MORNING: WHOM ARE YOU SERVING? / Do not let any part of your body become an instrument of evil to serve sin. Instead, give yourselves completely to God. Romans 6:13 NLT / Although Paul needed to help the church in Rome sort out their beliefs, he also had to address their practices. How would the Roman Christians live each day in light of salvation in Christ? Considering that they were no longer dead in their sins, they should live differently because of God's power in their lives.

Today, ask yourself this question: Am I relying on God's power as I offer myself to His purposes in my life, or am I clinging to my own plans and desires?

Even when you've been saved by faith, your daily decisions matter a great deal—in your relationship with God and your ability to glorify Him.

EVENING: A SAFE PLACE? / *Even in laughter the heart may ache, and rejoicing may end in grief.* Proverbs 14:13 NIV / When beloved actor and comedian Robin Williams committed suicide in 2014, people were shocked. The man who had made so many laugh hadn't been willing to share his own problems—including severe depression and the effects of past drug and alcohol addiction—with the world. Ultimately, they overwhelmed him.

One of the church's biggest failures is that believers often fear they'll be judged if they admit to struggling or hurting. So we often hide our skeletons in the closet. But by ignoring the fundamental truth that we're *all* sinners in need of forgiveness, we make the church feel unsafe.

When the church is seen as a place of real healing, people will flock to it. Let's all do our part to throw the doors open.

DAY 221

MORNING: PRAYER CHANGES SITUATIONS / *The Sovereign* Lord *was calling for judgment by fire; it dried up the great deep and devoured the land. Then I cried out, "Sovereign* Lord*, I beg you, stop! How can Jacob survive? He is so small!" So the* Lord *relented.* Amos 7:4–6 niv / Just imagine what was going through Amos' mind when he found out that God's judgment on the nation of Israel had already begun. Amos loved his nation and its people, so his heart must have been breaking. Consequently, he got on his knees and pleaded on behalf of Israel. In response to Amos' prayers, "the Lord relented."

Do you know of a situation that needs to be changed? If so, go to God and offer Him specific prayers. Perhaps He is just waiting to change that circumstance before your eyes!

EVENING: GOD'S TOOLS TO SHAPE YOUR HEART / *You have thrown me into the lowest pit, into the darkest depths.* Psalm 88:6 nlt / First Chronicles describes Heman the Ezrahite—the author of this evening's psalm—as a multitalented Levite: a composer, musician, singer, worship leader, and prophet. Sadly, many such gifted men suffer from discouragement, depression, and despair.

Heman was no exception. Unlike every other psalm, Psalm 88 offers not even a hint of an uplifting note of hope, hallelujah, or inspiration.

A. W. Tozer admitted, "It is doubtful whether God can bless a man greatly until He has hurt him deeply." Often, discouragement, depression, and despair are God's tools to chip away at the faulty, rough, and wayward parts of your heart.

Like a world-class jeweler, the Lord wants to make you a million-dollar trophy of His loving-kindness, mercy, and grace—now and for eternity. Let Him!

MORNING: THE SOURCE OF TRUE FREEDOM / *Now the Lord is the Spirit, and where the Spirit of the Lord is, there is freedom. And we all. . .are being transformed into his image with ever-increasing glory.* 2 Corinthians 3:17–18 NIV / Paul was careful to say that both the law of Moses and the new covenant under Christ displayed the glory of God—Christ, however, has brought a deeper level of intimacy with God.

As we turn to the Lord and receive His Spirit, we are transformed into a new kind of freedom that empowers us to follow the lead of the Spirit. We aren't cut off from God's will or struggling to obey laws on our own.

God isn't waiting for us to get our act together. Rather, the Spirit gives us the freedom to dwell in God's presence and is transforming us into the image of Christ.

EVENING: HONESTY WITH GOD / *"I do believe; help my unbelief."* Mark 9:24 NASB / The words spoken in this evening's verse came from the mouth of a desperate man who wanted Jesus to heal his demon-possessed son.

How, you might wonder, *could a man who had heard so much about Jesus possibly doubt Him?* But maybe he didn't struggle with believing Jesus could heal people—maybe he just wondered if Jesus would help *him.*

The thought of being this honest with God scares many men. There are things, after all, you don't even want to admit to yourself, let alone to your Creator! But when you come to the end of yourself, this is just the kind of honesty He wants from you.

God can handle any doubts you confess to Him, and He can also open your heart and mind to what He has planned for you.

MORNING: REFUTING ARGUMENTS / *[Inasmuch as we] refute arguments and theories and reasonings and every proud and lofty thing that sets itself up against the [true] knowledge of God.* 2 Corinthians 10:5 AMPC / Paul often battled false philosophy. He "reasoned and argued" from the scriptures with the Jews in Thessalonica for three Sabbaths about the need for Jesus to die and rise from the dead (Acts 17:2 AMPC). Later, he encountered Epicurean and Stoic philosophers and engaged them in discussion.

The darkness is not pushed back with physical weapons. Instead, one of the ways it loses ground is when the people of God refute faulty reasoning.

Are you engaging in civil discussion with people who oppose your Christian worldview? You don't have to be a scholar. Simply preach Christ crucified and hold fast to the resurrection. God will be with you.

EVENING: WHEN GOD SEEMS SILENT / *O God, do not remain silent; do not turn a deaf ear, do not stand aloof, O God.* Psalm 83:1 NIV / At the end of World War II, the following was found scrawled on the wall of a Nazi concentration camp: *"I believe in the sun even when it's not shining. I believe in love even when I don't feel it. I believe in God even when He is silent."*

In the horrors of a concentration camp, it would probably be very easy to question God's existence. Yet this anonymous believer found the inner faith to continue believing.

Life is truly difficult sometimes, and you may find yourself occasionally questioning whether God cares about your struggles. Even psalm writers felt that way on occasion.

But the Lord still wants you to cast your cares on Him. He truly cares about you (1 Peter 5:7).

MORNING: GOD IS JUST / *This is what the Lord says: "For three sins of Damascus, even for four, I will not relent."* Amos 1:3 NIV / It's tough to see just how wicked our world is. Seemingly every day, the dishonesty and corruption and violence increase. Sometimes we only view the trouble on our screens. At other times, people's sin touches us and our loved ones personally.

If you ever feel overwhelmed by the injustice, know that God doesn't. He is fully aware of who's suffering and who's causing the trouble. And He has a plan to make everything right. Those of us who truly follow Jesus will be rewarded with rest. The troublemakers will be punished.

God is just. He will ultimately take care of everything—including you.

EVENING: HATING LIFE? / *"Anyone who. . .hates their life in this world will keep it for eternal life."* John 12:25 NIV / Have you ever heard a depressed person blurt out the words "I hate this life"?

When Jesus told His followers to "hate their life in this world," He didn't mean going through life lamenting that you're stuck here on earth. That's not the abundant life He promised those who love and faithfully follow Him (John 10:10).

Rather, Jesus wants you to remember that this life is nothing compared with what God has for you beyond the here and now: your forever home in a place Jesus called "paradise."

God has given you a precious life here on earth. You can express your gratitude by giving every day to Him as a sacrifice of praise and thanksgiving.

MORNING: DOES GOD HAVE YOUR ATTENTION? / *Do not be like the horse or the mule, which. . .must be controlled by bit and bridle. . . . Many are the woes of the wicked, but the LORD's unfailing love surrounds the one who trusts in him.* Psalm 32:9–10 NIV / C. S. Lewis wrote, "God whispers to us in our pleasures, speaks in our conscience, but shouts in our pains: it is His megaphone to rouse a deaf world."

Sometimes, our pain and difficult situations can feel like a bit or bridle that drags us back to God. The solution, according to this psalm, is to understand and to trust God's unfailing love to surround us whether our lives are difficult or pleasant.

God's love doesn't force us to act in a particular way. Rather, it's always present and comforting, remaining faithful even when we wander.

EVENING: RECEIVING WISDOM / *Listen to advice and accept discipline, so that you may be wise the rest of your days.* Proverbs 19:20 NASB / One of many amazing things about God is that as long as you're committed to walking with Him, He never allows an experience to go to waste.

The apostle James had no doubt observed what many Christian leaders since the first century have seen: people don't always know how to respond wisely during difficult times. That is why he instructed the first-century believers, who lived during very perilous times, to seek God for wisdom and to be assured that He would give them what they asked for.

God promises to give wisdom—through His written Word, His Holy Spirit, life experiences, and other people—to anyone who asks for it.

Are you open to the different ways God can grant your request?

MORNING: BUILDING WITH GOD / *Commit your actions to the Lord, and your plans will succeed.* Proverbs 16:3 NLT / The devil often fights what men of God are doing, so you need divine assistance to bring your good works to completion. A solid Bible promise states, "Commit everything you do to the Lord. Trust him, and he will help you" (Psalm 37:5 NLT). He'll help you, that is, if the project was His will to begin with.

On the other hand, the Bible warns, "Except the Lord build the house, they labour in vain that build it" (Psalm 127:1 KJV). Too many men are spinning their wheels when they never checked for God's stamp of approval first. Whatever they're trying to accomplish, it won't succeed. Not for long, anyway.

Before you embark on any project, lay it before God for His blessing. And be sure to give Him space to say no.

EVENING: A SOURCE OF CONFIDENCE / *David inquired of the Lord, "Shall I pursue this raiding party?"* 1 Samuel 30:8 NIV / Have you ever felt a burden to do something important but wanted assurance that God approved?

Today's scripture records King David's prayer as he sought God's go-ahead to pursue an enemy who had committed atrocities against the city of Ziklag. David asked God a very specific question: Would a military venture against the raiders be successful? God's answer was a very clear yes, so David launched the campaign. In the end, it was one of David's finest hours.

None should launch out on life-altering ventures without first seeking a green light from God. He promises to hear your prayers and act on your behalf—that includes giving you approval for plans that align with His will.

MORNING: HIS WAYS ARE RIGHT / *Who is wise? Let him understand these things. Who is prudent? Let him know them. For the ways of the Lord are right; the righteous walk in them, but transgressors stumble in them.* Hosea 14:9 NKJV / This morning's verse points us to true wisdom: the ways of our Father in heaven. It amplifies Solomon's words: "The fear of the Lord is the beginning of wisdom, and knowledge of the Holy One is understanding" (Proverbs 9:10 NIV).

In today's age of social media, people often prefer witty aphorisms over well-thought-out perspectives. But this worldly wisdom is almost always incomplete or false.

That's why God's words to Hosea are as important to us today as they were back then. God is our source of complete wisdom, and His ways are the best ways for us to follow, no matter what the world says.

EVENING: WITH JESUS—FOREVER / *"And if I go and prepare a place for you, I will come back and take you to be with me that you also may be where I am."* John 14:3 NIV / Jesus knew that His time on earth was short. He had spent the past three years healing the sick, feeding the hungry, and delivering life-changing teaching about the kingdom of God. But it wouldn't be long before He completed the most important task of His time on earth: dying on a cross and rising from the dead.

Before leaving His disciples behind to complete His work here on earth, Jesus promised them—and you—that He would prepare a place where they could be with Him. . .forever.

Loving someone means wanting to be with that person. Jesus wants to spend eternity with you!

MORNING: LOVE BEGINS WITH FAITH / *We love because he first loved us.* 1 John 4:19 NIV / Our image of God will determine how we treat others.

When John wrote about love, it was from the perspective of someone who saw God's love with tremendous clarity. Out of that deep reserve of love and acceptance, John found that he was able to extend grace to others.

In fact, the best way to gauge our relationship with God is how we treat others. If we love others, then we have experienced God's love. If we are fearful, angry, or uncaring, then we've most likely not encountered God for ourselves.

Showing love may require some effort on our part, but it most certainly begins with faith: believing that God loves us. That foundation of love makes it possible to love and accept others regardless of how they have treated us.

EVENING: WHAT ARE YOUR CREDENTIALS? / *Amos answered Amaziah, "I was neither a prophet nor the son of a prophet, but I was a shepherd."* Amos 7:14 NIV / Have you ever felt challenged to get more involved in a ministry but thought, *I don't know how much help I can be. I don't have any kind of education or credentials.*

Men tend to put a lot of stock in credentials. They see the highly educated or accomplished as somehow more qualified or trustworthy. But as someone once said, "God doesn't call the qualified; He qualifies the called."

God doesn't look first at your credentials but rather your willingness to obediently step out and be used by Him to influence your part of the world for His kingdom.

As long as you're willing, you don't need a doctorate in theology—the qualifications He gives will be more than enough!

MORNING: A BIBLICAL ANATOMY LESSON / *Just as a body, though one, has many parts, but all its many parts form one body, so it is with Christ.* 1 Corinthians 12:12 NIV / In 1 Corinthians 12, the apostle Paul likens the church to the human body, which consists of many individual parts—some big and some small—that work wonderfully together for one purpose: to keep you alive and moving.

If Paul were writing to the different church bodies today, he'd tell them the same thing. Each member has a part to play for the greater good of the church.

God doesn't intend for you to attend church services every week just to warm a pew. On the contrary, He has given you special gifts and abilities so that you can serve this wonderful organism called the body of Christ.

EVENING: THE ULTIMATE BANQUET / *On this mountain the Lord of Armies will prepare for all people a feast with the best foods, a banquet with aged wines, with the best foods and the finest wines.* Isaiah 25:6 GW / A time is coming when God's people will attend a feast made possible by Jesus the Messiah. It'll be an all-inclusive feast, for both the Jew and the Gentile who has called on the name of Jesus.

It should be no surprise that as you currently break bread with friends and family, it leads to some of the most intimate conversations you experience. When you sit down with the intention of pulling away from the cares of this world, you are freer to focus on the people around your table. Imagine having such an experience with the "Lord of Armies"—it will be the ultimate banquet!

MORNING: GOD WITH YOU / *David. . .became more and more powerful, because the LORD God Almighty was with him.* 2 Samuel 5:9–10 NIV / The biblical story of David is amazing. He rose from humble beginnings to a position of great power and prestige in the ancient world. Yet David didn't grow in power because of his own wisdom and strength, let alone because he was perfect in all his ways—in fact, he was far from it. Rather, he grew in his power for one reason: God was with him.

God may not have planned to make you powerful, famous, or rich. But His plans for those He loves are perfect, and you can place yourself in the middle of those plans when you align your desires with His.

EVENING: GREATLY BELOVED / *Then again, the one having the likeness of a man touched me and strengthened me. And he said, "O man greatly beloved, fear not! Peace be to you; be strong, yes, be strong!"* Daniel 10:18–19 NKJV / Earthly fathers who want to raise confident, courageous children can take a huge step toward making that a reality when they let their children know one thing: they are genuinely loved.

Similarly, God prompted Daniel toward courage by starting with the words, "O man greatly beloved." And because he embraced his value in God's eyes, Daniel went on to accomplish powerful things.

As a Christian, you can think of yourself as many things in God's eyes: saved, redeemed, blessed, set aside, and so much more. Don't forget, however, that you are all those things because you are, above all, *greatly beloved.*

MORNING: A CLEAN CONSCIENCE / *But after he had taken the census, David's conscience began to bother him.* 2 Samuel 24:10 NLT / Remember the old saying "Let your conscience be your guide"? That's actually good advice for a Christian man. Your conscience, when it's in tune with the Lord, can keep you out of trouble and alert you to unconfessed sin.

King David made a huge mistake when he ordered one of his servants to count all the people of Israel—an act the law of Moses prohibited. David later realized he had sinned against God, and he confessed his wrongdoing.

Living unshakably requires that you keep your conscience clean and sensitive to what God is saying to you through both His written Word and His Holy Spirit. When your conscience tells you that it's time to make things right with your heavenly Father, listen and obey!

EVENING: THE JOY OF GROWING STRONGER / *Consider it pure joy, my brothers and sisters, whenever you face trials of many kinds, because you know that the testing of your faith produces perseverance.* James 1:2–3 NIV / Everyone wants to experience "pure joy," but not many people would think of a trial or test of faith as an opportunity to experience it.

What was James thinking?

For starters, James was looking at the big picture. He saw the whole of life stretched before him, continuing into eternity—where God will reward those who have remained faithful. All believers will face difficulties, so trusting God in today's trials will prepare them to remain faithful in future challenges.

If our difficulties help us remain close to Christ, then we can trust that even the most disappointing setbacks will help our faith leap forward.

MORNING: SHOWING RESPECT / *Show proper respect to everyone, love the family of believers, fear God, honor the emperor.* 1 Peter 2:17 NIV / It may come as a surprise to many Christian men, but God calls each of His people to show respect for others, no matter their beliefs or lifestyles. That's not always easy, especially when people show disregard for the truths revealed in God's Word. But the actions of others don't relieve you of your responsibility to treat them with respect.

Respect doesn't mean giving approval to sinful lifestyles—it simply means seeing and treating people as valued creations made in the image of God.

Your role as a Christian is to be an example of God's love and grace. You move yourself closer to that goal when you show love and respect for all.

EVENING: INTERNAL RENEWAL / *Though outwardly we are wasting away, yet inwardly we are being renewed day by day. For our light and momentary troubles are achieving for us an eternal glory that far outweighs them all.* 2 Corinthians 4:16–17 NIV / Paul knew his time on earth was short. If he didn't die from an ailment, beatings, drowning, or starvation, he knew he would die for His faith. Even so, he referred to his extreme hardship as "light and momentary" in light of the fact that his soul was being renewed day by day.

If you're over the age of thirty-five, you probably know exactly how Paul felt when he spoke of wasting away outwardly—aches, pains, and losses start to accumulate very quickly. But, praise God, the more a Christian wastes away outwardly, the more he's being renewed inwardly as the Holy Spirit transforms him.

MORNING: GOD'S TIMING / *When Mary reached the place where Jesus was and saw him, she fell at his feet and said, "Lord, if you had been here, my brother would not have died."* John 11:32 NIV / When Lazarus' sister Mary first met Jesus after her brother's death, she voiced a measure of faith. However, she also protested that if Jesus had only come sooner, Lazarus would still be alive. You can feel her profound sense of grief and disappointment.

In the end, however, Mary and her sister, Martha, saw God glorified when Jesus brought their brother back to life. Many others also witnessed this miracle and put their faith in Jesus.

Are you facing a situation where you think God has failed you? If so, hold to your faith and wait. Maybe God has a great miracle planned—one that will benefit you, glorify God, and bring others to belief.

EVENING: OUR SOURCE OF UNDERSTANDING / *Daniel replied, "No wise man, enchanter, magician or diviner can explain to the king the mystery he has asked about, but there is a God in heaven who reveals mysteries."* Daniel 2:27–28 NIV / After having a troubling dream, the Babylonian king Nebuchadnezzar turned to his astrologers and magicians. But they couldn't help him. That's when he turned to Daniel, the man of God.

With the Lord's help, Daniel solved the mystery of the king's dream. But first, he imparted some wisdom that's still important to us today: God had given Nebuchadnezzar his dream, and only God could explain what it meant—not wise men, enchanters, magicians, or diviners.

It's sometimes tempting to turn to sources of worldly wisdom when we're desperate for answers. But if we're truly seeking understanding, we should always trust God. And His answer will always agree with His written Word.

MORNING: HONESTY / *"Use only honest weights and scales and honest measures."* Ezekiel 45:10 NLT / The Bible makes a big deal about honesty in every part of our lives, including our work and business practices. Even most non-Christian businessmen understand that honesty is the best policy. After all, a shady reputation can quickly lead to business failure.

Of course, honesty is all the more important for the man who follows Christ, simply because that's the way God calls us to be.

How important is honesty to you? Do you always try your best to speak truthfully? Do you always make sure you don't waste your company's time when you're on the clock? Do you always treat business clients scrupulously?

You demonstrate your love for God—and for your neighbor—when you practice integrity and honesty in every area of your life.

EVENING: IN JESUS' NAME / *"At that time you won't need to ask me for anything. I tell you the truth, you will ask the Father directly, and he will grant your request because you use my name."* John 16:23 NLT / You've no doubt heard ministers and laypeople alike end prayers with the words "In Jesus' name, amen!" This evening's scripture passage shows that this isn't just a platitude. These words are very powerful.

Jesus told His followers that when they prayed using His name, they would receive what they asked for—all because of the world-changing work He did when He died on the cross and then rose from the dead three days later. From that time forward, they had full access to God the Father through Jesus. So do you!

When you pray, remember whose you are—and then make your requests in His powerful, wonderful name.

MORNING: STOPPING ANGER IN ITS TRACKS / *My dear brothers and sisters, take note of this: Everyone should be quick to listen, slow to speak and slow to become angry, because human anger does not produce the righteousness that God desires.* James 1:19–20 NIV / When we believe we've been insulted, it's easy to jump to conclusions and offer a biting, ready-made reply. Once this happens, practically nothing can stop the argument from spiraling out of control.

Listening is the best defense against unhelpful and unrighteous anger—that's why James wisely counsels us to be quick to listen. James doesn't tell us to stop being angry; rather, he tells us listening first keeps us from becoming angry for the wrong reasons.

Perhaps if we prioritize listening, we'll also begin to hear the still, small voice of God speaking into our lives.

EVENING: LONE RANGER CHRISTIANITY / *All the believers devoted themselves to the apostles' teaching, and to fellowship, and to sharing in meals (including the Lord's Supper), and to prayer.* Acts 2:42 NLT / Several polls show that more and more people—including many professing Christians—say they don't go to church services regularly, if at all.

One of the most common alibis for skipping church is "I don't have to go to church to be a Christian." While that may technically be true, it's also true that in order to grow in your faith, you need the teaching and fellowship you receive when you gather for worship and Bible study—as seen by this evening's verse.

God never intended for you to be a Lone Ranger Christian. That's why it's a good plan for you to find a church that provides sound teaching and then commit to attending regularly.

MORNING: THE FRAGRANCE OF CHRIST / *In the Messiah, in Christ, God leads us from place to place in one perpetual victory parade. Through us, he brings knowledge of Christ. Everywhere we go, people breathe in the exquisite fragrance.* 2 Corinthians 2:14–15 MSG / As Paul traveled from place to place, the gospel was having its way with people—so much so that he referred to his travels as a perpetual victory parade. Of course, he faced hardship in his missionary journeys. But the gospel still prevailed, bringing in the fragrance of Christ, much like the scent of perfume follows a woman wherever she goes.

Would you describe your own travels as a perpetual spiritual victory parade? Does the fragrance of Christ follow you into worship? Into local cafés? Into work?

Make no mistake: if you truly belong to Christ, it will.

EVENING: COME HOME / *Your love has always been our lives' foundation, your fidelity has been the roof over our world.* Psalm 89:2 MSG / The foundation of your spiritual life is God's love. The roof? His faithfulness. God keeps you both steady and protected. Now you can face spiritual earthquakes and tornadoes with confidence.

But there's more. God wants you to stop believing that if things are going to get done it will be due to your own effort, planning, and personal experience.

Throughout biblical history, men who trusted God often stopped consulting Him like they once did. Many ultimately chose a path leading away from the foundation and roof of God's love and faithfulness. Just think of mighty King Solomon and Judas Iscariot, for instance.

But your life doesn't have to end this way. God always works to remind you of the place where love and faithfulness invite you home.

MORNING: ATTENTION TO DETAIL / *The L*ORD *said to me, "Son of man, take careful notice. Use your eyes and ears, and listen to everything I tell you about the regulations concerning the L*ORD*'s Temple. Take careful note of the procedures for using the Temple's entrances and exits."* Ezekiel 44:5 NLT / Often, online job listings include the qualification "attention to detail." That usually means that the job requires the worker to pay close attention to the little things.

God gave Ezekiel some detailed instructions for the Jewish priesthood when the Jews returned to Jerusalem after the Babylonian exile. That's why He told the prophet, "Take careful notice."

There may be times in your walk with the Lord—and in your daily Bible readings—when He seems to be telling you, "Pay close attention. This is very important!"

And if God says it's important, you'd do well to listen closely.

EVENING: SOMETHING EVERY GUY NEEDS / *So God replied, "Because you have asked for wisdom in governing my people with justice. . .I will give you what you asked for!"* 1 Kings 3:11–12 NLT / A New Testament verse begins with these words: "If you need wisdom. . ." (James 1:5 NLT). Maybe it's good to personalize this verse by imagining it saying, *"When I need wisdom."* Between work, family, ministry, and other important duties, you have a lot on your plate. In order to live an unshakable life, you need wisdom every day—every guy does.

The good news is that God wants to give you His wisdom—just like He did for Solomon. He'll never look down on you when you ask for wisdom, and He'll always provide it—so you can flourish in every area of your life.

MORNING: LIVING BY FAITH / *Who may ascend the mountain of the* L*ORD? Who may stand in his holy place? The one who has clean hands and a pure heart, who does not trust in an idol or swear by a false god.* Psalm 24:3–4 NIV / When the writer of this psalm says that those who stand in God's holy place will not trust in an idol or swear by a false god, we would do well to remember that idols and false gods weren't just passing fads: they were often trusted to provide essentials for life—rain for crops, fertility, and so on.

Those who live by faith in God, however, place their trust in Him alone—not personal influence, wealth, or relationships—for their daily needs, believing that their obedience will not be in vain.

Are you living by faith today?

EVENING: YOU NEED GOD'S CORRECTION / *I know,* L*ORD, that our lives are not our own. We are not able to plan our own course. So correct me,* L*ORD, but please be gentle.* Jeremiah 10:23–24 NLT / In the midst of the destruction of his homeland, the prophet Jeremiah saw the fragility of life firsthand. But under the crushing loss of his country, he entrusted himself to God.

We rarely face that kind of devastation and heartbreak, but we may see our plans, hopes, and dreams unravel in an instant. We're surrounded by people whose choices can dramatically impact the course of our lives.

In the midst of this uncertainty, you can join with Jeremiah in placing your trust in God. We can all look to the Lord for correction, instruction, and guidance.

MORNING: REMEMBER THE DAYS OF LONG AGO / *I remember the days of long ago; I meditate on all your works and consider what your hands have done.* Psalm 143:5 NIV / While David was running from Absalom's rebellion, he began recalling the days of old when God continually delivered him from Saul's hands. And in remembering God's faithfulness, he entered worship mode, lifting his hands to the Lord and writing this psalm.

Are you going through a trial that feels familiar—like one you've endured in the past but hoped never to have to face again? If so, consult your journal or talk to the person who prayed and walked with you through the trial the first time.

Doing so will remind you of the little ways God provided. It will fill you with great hope and lead you into a spirit of worship for what God has already accomplished.

EVENING: LIFE CHANGE / *Jesus said to him, "I am the way, the truth, and the life. No one comes to the Father except through Me."* John 14:6 NKJV / Positive life change. Most people want it; some go to great lengths to find it.

You may have explored self-help methods, behavior modification, multiple steps to success, or changing your network of friends. But none of these things bring lasting change. There's only way to reach the truly abundant life—*Jesus*.

Only He can save you from the penalty of sin, separation from God, and life without direction. Only He provides *real* life change. And He's just waiting for you to call.

MORNING: A GOD OF THE IMPOSSIBLE / *I saw a great many bones on the floor of the valley, bones that were very dry. He asked me, "Son of man, can these bones live?" I said, "Sovereign LORD, you alone know."* Ezekiel 37:2–3 NIV / When God showed the prophet Ezekiel a vision of a valley filled with dry bones, He asked him a single question: "Can these bones live?"

Ezekiel knew that God could do the impossible, and the vision ended with these dry bones covered with flesh and coming to life.

Today, God is showing each of us our own valleys filled with dry bones—the people in our lives who don't know Jesus—and asking us, "Can these bones live?"

The answer, of course, is *Yes, they can!* Our part in making that miracle happen is to speak the words of life we know as the gospel of Jesus Christ.

EVENING: NO HARM OR DISASTER / *If you say, "The LORD is my refuge" and you make the Most High your dwelling, no harm will overtake you, no disaster will come near your tent.* Psalm 91:9–10 NIV / As you read this evening's scripture passage, you might find yourself thinking, *How can this be? A lot of godly men have faced harm and disaster! Is there some kind of typo in these verses?*

Jesus once warned His followers, "In this world you will have trouble" (John 16:33 NIV). But He also promised in that same verse, "I have overcome the world."

In light of that, you can interpret this evening's scripture reading to mean that while you'll encounter many difficulties in this life, if you make the Lord your refuge you'll ultimately never be defeated.

MORNING: OUR DAILY BREAD VS. OUR ETERNAL BREAD / *"Do not work for food that spoils, but for food that endures to eternal life, which the Son of Man will give you."* John 6:27 NIV / Jesus didn't instruct His disciples to pray for storehouses of grain or reserves of coins; rather, He told them to ask God for a much more temporary provision—their daily bread.

It's almost maddening to think that a God with limitless resources would instruct us to ask for so small a provision. But perhaps Jesus knew of our tendency to rely on possessions rather than God.

Our strength, finances, and relationships will fail us when we need them the most, but the presence of Christ in our lives will never let us down. The only sure "long-term" bet is the eternal bread of Jesus Himself, nourishing us and providing for our needs day by day.

EVENING: IS TRUSTING GOD A "RISK"? / *Those who live in the shelter of the Most High will find rest in the shadow of the Almighty. This I declare about the* Lord: *He alone is my refuge, my place of safety; he is my God, and I trust him.* Psalm 91:1–2 NLT / What does it mean to dwell in God's shelter? Perhaps it means releasing control over a specific life circumstance. For others, it may be taking a step of faith. The irony is that trusting God as your sole refuge can often feel more like a risk.

As you grapple with your desire for safety, ponder the words of this psalm. How does it feel to have God as your refuge and stronghold? Does it feel like a risk right now? Are there ways you can learn to grow deeper in your trust in God today?

MORNING: COME, LORD JESUS! / *It will happen in a moment. . .when the last trumpet is blown. For when the trumpet sounds, those who have died will be raised to live forever. And we who are living will also be transformed.* 1 Corinthians 15:52 NLT / In this morning's verse, the church is promised resurrection. A trumpet will sound and the dead in Christ shall rise to be transformed into a resurrected body. Those who are still living will also be transformed.

"And cannot the same power now change us into saints in a moment?" John Wesley asked in his commentary. Surely it can. The promise of resurrection should help us determine how we will spend our time, money, and energy right now.

Knowing that the final trumpet can sound at any minute, it's time to get busy doing kingdom work and leave the foolish pursuits of this world behind.

EVENING: LIFE IN THE REARVIEW MIRROR / *God guaranteed his covenant with me, spelled it out plainly and kept every promised word.* 2 Samuel 23:5 MSG / As David, Israel's most famous king, neared the end of his life, he could have lamented his poor choices, impulses, and personal example. Conversely, he could have focused on his personal achievements, adventurous life, and winner-take-all battle with the giant, Goliath. But he didn't.

Instead, David spent most of his final words recounting God's faithfulness. He recalled the bad days and the God who made them good. He saw the value of following the God of both mercy and justice.

If this resonates with you as an "I-want-that-too" kind of life, take courage! Always remember the goodness of God. It will bring the contrast that's needed to pull you out of bitterness, revenge, or an unforgiving spirit. *This thinking changes a man.*

DAY 243

MORNING: A NEW HEART / *"I will remove from you your heart of stone and give you a heart of flesh."* Ezekiel 36:26 NIV / On December 3, 1967, at Groote Schuur Hospital in Cape Town, South Africa, a large team led by surgeon Christiaan Barnard performed the world's first human-to-human heart transplant.

As incredible as this medical event was, God did something even more amazing when He saved you. At the moment you humbled yourself before Him, He replaced your old, stony heart with a new, soft heart. This spiritual heart transplant changed you in every way: you actually became a completely new person (2 Corinthians 5:17).

Through the work of His Holy Spirit, God gave you a new, undivided heart that can hear Him and respond to what He says to you. This new heart will never need to be replaced again.

EVENING: THRILLED! / *You thrill me, Lord, with all you have done for me! I sing for joy because of what you have done.* Psalm 92:4 NLT / Can you remember a time you worshipped God with everything you had, then felt overwhelmed with joy?

While you shouldn't base your relationship with God on emotion alone, you can still enjoy those moments when your heart feels overwhelmed with love and gratitude toward your heavenly Father. He's more than worthy of all the praise you can give Him.

When you think deeply about who God really is, and then about the wonderful things He has done for you (starting with your eternal salvation), you'll find yourself feeling deep gratitude and speaking words of praise to your heavenly Father.

That's what being *thrilled* with God looks like.

MORNING: HOPE FOR DOUBTERS / *He said to them, "How foolish you are, and how slow to believe all that the prophets have spoken!". . .He explained to them what was said in all the Scriptures concerning himself.* Luke 24:25, 27 NIV / At one point or another, we all struggle through situations that test our faith or cause us to question the goodness of God.

In this morning's passage, we find two followers of Jesus who had essentially given up. They were confused and fearful, having fled Jerusalem for fear of losing their lives. So far as we can tell, they believed Jesus' movement was finished. But despite their doubts, Jesus still showed up and eventually revealed Himself to them.

Whenever you're looking for Jesus or just wandering in confusion, remember: all is not lost. He's more than willing to show up and lead you back to faith.

EVENING: WHY JESUS IS MERCIFUL / *This High Priest of ours understands our weaknesses, for he faced all of the same testings we do, yet he did not sin.* Hebrews 4:15 NLT / Sometimes, it's hard to acknowledge our weaknesses or our need for help. We live in a self-sufficient culture, so it may come as a shock to read that Jesus spent time on earth in order to feel your weaknesses and to show mercy to you.

If you struggle with sin or don't think you can set your life right, know this: Jesus felt your fears, inadequacies, and weaknesses. He knows that you're tempted and that you won't always make the best choices. Yet He's merciful, and He wants you to come to Him in your failure.

Acknowledging our weaknesses is the first step toward restoration.

MORNING: THE LEAST / *For I am the least of the apostles, who am not worthy to be called an apostle, because I persecuted the church of God. But by the grace of God I am what I am.* 1 Corinthians 15:9–10 NKJV / Paul's background wasn't a secret. Prior to his conversion, he persecuted the church and even watched approvingly as Stephen was stoned (Acts 22:20). It's no wonder Paul considered himself the least of the apostles—it's difficult to have an inflated ego when you have such a checkered past.

Do you consider yourself the least of the men at your church or in your Bible study? Or have you gotten so comfortable in your faith that you're feeling puffed up?

Paul had quite the religious background (Philippians 3:3–6), but he had no confidence in his post-conversion flesh. Neither should we.

EVENING: WORLD-CHANGING OBEDIENCE / *"As you sent me into the world, so I have sent them into the world."* John 17:18 ESV / Nothing escapes Jesus' attention. He knew the troubles and persecutions His disciples would face once He returned to God. All the more, He needed them to know they were receiving a commission from His heavenly Father, who wanted to use them to shake the Roman empire.

Jesus knew that as His disciples were increasingly transformed, they would be more and more useful in helping change the hearts, minds, and lives of those who never met Him face-to-face. Jesus longed for the societal changes that would bring His wisdom and purpose to the top of mankind's list of choices.

The world changed because Jesus obeyed. Today, the world continues to change because His followers obey.

Are you shaking the world for Jesus?

MORNING: RIGHTLY MOTIVATED / *"For with their mouth they show much love, but their hearts pursue their own gain."* Ezekiel 33:31 NKJV / As a Christian man, you probably attend church services regularly. That's a good thing. You might go to a weekly men's Bible study. That's also a positive. And you might even give till it hurts to your church or other ministry. God approves!

But how often do you take the time to examine your real motives for the things you do? How often do you look into your heart to make sure that the things you do and say are truly motivated out of true love for God and not out of what you consider proper religious duty?

God sees our hearts first, not our outward religious acts. That's why it's important to not just do the right things but do them for the right reasons.

EVENING: LET GOD BE GOD / *O Lord God, You to Whom vengeance belongs. . .shine forth! . . . Lord, how long shall the wicked, how long shall the wicked triumph and exult?* Psalm 94:1, 3 AMPC / Do you ever look at all the sin and injustice in the world around you and wonder why God doesn't just come down and set things right?

The psalmist seemed to wonder the very same thing, pointedly asking God how He could allow evil men to continuously prosper. But he starts out his complaint by acknowledging one important fact: all vengeance belongs to the Lord. Recompence for sin and injustice does not belong to us—it's in the hands of a God who possesses perfect wisdom.

So let God be God—and live unshakably in the knowledge that He has everything under control.

MORNING: THE BLESSING OF AN ENDING / *Teach us to number our days, that we may gain a heart of wisdom.* Psalm 90:12 NIV / Aging sparks no end of troubling moments. If anything, we may find less wisdom and more regret and recklessness as yet another year passes by. Each crisis of aging is rooted in the terrifying realization that we will all face death one day.

However, the psalm writer assures us that numbering our days can actually lead us to greater wisdom. After all, once we view our days as limited, aren't we compelled to consider how to use them best? Doesn't each day we have become all the more valuable?

By numbering our days with an awareness of their limited supply, we'll have greater clarity when discerning our priorities, and we'll find greater peace in the knowledge of God's presence.

EVENING: HOW WE GROW / *So get rid of all evil behavior. Be done with all deceit, hypocrisy, jealousy, and all unkind speech. Like newborn babies, you must crave pure spiritual milk so that you will grow into a full experience of salvation.* 1 Peter 2:1–2 NLT / Peter seems to have taken Jesus' instructions about becoming like children a step further: he tells his readers to become like infants.

Just as infants have a simple, single-minded dependence on their mothers for milk, we should depend entirely on God's nurturing care for us. Failing to do so leads to envy, hypocrisy, criticism, and deceit as we strive harder and harder to overcome our many spiritual struggles.

Don't waste your life longing to become more spiritual—long for the presence of the Lord instead. Once you've tasted the goodness of the Lord, you'll find deliverance from your greatest struggles.

MORNING: FLEE FROM HER / *I discovered that a seductive woman is a trap more bitter than death. Her passion is a snare, and her soft hands are chains.* Ecclesiastes 7:26 NLT / If any man was qualified to warn other men about seduction, it would be Solomon. He had seven hundred wives and three hundred concubines, and they turned his heart away from the Lord to worship Ashtoreth and Molech (1 Kings 11:3–5).

If you could see what God has recorded about your dealings with worldly women, what would you find? Would you see that you've pleased Him by escaping such snares? Or would you discover that their soft hands were like chains, binding you and keeping you from walking in the Spirit?

Those who are pleasing to God will escape the seductress before she turns their hearts away. It's never too late to trust in God's power and run.

EVENING: FICKLE AND FAITHLESS / *They slapped him in the face.* John 19:3 NIV / Cheers billowed over Jerusalem like smoke from a fire. But as the days passed, the voices grew silent and then surly. The once adoring crowd began shouting insults at the Messiah and demanded His death. Their enthusiastic worship turned to bitter scorn as Roman soldiers slapped Jesus' face.

Like the fickle crowd, we were born in need of the grace that Jesus died to bring.

We can follow God and act like He's the enemy, say we want to be more like Christ and act like we're unteachable, or sing God-songs and never let the words speak life to our spirit. None of these will lead to the transformation that God offers.

If you refuse to cooperate, you could find yourself singing praise one moment and denying you know Him the next.

MORNING: WHEN OTHERS SPEAK WELL OF YOU / *Son of man, say to the ruler of Tyre, "This is what the Sovereign LORD says: 'In the pride of your heart you say, "I am a god; I sit on the throne of a god in the heart of the seas." But you are a mere mortal.' "* Ezekiel 28:2 NIV / One of the biggest dangers in accomplishing great things is the praise people heap on you. If you're not careful, their words can go to your head.

That happened to the king of Tyre, a talented and wise leader who built his city into one of the richest and most beautiful in the world. It can happen to us today too.

When people say good things about you, don't reject their compliments. But it's always good to also remind them—and yourself—that God deserves all credit for everything you do.

EVENING: HUMBLE WORSHIP / *Come, let us worship and bow down. Let us kneel before the LORD our maker, for he is our God. We are the people he watches over, the flock under his care.* Psalm 95:6–7 NLT / The first seven verses of Psalm 95 are some of the most beautiful expressions of praise in the whole Bible. The writer clearly felt an overwhelming sense of awe at the greatness of God. . .and an even more overwhelming sense of gratitude for his Creator's goodness and love toward His people. The psalmist is so humbled, in fact, that he encourages his readers to worship, bow down, and kneel before the Lord.

When you focus on the greatness of God and His goodness toward you, there's nothing for you to do but humbly worship Him. He really is worthy!

MORNING: WHEN GOD WORKS AMONG US / *"Go back and report to John what you have seen and heard: The blind receive sight, the lame walk, those who have leprosy are cleansed, the deaf hear, the dead are raised, and the good news is proclaimed to the poor."* Luke 7:22 NIV / John had expected Jesus to destroy the Roman occupiers of Israel with His "winnowing fork." So when Jesus limited His power to healing the sick and demon-possessed, John was tempted to write Him off.

John's story is a powerful reminder of the ways our own agendas can cloud our perspective. God might perform mighty works in our lives, but it's easy to miss them when they don't match our expectations.

Sometimes, faith means learning to see where God is working right now in the moment, rather than asking Him to show up on our terms.

EVENING: TEMPORARY DESPERATION / *As the deer longs for streams of water, so I long for you, O God. I thirst for God, the living God. When can I go and stand before him?* Psalm 42:1–2 NLT / Streams were few and far between in the land of Israel. Consequently, the deer of the land were often hard-pressed to find water. In a season of drought, it may have seemed nearly impossible to find a stream.

This intense thirst for a scarce water supply captures the spirit of desperation that the writer of this psalm shares while waiting on God's deliverance. Although God remains alive and well, seasons of doubt or isolation can leave you desperate.

But remember: your times of trial, uncertainty, and longing for God's presence won't last forever. God will always show up with much-needed spiritual water whenever the time is right.

MORNING: PROCLAIMING THE LORD'S DEATH / *For whenever you eat this bread and drink this cup, you proclaim the Lord's death until he comes.* 1 Corinthians 11:26 NIV / Communion is the most somber of celebrations because the church looks back on what Christ did for us, recognizing that our sins led to His death while also recognizing that His death led to our redemption. So Christians of all denominations partake in faith, and the mere act proclaims the Lord's death to a lost and dying world.

Regardless of how often your church celebrates communion, stir yourself up to earnestly desire participation in it. It's a glorious opportunity to wipe your slate clean and start fresh, and it also encourages unbelievers who might be seated around you—if they see that the church is serious about their own sin—to do the same.

EVENING: DRINK DEEP / *"If you'll hold on to me for dear life," says God. . . "I'll. . .give you a long drink of salvation!"* Psalm 91:14, 16 MSG / Take stock of your life. Behold the imperfections, the bitterness, the broken dreams, and the hands stained with evil deeds and missed opportunities. Inside clangs a hard heartbeat like a pickax against stone.

You fixate on your own worst efforts. You promise better behavior. You choose to punish yourself, insisting that even if you get it right this time, you'll never be acceptable to God.

God helped the psalmist understand that personal effort is no substitute for grasping the coattails of His perfection. Working harder to please God will never satisfy a parched soul. Rather, being transformed takes holding on to God for dear life.

This is a choice that restores a broken man. This is rescue—drink deep.

MORNING: BEING AN INTERCESSOR / *"I looked for someone who might rebuild the wall of righteousness that guards the land. I searched for someone to stand in the gap in the wall so I wouldn't have to destroy the land, but I found no one."* Ezekiel 22:30 NLT / Over the last few years, the news has become increasingly more depressing.

For the Christian man, however, seeing bad news is just another opportunity to engage in what is called "intercessory prayer." That's the kind of prayer in which someone "stands in the gap" before God and pleads for His mercy and intervention on behalf of another—including friends, family members, and leaders.

God has given each of us an amazing privilege—to be men who plead fervently with Him on behalf of others. Who can you begin praying for today?

EVENING: FEELING ALL ALONE / *He replied, "I have been very zealous for the LORD God Almighty. The Israelites have. . .put your prophets to death with the sword. I am the only one left, and now they are trying to kill me too."* 1 Kings 19:14 NIV / Shortly after performing an incredible miracle that showed the Israelites God's power (1 Kings 18:16–40), Elijah found himself alone, fleeing a threat on his life.

Elijah was so depressed and discouraged that he believed he was the only true prophet of God left in Israel. He wasn't truly alone, of course. But in his discouragement, Elijah *felt* alone—just as we all do sometimes.

When you feel alone, don't try to hide your emotions from God. Be honest with Him and ask Him to encourage you—both with His presence and the input of godly friends.

MORNING: DIRECTED BY OUR DELIGHTS / *Blessed is the one. . .whose delight is in the law of the L*ORD*, and who meditates on his law day and night.* Psalm 1:1–2 NIV / We are delighted by a visit with friends or by spending time with family, but the source of our delights can have a far more significant spiritual meaning.

God isn't interested in shutting down our delights. But He does want to redirect our delights toward their most certain source.

Mockers and sinners will certainly find their own kinds of delight, but those delights will last only as long as the last punch line. Those who delight in communing with God will find a deeper, lasting delight that will carry them through the best and the worst that life has to offer.

EVENING: LETTING GO OF GRUDGES / *"So if you are presenting a sacrifice at the altar in the Temple and you suddenly remember that someone has something against you, leave your sacrifice there at the altar. Go and be reconciled to that person. Then come and offer your sacrifice to God."* Matthew 5:23–24 NLT / Your worship and your treatment of others are linked. Broken fellowship with a friend can get in the way of your worship of God, and your only path to freedom is through confession and forgiveness.

Perhaps your own pride has offended another person or a grudge has poisoned your relationship. Whatever you're holding on to, your ability to pray and to worship freely will be damaged by the same things that damage your relationships.

Do your interactions or relationships indicate that you think too highly of yourself? If so, what steps can you take to remedy that?

MORNING: HUMILITY AND UNITY / *Behold, how good and how pleasant it is for brethren to dwell together in unity!* Psalm 133:1 NKJV / In the middle of his letter to the Ephesian church, Paul told the people to be humble and diligent to preserve their unity (Ephesians 4:2–3). Unity among Christians is based on Jesus' own humility (Philippians 2:1–11).

When Christians bicker, what's the problem? Pride. When disagreements turn into disputes of "I'm right, you're wrong," men are pouring out their contempt. The opposite of contempt is respect.

Respect embraces the truth that everyone is made in the image of God. Brothers in Christ are to be loved and respected. And your church's leaders deserve the highest respect. Great authority comes from great humility.

Humility is healing. It alone releases the power and blessing of God among believers.

EVENING: UNSHAKABLE GENEROSITY / *All the believers were one in heart and mind. No one claimed that any of their possessions was their own, but they shared everything they had.* Acts 4:32 NIV / That first generation of Christians living in Jerusalem set many amazing examples for believers today. This evening's scripture says that they were united in their love for Jesus and committed to sharing their possessions and financial assets.

That's love in action! Because they realized that God owned everything they had, they were able to let go of their possessions and money for the good of others.

When you share out of a heart of loving generosity, you meet the needs of others, glorify God, and put yourself in a position to receive His blessings.

That's a big win for everyone involved.

MORNING: BUILDING FROM THE DUST / *The LORD is like a father to his children, tender and compassionate to those who fear him. For he knows how weak we are; he remembers we are only dust.* Psalm 103:13–14 NLT / Do you feel pressure to appear capable, strong, or holy? Have you ever feared being "found out" because you struggle privately?

Our masks always fall off in God's presence. While that may be humiliating, God knows it's for our benefit. We will find freedom only when we see with clarity that although we're little more than dust, God still cares for us like a father cares for his children. This is the only identity we have to claim.

Only an admission of weakness and dependence can open us up to God's strength—and enable us to share it with others.

EVENING: NEVER FORSAKEN / *"May the LORD our God be with us as he was with our ancestors; may he never leave us or abandon us."* 1 Kings 8:57 NLT / History's wisest king wanted assurance that God would never leave or abandon his people, and he wanted God to give those people a desire to obey.

You can't move mountains, turn hard hearts soft, or rescue yourself from even one sinful choice. Then again, what you can't do, God has already done.

First Corinthians 10:13 (MSG) says, "God will never let you down; he'll never let you be pushed past your limit; he'll always be there to help you come through it."

You can't go where God is not (Romans 8:38–39). When your heart is shattered, He's close (Psalm 34:18). When you need to get out of the storm, He's your refuge (Psalm 46:1).

MORNING: HOW DO WE REPENT? / *But Zacchaeus stood up and said to the Lord, "Look, Lord! Here and now I give half of my possessions to the poor, and if I have cheated anybody out of anything, I will pay back four times the amount."* Luke 19:8 NIV / The story of Zacchaeus provides a powerful picture of true repentance in action. Zacchaeus didn't just commit to follow Jesus—he recognized that following Jesus meant he had to completely change his life according to divine priorities.

Zacchaeus didn't just stop cheating people. He vowed to right the wrongs he had committed, pledged to give generously to the poor, and promised to provide justice to those he'd exploited as a tax collector for Rome.

Zacchaeus repented by not only changing his future but by repairing his past.

EVENING: GOD'S HEART FOR SINNERS / *"Do I take any pleasure in the death of the wicked? declares the Sovereign LORD. Rather, am I not pleased when they turn from their ways and live?"* Ezekiel 18:23 NIV / Have you ever found yourself secretly condemning certain people as beyond God's reach?

Humanly speaking, it's hard to understand how God could save what we consider the vilest of sinners. But God has been doing just that from the very beginning.

As the apostle Peter wrote, "The Lord is not slow in keeping his promise, as some understand slowness. Instead, he is patient with you, not wanting anyone to perish, but everyone to come to repentance" (2 Peter 3:9 NIV).

Today, let God be God and pray that He does the same kind of miracles in others as He did when He saved you.

MORNING: BEYOND COMPREHENSION / *"God thunders marvelously with His voice; He does great things which we cannot comprehend. For He says to the snow, 'Fall on the earth'; likewise to the gentle rain and the heavy rain of His strength."* Job 37:5–6 NKJV / In Job 36–37, Elihu did a good job of describing God's majesty, pointing out His absolute control over nature to show that nothing goes unnoticed with Him. God tells rain and snow to fall on the earth, and they do.

Just as your survival depends on the ecosystem, the ecosystem wholly depends on the weather. And God is sovereign over both.

So don't complain about the weather. Instead, consider observing it so you can be just as wowed by God's handiwork as Elihu was. Then praise God for the snow and rain, letting Him know you trust that He provides everything you need.

EVENING: THE STRESS OF DOUBTING / *When doubts filled my mind, your comfort gave me renewed hope and cheer.* Psalm 94:19 NLT / In any state of transition, belief and doubt seem to coexist. When you move to a new town, accept a new job, or buy a new home, you can believe it's a good decision yet occasionally doubt you made the right choice.

God never intended to leave His family in doubt. Whenever the psalmist admitted misgivings, God sent reassurance that brought about hope and encouragement. Similarly, though you will not be commended for doubting God, you may unintentionally be putting yourself in line for a divine reminder of God's faithfulness.

God's kindness resolves the tension between a life without Jesus Christ and one that answers Jesus' call to "Follow me" (Matthew 8:22 NLT).

MORNING: HUMBLE GIFTEDNESS / *"Your fame spread among the nations on account of your beauty, because the splendor I had given you made your beauty perfect, declares the Sovereign Lord."* Ezekiel 16:14 NIV / The words above were addressed to a very gifted, very blessed people: God's chosen nation, Israel. But in the following twenty verses, the Lord chided them because they had somehow forgotten that everything they had was a gift from Him.

This part of Israel's story should remind us to heed the words of the apostle Paul: "What do you have that you did not receive? And if you did receive it, why do you boast as though you did not?" (1 Corinthians 4:7 NIV).

Confidence isn't a bad thing, but it must be tempered with an awareness that everything we have comes from the hand of our generous heavenly Father.

EVENING: ASKING BIG / *When they had crossed, Elijah said to Elisha, "Tell me, what can I do for you before I am taken from you?" "Let me inherit a double portion of your spirit," Elisha replied.* 2 Kings 2:9 NIV / Elisha knew two things: Elijah, his friend and mentor, would soon be leaving him, and Elisha would take his place as Israel's leading prophet.

Knowing he would need great power to serve as mightily as Elijah had, Elisha made one request before Elijah was taken up to heaven—he asked Elijah for a "double portion" of his spirit after he left. Elijah agreed and then was taken to heaven.

Because Elisha had summoned up the courage to make such an audacious request, God empowered him to become a unique, miracle-working servant of the Lord.

Do you believe God has great plans for you? Then don't be afraid to ask big!

MORNING: FORGIVE AND FORGET / *Lord, if you kept a record of our sins, who, O Lord, could ever survive? But you offer forgiveness, that we might learn to fear you.* Psalm 130:3–4 NLT / Toward the end of summer break, a college student in Chicagoland handed his parents a four-page handwritten letter that detailed all the ways he had sinned against them and the Lord.

When they finished reading the letter, the father stood up, walked over to a gas grill and burned the letter inside. After erasing all record of his son's wrongdoings, the parents hugged their son and shed tears of both grief and joy. Beyond words, the college student knew all was forgiven.

This is a picture of the way God forgives us. This is a picture of the way we should forgive others.

EVENING: THE ULTIMATE PAYBACK / *Don't repay evil for evil. Don't retaliate with insults when people insult you. Instead, pay them back with a blessing.* 1 Peter 3:9 NLT / In the heat of an argument—especially on social media—it's hard to resist trading insults or sharing a piece of your mind. We often experience the worst parts of our anger without the filter of empathy or understanding.

Peter, however, knew that we gain very little from retaliation. That's why he challenged us to *bless* those who insult us.

Even receiving an insult can be good for you. Although it may undermine your ego, the act of releasing your anger and handing over a blessing is positive. It will bring the other person one step closer to God while reminding you of where your true identity lies.

MORNING: THE END OF PAIN / *I heard a loud voice from the throne saying, "Look! God's dwelling place is now among the people. . . . 'He will wipe every tear from their eyes. There will be no more death' or mourning or crying or pain."* Revelation 21:3–4 NIV / When we hear about or experience tragedy, it's tempting to think that grief and sorrow have no end.

However, God's final revelation will end all death, crying, and pain. Our future is leading toward a day when God dwells among us, bringing us the comfort we have longed for all our lives. The Bible points us consistently in this direction: from the days of the tabernacle to the temple to the coming of the Spirit at Pentecost, God has consistently moved closer to us, not farther away.

And in the light of God's presence, darkness can't help but flee.

EVENING: THE INVITATION / *Today, if you hear his voice, do not harden your hearts.* Psalm 95:7–8 ESV / Every day, hour, and minute, God is extending an invitation to new life.

Second Corinthians 6:2 (NLT) says, "The 'right time' is now. Today is the day of salvation." Because it's the right time, take a moment to review this evening's verse. Again, it says, "If you hear his voice, do not harden your hearts."

You may not always understand what God is saying. So get quiet and focus. Once you hear His message, make obedience your first response.

To harden your heart is to resist God's will and insist you know more than Him. It would be like an army private arguing with a five-star general.

God knows more than you can even imagine—never resist His call.

MORNING: TURNING FROM IDOLS / *"Therefore say to the people of Israel, 'This is what the Sovereign* Lord *says: Repent! Turn from your idols and renounce all your detestable practices!' "* Ezekiel 14:6 NIV / Christians today don't think or speak much about idols or idolatry. To most of us, that's Old Testament stuff. Besides, we don't worship literal idols like people in ancient times did.

Sounds like we have this idolatry thing licked, doesn't it?

In reality, though, idolatry is as much of a danger for the man of God today as it was in Old Testament times. We may not worship statues or other lifeless objects, but the world offers all kinds of temptations toward idolatry—money, position, social standing, and a host of other things.

What things do you find yourself tempted to "worship"? Are you making sure God alone is your object of adoration?

EVENING: OBEY GOD FIRST / *But Peter and the apostles replied, "We must obey God rather than any human authority."* Acts 5:29 NLT / The Bible is clear that Christians are to obey earthly authorities (Romans 13:1–2). However, when Jewish religious leaders warned the apostle Peter and some of his friends to stop talking to people about Jesus, Peter's response was clear: "We must obey God rather than you." In saying that, Peter showed incredible courage and set an example for all men of God to follow.

You should respect, obey, and pray for earthly authorities because God has placed them in their positions. But when these authorities contradict or oppose the laws of God, it is your duty to respectfully speak up and even disobey.

But before you do that, seek God and ask for wisdom in making the best decision.

MORNING: HOW OUR JOURNEYS BEGIN / *Then Jesus came from Galilee to the Jordan to be baptized by John.* Matthew 3:13 NIV / The muddy waters of the Jordan River were no place for a King to begin His reign. Even a powerful army commander thought these waters were beneath him. But at the start of His ministry, Jesus humbly sought baptism under John in order to fulfill all righteousness, placing Himself alongside the people among whom He planned to minister.

For all that Jesus accomplished in His ministry, He didn't begin by rising to the top. He began by descending to the lowest point so that He could reach all people.

Are you willing to take a step down to begin a new season of your life? It's one thing to read about starting small and working your way up, but it's another thing to step out in faith and *do it*.

EVENING: FINDING GOD EACH DAY / *How amazing are the deeds of the Lord! All who delight in him should ponder them.* Psalm 111:2 NLT / Today's psalm should encourage you to pause and ponder the works of God around you. Each moment is an invitation to draw near to God and become aware of His presence.

It's easy to run from one task to another and then, in the evening, wonder where God was throughout the day. While scripture assures you that He's always with you, you can surely overlook His presence and gifts unless you take time—alone or with a group of His people—to see them.

And remember: whenever you hit a place of stability, someone in your circle will probably need a reminder of God's care too. It's impossible to truly enjoy God without sharing His joy with others.

DAY 263

MORNING: GOD'S DELIGHT / *God in his wisdom took delight in using what the world considered stupid—preaching, of all things!—to bring those who trust him into the way of salvation.* 1 Corinthians 1:21 MSG / One day, a woman criticized D. L. Moody, one of the nineteenth-century's greatest evangelists, for his methods. Moody's reply: "I agree with you. I don't like the way I do it either. Tell me, how do you do it?"

The lady answered, "I don't do it."

Moody replied, "Well, then, I like my way of doing evangelism better than your way of not doing it."

True, public evangelism isn't solely locked into preaching—so if you're not a public proclaimer, you still have plenty of options. But at the end of the day, it's what God loves to use "to bring those who trust him into the way of salvation."

EVENING: SPIRITUAL DROUGHT / *Elijah the Tishbite, of the inhabitants of Gilead, said to Ahab, "As the LORD God of Israel lives, before whom I stand, there shall not be dew nor rain these years, except at my word."* 1 Kings 17:1 NKJV / King Ahab's choices to defy God exceeded any king before him. He provoked the Lord and followed the non-god Baal. That's why God sent the prophet Elijah to tell Ahab that the rains would stop—maybe he would see a reflection of his heart in the dry and barren land.

Like Ahab, you may need to go through personal and spiritual drought to get to the place where you will admit your rebellion and ask God for help.

Are you thirsty? He offers living water. *Are you hungry?* His Word offers fine meat. *Are you in need of rescue?* His kindness introduces salvation.

MORNING: HURTING GOD? / *"Then when they are exiled among the nations, they will. . .recognize how hurt I am by their unfaithful hearts."* Ezekiel 6:9 NLT / You probably already know that the Bible teaches God can be angered at the sinful actions of His people. But did you ever consider that He can also feel emotional pain when we stop following Him?

Genesis 1:27 tells us that God created humans in His own image. He wanted a created being that He could love and that could choose to love Him in return. So when that object of God's love chooses another, He feels heartbreak in much the same way a husband does when his wife leaves him for another man.

God has given each of us a choice—and the right one is to choose to love Him with everything within us.

EVENING: NO TURNING BACK / *"But our ancestors refused to obey him. Instead, they rejected him and in their hearts turned back to Egypt."* Acts 7:39 NIV / Many Bible scholars believe that the Israelites didn't literally want to go back to the land of Egypt; instead, they wanted to resume the idolatrous practices of the Egyptians—practices God wanted them to leave behind as they began their journey to the promised land.

Though God had miraculously freed the Israelites from slavery, their hearts were inclined to return. Many Christian men still face this temptation today.

The Bible teaches that those who don't know Jesus are enslaved to sin, but the apostle Paul wrote, "You have been set free from sin and have become slaves to righteousness" (Romans 6:18 NIV).

God has set you free, so don't go back to your own personal Egypt—keep moving forward to your promised land!

MORNING: JOY IN PAIN / *We are hard-pressed on every side, yet not crushed. . .always carrying about in the body the dying of the Lord Jesus, that the life of Jesus also may be manifested in our body.* 2 Corinthians 4:8, 10 NKJV / Standing up for your faith can be hard. For some people—such as the apostle Paul—"hard" means being conspired against, arrested, beaten, imprisoned, and even stoned on a semi-regular basis. For most of us, however, it simply means going against the flow.

But don't let the distance between these two extremes fool you—hard is still hard, no matter what form it takes. Through the Spirit's help, though, Paul mastered the art of being unfazed in disaster. In fact, he was even *consoled* by the pain, knowing that he was following his Savior's example.

Next time you face persecution, remember that Jesus knows exactly how you feel—and that He's cheering every step you take.

EVENING: ADMIT YOUR DISAPPOINTMENT / *Martha said to Jesus, "Lord, if only you had been here, my brother would not have died. But even now I know that God will give you whatever you ask."* John 11:21–22 NLT / When have you felt hopeless or disappointed in God? Were you afraid to say exactly what you were thinking? Perhaps you didn't feel God would ever listen to your prayers again if you did.

At her lowest point, Martha spoke her mind to Jesus. She didn't hold back but rather embraced the tension between Jesus' power and her overwhelming disappointment.

Sometimes, voicing your disappointment to God could be a greater act of faith than keeping yourself from saying what you really think.

What do you need to speak to God about with complete transparency today?

DAY 266

MORNING: GOD JOURNEYS WITH YOU / *Where can I find help? My help comes from the* Lord, *the maker of heaven and earth.* Psalm 121:1–2 GW / Psalm 121 is the second "psalm of ascents" sung by pilgrims traveling to Jerusalem for the annual Jewish feasts. In this psalm, you join them on the journey.

Mountain ranges could be challenging to travelers: "I look up toward the mountains," the psalm begins. "Where can I find help?" (121:1). Yet the writer was quick to add, "My help comes from the Lord, the maker of heaven and earth."

God won't let anything stop you from doing His will. Instead, He will keep you, shade you, and guard you as you travel.

EVENING: EXPERIENCING GOD'S LOVE ANEW / *Those who trust God's action in them find that God's Spirit is in them—living and breathing God! . . . Attention to God leads us out into the open, into a spacious, free life.* Romans 8:5–6 MSG / Slow down and take a minute to carefully reread the scripture verses above. Isn't that the kind of life you want to experience?

Sadly, many men think God doesn't look on them with love, favor, or delight. In their heart, they feel God is angry at them. . .or at best, distant and uncaring. They certainly don't trust what He does in their lives. This is a great disconnect—and the Father wants to erase it from our hearts.

When you trust and embrace God's deep love for you, you become better able to love others in return. Loving what God loves is the key—and yes, He absolutely loves you.

MORNING: JESUS: TRANSFORMED / *"God raised [Jesus] from the dead, freeing him from the agony of death, because it was impossible for death to keep its hold on him."* Acts 2:24 NIV / In the beginning, Jesus was with God the Father (John 1:1). He was the Creator of all (Colossians 1:16). He is God's Son (Matthew 3:17). When the "Always Was" stepped into this world, humanity would never be the same.

Jesus came to bring life (John 1:4), light (John 8:12), and love (1 John 4:19). He offered acceptance, forgiveness, and restoration. He was praised and then rejected, being sentenced to death by His creation.

This sacrifice provided the only sin payment God would accept. And on day three, "God released him from the horrors of death and raised him back to life, for death could not keep him in its grip" (Acts 2:24 NLT).

Jesus was transformed to be your Savior.

EVENING: WILLING TO SPEAK UP / *"Nevertheless if you warn the righteous man that the righteous should not sin, and he does not sin, he shall surely live because he took warning; also you will have delivered your soul."* Ezekiel 3:21 NKJV / Many Christians are reluctant to speak up when they see a professing brother or sister in Christ drifting away from the faith. The reason? They don't want to be seen as "judgmental."

God, however, has designed the Christian faith so that we believers need one another. We are to hold one another accountable, even when doing so makes us uncomfortable. God calls us to love our brothers enough to tell them difficult truth.

The life direction of someone you care about could be changed if you choose to speak up. Are you willing?

MORNING: RADICAL FORGIVENESS / *As they stoned him, Stephen prayed, "Lord Jesus, receive my spirit." He fell to his knees, shouting, "Lord, don't charge them with this sin!" And with that, he died.* Acts 7:59–60 NLT / It's one thing to love, forgive, and pray for those who love you, but Jesus called His followers to take their love and forgiveness to a radical new level. He set the ultimate example when He hung from the cross, suffering unimaginable agony, and pleaded with His Father to forgive His tormentors (Luke 23:34).

Stephen, the first of many people who would die for serving Jesus, followed this example. As he died a grisly, agonizing death, Stephen asked God to forgive the men who were killing him.

When people do you wrong, follow Jesus'—and Stephen's—example by loving your enemies deeply enough to pray earnestly for them.

EVENING: NARROW-MINDED / *"Enter by the narrow gate."* Matthew 7:13 NKJV / The world is webbed with highways and byways, but there are only two roads that ultimately matter—the one that leads to destruction and the one that leads to life.

Most maps don't even mark the narrow path. "It's too narrow," the world says. Those who travel the path are often accused of being narrow-minded, but that's okay—Jesus, who blazed that trail, said, "I am the way and the truth and the life. No one comes to the Father except through me" (John 14:6 NIV).

Some call such narrowness "hateful," "exclusive," and "bigoted." Maybe it is: it hates hell, excludes sin, and welcomes only those willing to follow Jesus.

But it also calls *all* to follow, and it leads to eternal life—ultimately, there's nothing wider than that!

DAY 269

MORNING: RECEIVING GOD'S MERCY / *"I entered this world to render judgment—to give sight to the blind and to show those who think they see that they are blind."* John 9:39 NLT / If you feel like you can't figure out how to draw near to God or if you struggle with particular sins, then you're right where Jesus can help you. In fact, you'd be worse off if you thought you had your act together and had no need of His mercy.

Jesus came to reveal your true spiritual state. You can resist His offer of mercy, claiming that you're good enough on your own, or you can stop pretending and fully admit your need.

Jesus knows how blind and lost we are. But if we come to Him with honesty and dependence on His mercy, we will receive His help and experience true restoration.

EVENING: "FRIEND OF GOD" / *So now we can rejoice in our wonderful new relationship with God because our Lord Jesus Christ has made us friends of God.* Romans 5:11 NLT / Have you ever thought of yourself as a friend of God?

Maybe you think this title is reserved for great men like Abraham (2 Chronicles 20:7; Isaiah 41:8; and James 2:23) and Job (Job 29:4). However, James 4:4 and Romans 5:11 make it clear that any man can be a friend of God if he repents, trusts Jesus Christ, and loves the Lord wholeheartedly.

This isn't "friend" in the Facebook sense. Instead, the apostle Paul describes it as "our wonderful new relationship with God."

Do you believe this truth enough to say it aloud? Say it first in prayer to God. Then feel free to proclaim it to others.

MORNING: WHAT YOU BELIEVE / *The Lord is good; his steadfast love endures forever, and his faithfulness to all generations.* Psalm 100:5 ESV / If what you believe can change your thinking, it can also change the way you act.

Consider this: if you believe that looking out for your own interests is your highest priority, you'll never go out of your way to help another person—because no one will be more important in your thinking than you.

However, if you believe God is good, that His love never fails, and that He has never once given up the title of "Faithful and True," then His commands will start overriding your personal ambitions. Other people will become more important than your handcrafted bucket list.

Belief always transforms thinking. Thinking always determines actions. Actions always speak the truth about what you believe.

EVENING: PEACE IN TIMES OF CRISIS / *Because of the Lord's great love we are not consumed, for his compassions never fail. They are new every morning; great is your faithfulness.* Lamentations 3:22–23 NIV / As the prophet Jeremiah looked around the smoldering rubble of the once-great city of Jerusalem, his heart was filled with crushing sorrow. Yet in the midst of the horrors of the Babylonians' destruction, he was still able to thank God for His love, compassion, and faithfulness.

When catastrophe strikes—the loss of a loved one, a financial crisis, a divorce, or a bad medical diagnosis—how will you respond? It's not easy to keep praising and trusting God during these times, but it's the key to finding peace when your world is falling apart.

Today, start by praising God for who He is and how good He is to you.

MORNING: FAITH IN ACTION / *The child. . .said to his father, "My head! My head!"* 2 Kings 4:18–19 NIV / God is far beyond our understanding. A woman in a town called Shunem found that out when her son died.

She pursued Elisha, the prophet who sometimes stayed in her family's home. He agreed to return to her place and prayed, and God restored the child's life.

Maybe this seems far-fetched—God isn't raising people from the dead these days. But that's not really the point. This boy's mother believed God for something big. She put her faith in action and sought out a prophet to help.

At times, we'll face tough problems. Like the woman of Shunem, you can reach out for help—from praying friends and from God Himself. He may or may not resolve your issue in the way you hope. But you can be sure that His ways are always best.

EVENING: GOD'S LIGHT ERASES YOUR DARKNESS / *Do not remember the rebellious sins of my youth. Remember me in the light of your unfailing love, for you are merciful, O LORD.* Psalm 25:7 NLT / God's character defines how He interacts with you, not the other way around. If you had to be on your best behavior in order to receive God's mercy, you'd have no hope in the face of His holiness.

Fortunately, God doesn't look at your failures, hypocrisies, and faults. He sees you with compassion as His beloved child. It's this love that changes and transforms you, renewing you and drawing you near to Him on the merits of His unfailing love.

You don't have to bring anything to God—He desires to show mercy and compassion to you. In the warm glow of His light, your darkness is gone and you're free to be loved by Him.

MORNING: COACHES / *They became his advisers, to his undoing.* 2 Chronicles 22:4 NIV / In every sport, coaches make a difference. Poor coaches focus on their fame or fortune, but good coaches focus on helping their players and team improve. Smart players play for good coaches.

When Ahaziah inherited the throne at age twenty-two, he didn't dismiss the coaches his unsuccessful dad assembled around him. Instead, those same individuals "became his advisers, to his undoing." He reigned for only a year because he followed their miserable advice.

The same can happen to us if we're not careful.

Do the people around you put your improvement first, or are they more concerned about their reputations and the results of their leadership?

What kind of "coaches" do you have in your life?

EVENING: HELP! / *GOD, listen! Listen to my prayer, listen to the pain in my cries. Don't turn your back on me just when I need you so desperately. Pay attention! This is a cry for help!* Psalm 102:1–2 MSG / Repentance recognizes you've been running the wrong race and insists you turn around and switch tracks.

The psalmist wasn't saying, "Hey God, if You're not too busy, could You give me some advice?" No, the psalmist said, "This is a cry for help!" If you want to try to figure things out on your own, God will let you. Expect less than ideal results. But when God steps in, desperation becomes hope, crying turns to joy, and pain is treated with mercy.

When you don't know what to do, step back and invite God's solution. Transformation is not a do-it-yourself project. Accept God's help.

MORNING: STAND FIRM FOR JESUS / *Saul increased all the more in strength, and confounded the Jews who lived in Damascus by proving that Jesus was the Christ.* Acts 9:22 ESV / After Saul—who had made a habit out of persecuting and even killing Christians—experienced a dramatic conversion, the Holy Spirit started working in him, giving him a rock-solid resolve to tell others about the soul-saving message of Christ. Naturally, some of the disciples were afraid of him at first. But once they learned how boldly he was already living out his faith, they embraced him.

If Saul, who was also called Paul (Acts 13:9), could trust God with such resolution in his conviction to share Jesus with others, *any* believer can. As you go into your workplace today, don't hesitate to stand firm for Jesus. Tell others that anybody can be saved from their sins.

EVENING: HE'LL NEVER FORSAKE YOU / *"For Israel and Judah have not been forsaken by their God, the* LORD *of hosts, but the land of the Chaldeans is full of guilt against the Holy One of Israel."* Jeremiah 51:5 ESV / Israel and Judah had strayed from the Lord about as far as humanly possible, yet the Lord hadn't forsaken His people. At just the right time, the Lord promised to "stir up the spirit of a destroyer against Babylon" (Jeremiah 51:1 ESV), Judah's oppressor.

Does your sin ever cause you to feel distant from God? Do you even doubt His existence sometimes? If so, take heart: God never intended for you to live this way perpetually, regardless of what you've done.

No matter how distant you might feel from God right now, He stands ready to embrace you. Run toward Him and resolve to never leave His presence again.

MORNING: VAIN REPETITIONS / *"When you pray, do not use vain repetitions as the heathen do. For they think that they will be heard for their many words."* Matthew 6:7 NKJV / Buddhists have prayer wheels with mantras written on the outside of a cylindrical spindle. They believe that spinning the wheel will have the same effect as orally reciting the prayers over and over. The more the wheel turns, the greater the effect of the "prayer."

We are not to pray like that. We should definitely keep asking God until He answers our prayer, one way or another (Luke 18:1), but "vain repetitions" of words unconnected to our deepest heart desires are not helpful at all.

In the words of a treasured hymn: "What a friend we have in Jesus, all our sins and griefs to bear. What a privilege to carry everything to God in prayer."

EVENING: FAITH'S RESULT / *Let your unfailing love surround us, Lord, for our hope is in you alone.* Psalm 33:22 NLT / You can feel burdens of stress, strained relationships, and crammed schedules each day. As challenges pile up, you're weighed down by worries and obligations. Through it all, you may lose sight of God's provision.

That's why turning to God throughout the day is so important: it gives you your only lasting relief from these burdens.

Worries and cares may make it almost impossible to find God's concern for you. The more you focus on them the larger they become. But as you learn to trust in the Lord alone, you'll begin to see His loving-kindness with greater clarity, freeing you to realize that His love has remained unchanged—whatever your circumstances.

MORNING: CAUTION: GOD AT WORK / *The stone which the builders rejected has become the chief cornerstone. This was the LORD's doing; it is marvelous in our eyes.* Psalm 118:22–23 NKJV / On a scale of one to ten, how advanced is your theology of God?

God's ways are light-years higher than any of man's ways. So even if you scored yourself near 10, your theology still has a long way to improve. Most of the time, this process isn't easy.

C. S. Lewis once said, "When I invited Jesus into my life, I thought he was going to put up some wallpaper and hang a few pictures. But he started knocking out walls and adding on rooms. I said, 'I was expecting a nice cottage.' But he said, 'I'm making a palace in which to live.' "

When God starts dismantling your theology, will you be ready to listen?

EVENING: BROUGHT TOGETHER / *Many who were paralyzed or lame were healed. So there was much joy in that city.* Acts 8:7–8 ESV / The people of Samaria were not used to outside help, as the Israelites usually didn't associate with them. That's why—when the apostle Philip started moving through the Samaritan crowd healing people, answering their questions, and casting out demons—the people responded with amazement and joy. Suddenly, these left-out people were being brought together in Jesus Christ, regardless of name, ancestry, or skin tone.

God's rescue plan is not a test run, a limited time offer, or a first-come-first-served deal. It's available for everyone, even for those whom you'd never expect.

Never withhold God's rescue plan from people God never rejected. It's good news for you, and it will be for them.

MORNING: RESTORATION PLANS / *"Yet I will restore the fortunes of Moab in days to come,"* declares the LORD. Jeremiah 48:47 NIV / The Moabites were known as gross idolaters whose women seduced the Israelites into sexual immorality (Numbers 25:1–3).

Jeremiah 48 tells how Moab faced destruction. And yet, at the end of that chapter, the Lord said He would one day restore the fortunes of Moab. They hadn't done anything to warrant such favor. And yet God planned to restore them in some fashion.

Have you ever seen an enemy—either personal or national or of Christianity—get what he deserved? If so, don't rejoice. Instead, offer mercy and grace when none is warranted.

As you do, you'll show the world that Jesus really can restore and transform anybody.

EVENING: SECRET SAINTS / *"Your Father who sees in secret will Himself reward you openly."* Matthew 6:4 NKJV / God's people are called to be secret saints. Not necessarily hidden saints, but humble saints. We need to be careful that we don't do all the right things for all the wrong reasons: "Watch out! Don't do your good deeds publicly, to be admired by others, for you will lose the reward from your Father in heaven" (Matthew 6:1 NLT).

A secret saint doesn't even let his left hand know what his right hand is doing. He seeks God's glory, not his own. God rewards that kind of faith.

MORNING: FORGIVEN. . .COMPLETELY / *As far as the east is from the west, so far has he removed our transgressions from us.* Psalm 103:12 NIV / Perhaps nothing keeps a man of God from living an unshakable life of faith more than guilt. He may have confessed his sin and turned completely away from it, yet he still fears that God holds his misdeeds against him.

This morning's scripture shows the completeness of God's forgiveness. Consider this: If you were to begin traveling south from the northernmost spot on the globe, eventually you would start traveling north again. However, if you were to begin traveling east from any point on earth, you would continue going east forever.

The Bible says that when you confess your sins, God removes your sins from you and casts them as far as the east is from the west—an infinite distance!

EVENING: LESS TIME THAN YOU THINK / *"Watch therefore, for you do not know when the master of the house is coming."* Mark 13:35 NKJV / Jesus gives a rather stern warning that your time on earth could be far shorter than you expect. Whether He returns during your lifetime or you die by old age, accident, or disease, you can't take your time for granted.

You may have plans that fill your schedule each week and prompt you to put off the things that truly matter—spending time with your kids, community service opportunities, or church meetings, for example. Whatever you're putting off, remember that you don't have unlimited time.

While Jesus isn't disparaging rest, He does want His followers to adopt a spirit of awareness. The knowledge that you may well have less time than you expect should change how you plan for the future.

MORNING: WHEN LOSSES COME / *In the year that King Uzziah died, I saw the Lord sitting on a throne, high and lifted up, and the train of His robe filled the temple.* Isaiah 6:1 NKJV / Isaiah probably felt a double loss when King Uzziah passed away. The longest serving ruler of Judah, Uzziah had done much good. But in the end pride derailed him. Uzziah died a leper after offering incense in the temple, a job reserved for the priests. His moral failure and death were undoubtedly troubling to a faithful citizen like Isaiah.

But notice what God did. He gave an incredible vision of Himself to Isaiah. The old-time Bible teacher Matthew Henry wrote that "Israel's king dies, but Israel's God still lives. . . . King Uzziah dies in a hospital, but the King of kings still sits upon His throne."

Whatever losses come your way, know that your King is still in control.

EVENING: TRUE PURPOSE / *They followed worthless idols and themselves became worthless.* 2 Kings 17:15 NIV / When people today look for meaning in anything but God, they follow the same pattern as the kings and people of ancient Israel, who had seen God's great miracles but traded relationship with Him for idolatry. A meaningless existence inevitably follows.

The psalmist sums up the purpose of life well when he writes, "But from everlasting to everlasting the LORD's love is with those who fear him, and his righteousness with their children's children—with those who keep his covenant and remember to obey his precepts" (Psalm 103:17–18 NIV).

If some religious system, or money or success, or anything else promises the meaning you long to experience, then heed the lessons of the Israelites—only God gives true purpose.

MORNING: DO-GOODERS / *"Do good to those who hate you."* Matthew 5:44 NKJV / When wicked people lie on their beds and devise evil against us (as Micah 2:1 indicates), we are to lie on our beds thinking of ways to do them good.

Doing good deeds for those who do us wrong heaps "coals of fire" of conviction upon them (Proverbs 25:22 NKJV), and the Holy Spirit uses our good deeds to convict them of their own sin.

We are called in Christ to do good works, which He has prepared for us long before we saw the light of our first day (Ephesians 2:10). And when our enemies "take the heat" of the Holy Spirit's conviction, their hearts will expand to let Christ in, and their lips will open in praise and glory to our Father who is in heaven (Matthew 5:16).

EVENING: CONQUERING EVERY POWER / *No power in the sky above or in the earth below. . .will ever be able to separate us from the love of God that is revealed in Christ Jesus our Lord.* Romans 8:39 NLT / How often are you tempted to measure God's love by your difficult circumstances, guilt, or deflated sense of security?

Your desires and failures may lead you astray from within, and enemies will constantly assail you from without. Paul saw the powers of this world aligning themselves against believers, with demons and rulers straining themselves to pry you away from the love of God.

Still, God's love has been bonded to you in Christ Jesus, who has forever linked you to God the Father. You are His child, and there's no force in this world that can change that.

You can remain confident that your security in God is rooted in His unshakable love.

MORNING: PROUD OF THE GOOD NEWS / *I am not ashamed of the gospel, because it is the power of God that brings salvation to everyone who believes.* Romans 1:16 NIV / The apostle Paul was a master communicator who made frequent use of literary devices. So when he uses the phrase "not ashamed," he's really saying that he's "proud" of the life-changing gospel of Jesus Christ.

Ironically, when you cop out and never say anything, people are disappointed. Sometimes, they're outright offended that you don't stand up for the good news. They want to know what you believe—and expect that you believe it wholeheartedly. And when you boldly but graciously and courageously talk about your relationship with the Lord, they're often interested—even thankful.

You really have only three choices when it comes to sharing your faith: embarrassed, apathetic, or proud. Which will you choose?

EVENING: FORGET YOUR BIG PLANS / *"So forget about making any big plans for yourself. Things are going to get worse before they get better. But don't worry. I'll keep you alive through the whole business."* Jeremiah 45:5 MSG / Baruch, one of Jeremiah's scribes, apparently had plans—perhaps to advance to a higher office or to accumulate more wealth—that weren't in line with the way things were unfolding. Jeremiah, however, set him straight in this evening's verse.

What do you have your sights set on? Climbing the corporate ladder? Buying a nicer home? Moving to a better part of the city? What happens if God has other plans? Are you willing to submit?

God has a plan to take you through your times of lack. But you have to stay the spiritual course. Forget your big plans and seek Him instead.

He'll be your guiding light when darkness seems to surround you.

MORNING: FULL-TIME FAITH / *God "will repay each person according to what they have done."* Romans 2:6 NIV / God didn't hide His plan, conceal His will, or confuse His people. Instead, He offered generous helpings of truth and urged you to dig in, taste for yourself, and hold tight to the promise of being made a new creature (2 Corinthians 5:17).

Some stop short of accepting *all* of God's truth and only look to His Word for personally comforting quotes. But Christianity is more than a spectator faith—it takes being fully engaged to receive God's benefits.

Paul warns against pursuing a part-time gospel: "The time will come when they. . .will turn away their ears from the truth and will turn aside to myths" (2 Timothy 4:3–4 NASB).

Keep pursuing the reward of the faithful.

EVENING: SHOWING KINDNESS / *The men of Judah. . .told David, saying, "It was the men of Jabesh-gilead who buried Saul." David sent messengers to the men of Jabesh-gilead, and said to them, "May you be blessed of the LORD because you have shown this kindness to Saul your lord."* 2 Samuel 2:4–5 NASB / After David was anointed king of Israel in Hebron, he inquired about Saul's body, probably because he wanted to honor him with a proper burial. So when he learned that the men of Jabesh-gilead had buried King Saul, David sent a blessing back to them.

No matter how far Saul went astray, he was the Lord's anointed and worthy of respect. David firmly understood this concept, even when Saul was trying to take his life.

How do you respond when one of your enemies stumble? How does that compare with David's actions?

MORNING: REPENT AND BEAR FRUIT / *"Therefore, King Agrippa, I was not disobedient to the heavenly vision."* Acts 26:19 NKJV / The Damascus road conversion of Saul ranks among the most momentous proofs for the resurrection of Jesus Christ and the reality of the Christian faith. Luke included three separate retellings of the event in the book of Acts, not wanting his readers to miss its immense significance.

In addition to its apologetic value, Saul's conversion was important because it changed the expected trajectory of the early church. Its most fierce persecutor became its most dedicated evangelist, church planter, and apologist to the Jewish nation and to the Roman empire.

In other words, it wasn't Saul's conversion day, but the very conversion of his life. What Jesus said, Saul did—without fail—for the whole next generation.

EVENING: SERVE THE KING / *And Gedaliah. . .swore to them and their men, saying, Do not be afraid to serve the Chaldeans; dwell in [this] land and serve the king of Babylon, and it shall be well with you.* Jeremiah 40:9 AMPC / Gedaliah, the newly appointed governor over poor Judeans who hadn't been exiled, told his people basically what God had promised those who were in exile: if they dwelled in the land and served the king, things would go well with them.

Political leaders come and go. You'll agree with some and disagree with others. Vote your conscience, but never let a disappointing election discourage you from carrying on with your work. Continue living for the good of your family, neighborhood, and country, just as the people of Judah did.

Each Christian is called to a life of faithfulness, regardless of the ebb and flow of politics.

MORNING: YOU GROW BY BECOMING CHILDLIKE / *"I tell you the truth, anyone who doesn't receive the Kingdom of God like a child will never enter it."* Luke 18:17 NLT / If you listen to interviews of adults who grew up in poverty, you'll notice certain patterns. In most cases, they'll note that during their childhood they "never knew" they were poor, or that their parents found ways to make things work out. Even during their most challenging times, children found contentment and confidence in their family.

Whether you're comfortable or in great need today, a childlike dependence on God is where you'll find long-term contentment and security. You often hear of growing in wisdom or maturity in the Christian faith, and they certainly have their place. However, Jesus also expects you to grow more "childlike" if you're going to truly live in His kingdom.

EVENING: NO COMPROMISE / *For he held fast to the LORD. . . . And the LORD was with him; wherever he went out, he prospered.* 2 Kings 18:6–7 ESV / King Hezekiah was twenty-five years old when he began his reign in Judah, but his youth didn't stop him from doing what was right in God's eyes.

The Bible says, "He removed the high places, smashed the sacred stones and cut down the Asherah poles" (2 Kings 18:4 NIV). He even smashed the bronze serpent Moses had made—the one to which Israel had begun making offerings.

Doing what is right can make a man feel like he's all alone. But even if he ends up in jail—or worse—God is with him.

You should never compromise your faith in Christ, no matter how much pressure the world puts on you. Stay faithful to Him—He's always faithful to you.

DAY 284

MORNING: CUT IT OUT! / *"If your right eye causes you to sin, pluck it out and cast if from you; for it is more profitable for you that one of your members perish, than for your whole body to be cast into hell."* Matthew 5:29 NKJV / In the sci-fi zombie plague thriller *World War Z*, a courageous United Nations investigator cuts of the hand of a woman who has been bitten by a zombie to save her from the infection.

But in this morning's verse, Jesus isn't telling us to dismember ourselves. Rather, He is using strong, violent imagery to tell us how critical it is that we cut sin off at its root—by confessing to our brothers or by using some other radical method. After all, blinding ourselves to avoid lust will never cleanse our hearts—only Jesus can do that.

It may be hard to come clean. . .but look at the alternative!

EVENING: EXPECT HARDSHIP / *Can anything ever separate us from Christ's love? Does it mean he no longer loves us if we have trouble or calamity, or are persecuted, or hungry, or destitute, or in danger, or threatened with death?* Romans 8:35 NLT / Perhaps you've wondered how God can allow His own children to be persecuted, starved, or killed. Doesn't He promise to protect His followers (Job 5:11; Psalm 12:7; Proverbs 19:23)?

In some instances, God does intervene—offering physical protection to advance His kingdom. In other cases, He offers spiritual protection against the advances of the enemy. But sometimes, He allows hardship while preserving your soul.

This evening's verse reminds us of the hard truth that Christians face death every day for the sake of the kingdom. Hardship, however, can never separate you from the love of Christ.

DAY 285

MORNING: HIS STEADFAST LOVE / *"For he is good, for his steadfast love endures forever toward Israel."* Ezra 3:11 ESV / The melody has been lost to time. But we still know the powerful words: *God is good and His love for Israel endures forever.* Years had passed, but people who had endured captivity for most of their lives returned to the land of promise—and a song was born.

Sometimes, God allows us to be held captive as a result of our sinful choices. However, enduring this captivity often leads us to recall the God who has endured our own waywardness. That's when we learn that God's way was right from the beginning.

When you miss the companionship of your Maker, it's best to recall His faithfulness and say, "He is good, for His steadfast love endures forever."

EVENING: DESCENDANTS AND DESTINIES / *He remembers his covenant forever, the promise he made, for a thousand generations.* Psalm 105:8 NIV / Have you ever questioned the value of studying those genealogies in the Bible? If so, a few scripture passages provide reasons.

In Psalm 105, the poet uses the lineage of Abraham, Isaac, and Jacob to rehearse how God keeps His promises and to remind His children that they haven't been forgotten. First Chronicles also uses genealogy to show God's promise-keeping character and His interest in individuals. And Paul's sermon in Acts 13 traces the lineage of Jesus through Israel's history (Acts 13:14–34), reminding readers that God's promise of a Messiah was fulfilled in detail.

Never forget that this detail-oriented God knows and cares about every aspect of your life too.

MORNING: CONTINUE WITH THE LORD / *When [Barnabas] arrived and saw what the grace of God had done, he was glad and encouraged them all to remain true to the Lord with all their hearts. . . . A great number of people were brought to the Lord.* Acts 11:23–24 NIV / After Stephen was martyred, persecution in Jerusalem caused believers to scatter, preaching the Word wherever they went. Consequently, a great number of both Jews and Gentiles believed and turned to the Lord.

You have been scattered in a different fashion—in your workplace, campus, or community—and you have opportunities to tell others about Christ. No doubt, you will face opposition at times, but Barnabas would encourage you to "remain true to the Lord."

People will find eternal life in Christ as a result of what you do and say to them today.

EVENING: WORSHIP EXUBERANTLY / *"They shall come and sing aloud on the height of Zion, and they shall be radiant over the goodness of the Lord. . .their life shall be like a watered garden, and they shall languish no more."* Jeremiah 31:12 ESV / Some church observers believe men are singing less during worship services. Many reasons are cited, including a lack of fervor in Christian men, a modern tradition of more feminine songs, and the songs' keys being too high.

Whether these things are true or not, you should worship with all your heart—and lungs.

The New Testament equates "Zion" (which, in this morning's verse, refers to the city of David) to the church (1 Peter 2:1–6) and even to heaven (Revelation 14:1). How can the Christian man do anything but sing and exhibit joy over what Jesus has done for him?

MORNING: CITY ON A HILL / *"You are the light of the world. A city that is set on a hill cannot be hidden."* Matthew 5:14 NKJV / In the Old West, a gunslinger on the run might take to the desert and pray for nightfall to avoid a determined posse. But in the midst of a midnight sandstorm, the welcome light of another man's campfire always drew him in. At that wild and lonely campfire, coffee and hardtack were offered freely, and no man was an enemy.

The church, if it is doing the good works it is called to (Ephesians 2:10; John 14:10–12) will not hide the light of life from the fugitive in the desert. We will shine like stars in the night sky (Philippians 2:15), showing the way to life. Our campfire will signal shelter—eternal shelter—from the storm.

EVENING: DOCTRINAL INTEGRITY / *Likewise, exhort the young men to be sober-minded, in all things showing yourself to be a pattern of good works; in doctrine showing integrity, reverence, incorruptibility, sound speech that cannot be condemned, that one who is an opponent may be ashamed, having nothing evil to say of you.* Titus 2:6–8 NKJV / Doctrinal integrity doesn't mean perfection. It simply means living out truth as best you understand it, without walking in contradiction. For example, if you teach that anger is a sin, but everybody knows you as a hothead, your inconsistency signals to the next generation that you don't really believe what you say.

If you're older, are you teaching younger men in the faith? Do they see inconsistencies in your life, or do they see a repentant heart? If you're younger, how quick are you to accept the teaching of the older generation while acknowledging your own weaknesses?

MORNING: WHOM WE CAN CALL "BROTHER" / *"[Ananias] came and stood beside me and said, 'Brother Saul, regain your sight.' "* Acts 22:13 NLT / Imagine God asking you to call a murderer who has just been released after nearly twenty years in a maximum-security prison. When he answers the phone, what will you say?

"Brother" may not be the first word that comes to mind.

Yet Jesus consistently used the word "brothers" to describe his earthly half-brothers, His twelve apostles, all of His disciples, and even "the least of these" (Matthew 25:40 NLT). And in the book of Acts, this term broadens to include all men, even the most outspoken enemies of Jesus Christ (Acts 7:2; 22:1; 23:1, 5–6).

Calling an enemy brother may seem counterintuitive, but when you have the clear examples of Jesus Christ, the martyr Stephen, and the apostle Paul, it's best not to disagree!

EVENING: DON'T BE AFRAID OF THEIR FACES / *"Do not be afraid of their faces, for I am with you to deliver you,"* says the LORD. Jeremiah 1:8 NKJV / Guys don't like to admit they're afraid of anything. But almost everyone, everywhere, finds something frightening. And often that "something" is simply other people's reactions to us.

When God called Jeremiah to be a prophet, the young man claimed he was just a child. But God answered with the interesting words of this evening's scripture. You might think Jeremiah would be afraid of people's balled-up fists or maybe their karate-kicking feet. But the Lord specifically said, "Do not be afraid of their *faces*." How could their sneers or snickering harm Jeremiah? Especially when you consider that God was with him.

The smile of God far outweighs the frown of any human being.

MORNING: WORK IN PROGRESS / *Clothe yourselves with tender-hearted mercy, kindness, humility, gentleness, and patience. . . . Remember, the Lord forgave you, so you must forgive others.* Colossians 3:12–13 NLT / True humility allows you to recognize you're a sinner saved by God's grace—you're no better than other human beings. You have fallen short of God's perfect standard (Romans 6:23), yet God did the remarkable and offered a rescue plan so comprehensive it made you part of His family. He orchestrated His plan to encompass a restored relationship between a perfect God and an imperfect people.

As a Christian, you're asked to model the behavior of your Father God. He didn't love you because you deserved it. He loved you—period.

Because He offers all of these things to you, He wants you to do the same for others.

EVENING: STAY THE COURSE / *Some of the Jews, however, spurned God's message and poisoned the minds of the Gentiles against Paul and Barnabas. But the apostles stayed there a long time, preaching boldly about the grace of the Lord.* Acts 14:2–3 NLT / As Paul and Barnabas preached in a place called Iconium, the Jews worked against them. Some men might have become discouraged and left, but the apostles stayed there a long time, preaching boldly—and a great number of both Jews and Greeks were converted.

Are you facing spiritual resistance right now? Do you sense the Lord's power flowing through you, even though people you are trying to reach aren't necessarily receptive? Stay the course. You are only responsible for telling others about Christ. It's the Spirit's job to open their spiritual eyes.

Rest in that fact—and get to work!

DAY 290

MORNING: IMPROBABLE JOY / *"Blessed are those who are persecuted for righteousness' sake, for theirs is the kingdom of heaven."* Matthew 5:10 NKJV / Researcher David Barrett estimates that around seventy million Christians have died for the faith since the stoning of Stephen. Even in the modern West, Christian persecution seems to be increasing.

We are living in the day that Jesus spoke of when He told His disciples, "You will be hated by all nations because of me" (Matthew 24:9 NIV). So what does He command us to do? "Rejoice and be exceedingly glad" (Matthew 5:12 NKJV).

We know something that our persecutors don't—no matter what happens to us on earth here, heaven awaits! The kingdoms of this earth will all fall, but the kingdom of heaven will last forever. And so will our rewards.

EVENING: WORK, REST, AND PRAY / *Be still in the presence of the LORD, and wait patiently for him to act. Don't worry about evil people who prosper or fret about their wicked schemes.* Psalm 37:7 NLT / Being still in the Lord's presence means more than simply not moving—it's about being content in God, silencing the tongue from all murmuring and complaint. That doesn't mean you can't ask Him to act, but it does mean there should be times when you meet with Him without making requests.

The real test comes when evil people appear to prosper. Shouldn't a Christian fret then? "No," this evening's verse says. Instead, we should wait patiently for the Lord to act.

Isn't it nice to know that the success of God's kingdom and the responsibility to topple evil don't rest in your hands? You're called to work, rest, and pray—always trusting in Him.

MORNING: MYSTERY / *Now we see only a reflection as in a mirror; then we shall see face to face. Now I know in part; then I shall know fully, even as I am fully known.* 1 Corinthians 13:12 NIV / *Mystery*. It's a dirty word to many people. But if we can't live with some mystery, we're likely to be uncomfortable in the kingdom of God.

Partly, it's a personality trait. Some of us are just left-brained, mathematically and mechanically inclined, and always reaching toward certainty. Others are right-brained, poetic, emotional thinkers. But when it comes to faith, there are some things that are just impossible to know.

As Paul said, "We see only a reflection as in a mirror." If the theological genius who wrote Romans learned to live with God's mysteries, how much more should we?

EVENING: BECAUSE OF WHO HE IS / *Yet he saved them for his name's sake, to make his mighty power known.* Psalm 106:8 NIV / God reverses human mistakes. It's part of who He is.

The children of Israel, as they labored as slaves in Egypt, struggled every day as a result of their sin in prioritizing other things over God (Psalm 106:6). But because of who He is, God reversed the situation and gave them the promised land.

Similarly, When King Saul died because he "did not inquire of the Lord," God "turned the kingdom over to David" (1 Chronicles 10:14 NIV) and reversed a bad situation for the nation of Israel.

Because of God's character and everlasting love, He has fixed countless mistakes that His children have made throughout history. He can still do the same for you.

MORNING: A SPIRIT OF GRATITUDE / *I spoke to you in your [times of] prosperity, but you said, I will not listen!* Jeremiah 22:21 AMPC / The prosperous often believe they don't need God. They can meet all their own needs and many of their wants, so obedience to God isn't high on their priority list. While this isn't always the case, it certainly was in this morning's passage regarding God's people. God spoke but they disobeyed, just as they'd done since their youth.

So what's a believer supposed to do during times of prosperity? Pray for lack? No. But maintaining a spirit of gratitude to God—understanding that He is the source of every good and perfect gift (James 1:17)—will go a long way toward keeping you humble and willing to obey Him, whatever your financial situation.

EVENING: DESPERATE PRAYERS / *God delivered the Hagrites and all their allies into their hands, because they cried out to him during the battle.* 1 Chronicles 5:20 NIV / As the Reubenites, Gadites, and half the tribe of Manasseh waged war against the Hagrites and others, they cried out to God—and He answered them because they trusted in Him. God's people ended up defeating their enemies and seizing all their livestock. Because they didn't waver in their faith, the Lord delivered them.

Prayers of desperation are often likened to a "Hail Mary" pass in football. But unlike the player who makes a desperate toss across the field, believers don't leave the situation to chance. God hears His people, and He answers them.

What are you praying for right now? Don't give up!

MORNING: PEACEMAKERS / *"Blessed are the peacemakers, for they shall be called sons of God."* Matthew 5:9 NKJV / Samuel Colt, inventor of the first revolving cylinder handgun once said, "The good people in this world are very far from being satisfied with each other, and my [guns] are the best peacemaker." When Colt died from a sudden illness in 1862, his wife took over the gun business and developed the famous Colt .45, still known today by its nickname, "The Peacemaker."

When Jesus said, "Blessed are the peacemakers," however, He didn't have guns in mind. His peace came not through bullets but through love. God's love disarms the heart of man, and His kindness, forbearance, patience, and goodness lead us to repentance (Romans 2:4). Jesus shed His blood to make peace between God and humankind—and between man and man (Colossians 1:20).

How will you keep peace in your interactions today?

EVENING: STAY ALERT / *Watch out that you do not lose what we have worked so hard to achieve. Be diligent so that you receive your full reward.* 2 John 8 NLT / If you knew your car might veer off a mountainside at any moment, you'd be on heightened alert. Your radio would be off, your hands would firmly grip the steering wheel, and your eyes would be locked on the road ahead.

Spiritual diligence works in a similar fashion.

When the apostle John wrote his second epistle, many were denying that Jesus had come in an actual physical body (2 John 7). This was ultimately, John said, a rejection of Christ, and those who fell for it risked losing their heavenly reward and their relationship with God (verse 9).

In light of such consequences, be diligent in your fight against the devil's lies!

MORNING: WELL-SEASONED SPEECH / *Conduct yourselves with wisdom toward outsiders, making the most of the opportunity. Let your speech always be with grace, as though seasoned with salt.* Colossians 4:5–6 NASB / The prophets and disciples of the scriptures weren't like the hermit sages living on mountaintops dispensing clever sayings. They weren't concerned with answering every philosophical question people raised—they were focused on changing lives. They knew that right living makes a person wise, so they spoke truth to help people understand their choices.

Like the prophets of the Bible, we are surrounded by people who do not "see" the kingdom of God. They need spiritual truths explained. So we will always be surrounded by opportunities to share our hope if we are prepared—not with clever sayings, a rehearsed speech, or even theological arguments, but with gracious and practical words.

EVENING: REPURPOSING / *Save us, Lord our God, and gather us from the nations, that we may give thanks to your holy name and glory in your praise.* Psalm 106:47 NIV / When Paul talked with philosophers in Athens, he pointed out the irony in their thinking about idols: "Since we are God's offspring, we should not think that the divine being is like gold or silver or stone—an image made by human design and skill" (Acts 17:29 NIV).

Paul knew that humans tend to recreate God in their image, so he repurposed their idols to better connect the good news with that particular city's cultural bent.

Are there things in your life that take priority alongside your fellowship with God and His children? If so, repurpose those things so they can become ways of sharing Jesus Christ with your culture.

MORNING: STAYING FAITHFUL / *"But my people are not so reliable, for they have deserted me; they burn incense to worthless idols."* Jeremiah 18:15 NLT / In many ways, America has been both the easiest country to be a Christian in and the most difficult. Easy because of the freedom. Difficult because of the comfort.

Pastor and author John Piper once discussed the challenge: "You go to church, the music is nice, the AC is nice, the lighting is nice, the friends are there, the children have something fun to do, the sermon is more-or-less interesting, and we can go home saying that we've been Christians." This would change if persecution pushes the church underground. But it doesn't need to come to that.

Today, make a specific commitment to God to honor Him in all that you do. Ask Him to keep you faithful at all times, whether in ease or persecution.

EVENING: SEEKING GUIDANCE / *So Saul died for his breach of faith. He. . .did not keep the command of the Lord, and also consulted a medium, seeking guidance. He did not seek guidance from the Lord.* 1 Chronicles 10:13–14 ESV / King Saul serves as an example of how *not* to live the life of faith. He didn't wait for Samuel, offered an unauthorized sacrifice, and spared the Amalekite king when he had been instructed to kill him. This evening's verses add another grave sin to the list: he consulted a medium rather than seeking the guidance of the Lord.

A Christian man would do well to ask himself if there's any scriptural command that he's willfully disobeying. Your consequences might not be as severe as Saul's, but they might cost you more than you would ever dream of in your relationships, employment, or health.

MORNING: PURE HEART / *"Blessed are the pure in heart, for they shall see God."* Matthew 5:8 NKJV / In 1966, the Rolling Stones released a single called "Paint It Black," a somber song sung by a young man whose girlfriend has died. With her death, the color went out of his life: "I look inside myself and see my heart is black."

Jesus said, "If your eye is bad, your whole body will be full of darkness" (Matthew 6:23 NKJV). If our eyes are on worldly things, then we're not looking to the Light—and the light that we think is in us is actually darkness!

How does a man walk in the light? By being honest about the state of his own heart (1 John 1:8–9). Only the blood of Jesus can wash away sin's dark stain and purify our hearts. Then we enjoy true fellowship with God and one another.

EVENING: POOR CHOICES, GOOD CHOICES / *"The Lord delivered you into my hand today, but I refused to stretch out my hand against the Lord's anointed."* 1 Samuel 26:23 NASB / When Saul heard that David was hiding from him in the wilderness of Ziph, Saul took three thousand men in search of him. David outfoxed him, however, and showed up at Saul's camp early one morning while everybody was sleeping. His cousin Abishai wanted to kill Saul on the spot, but David recognized that Saul was God's anointed. To kill Saul would have meant being unfaithful to God, and David wouldn't do that.

At some point, we'll all be tempted to make a decision that would mean unfaithfulness to God. This evening, pray that He will protect you from such poor choices.

MORNING: TROUBLES? PRAY! / *Then they cried out to the LORD in their trouble, and He saved them out of their distresses.* Psalm 107:13 NKJV / From his grimy prison cell, King Manasseh looked back upon years of unspeakable crimes—worshipping the stars and sun in God's temple, shedding the blood of innocent people, and sacrificing his own sons to idols. Once he realized his rebellion had brought nothing but pain to himself and others, he looked up to God and cried out for help (2 Chronicles 33:1–20).

Even God's prophets must have thought Manasseh was too far gone. Yet his repentance was real. He immediately began tearing down pagan altars, restoring the temple, and worshipping the Lord publicly.

We can't always undo the damage of our actions. Yet our sins are never so great that God can't forgive us and grant us a new start.

EVENING: NO SALE PRICES HERE / *But King David replied to Araunah, "No, I insist on paying the full price. I will not. . .sacrifice a burnt offering that costs me nothing."* 1 Chronicles 21:24 NIV / Human cultures tend to champion frugality as a costume for selfishness. Few people are willing to pay the price that repentance exacts.

When David's disobedience hurt the people around him, he attempted to purchase a threshing floor to sacrifice a burnt offering. When the owner offered it freely, David surprised him by saying he would not offer a sacrifice that cost him nothing. David knew the harm he'd brought on others exacted a heavy price.

When you've wronged someone, do you try to get by with sacrificing as little time or money as possible? Or, like David, do you recognize the deeply personal nature of your offense and pay the full price?

MORNING: CORRECT ME, O LORD / *Correct me, O Lord, but in justice; not in your anger, lest you bring me to nothing.* Jeremiah 10:24 ESV / Hiding and running from God is the norm for people who have sinned and damaged their relationship with God—just ask Jonah or Adam and Eve.

In this morning's verse, however, a remnant of God's people not only refused to run from Him, they asked for His correction—not in His anger, lest He crush them, but in His justice. It's similar to a teenage son who makes a poor decision and, rather than hiding from his dad, picks up the phone and confesses, asking for mercy.

How can you do anything less after you've sinned? We'll not only restore our broken fellowship with God—we'll be made white as snow.

EVENING: A HUNGRY MAN / *"Blessed are those who hunger and thirst for righteousness, for they shall be filled."* Matthew 5:6 NKJV / When Jesus said this, He wasn't peddling burgers and beer to a TV audience munching potato chips. He was addressing men and women who intimately understood hunger and thirst.

In Jesus' day, the daily wage was equivalent to three cents; nobody got fat on that. Israeli working men—never far from real hunger or actual starvation—ate meat once a week. And thirst was worse; few besides the Romans had water in their homes.

In reality, this beatitude is a stark challenge: Do you want righteousness as much as a starving man wants food or a parched man needs water? How intense is your desire for God, for His goodness and glory?

Only God and His Word can fill us for following Jesus.

MORNING: LEADING AN INHERITANCE / *A good man leaves an inheritance to his children's children, and the wealth of a sinner is stored up for the righteous.* Proverbs 13:22 NASB / As you head off to start your day this morning, you may have a sense of weariness. But today matters. So does tomorrow. You're providing for your family—and hopefully being thrifty enough to store up an inheritance for your children and grandchildren.

Bible commentator Adam Clarke, in his exposition of this morning's verse, goes a step further: he says that such a man "files many a prayer in heaven in their behalf, and his good example and advices are remembered and quoted from generation to generation."

The point of this morning's verse is to think far beyond today, this week, this month, or even this year. Everything you do should be done with the spiritual well-being of future generations in mind.

EVENING: A TRUSTING HEART / *One woman, Lydia, was. . .known to be a God-fearing woman. As she listened with intensity to what was being said, the Master gave her a trusting heart—and she believed!* Acts 16:14 MSG / The world's greatest miracle? Hands down, it's God's gift of a faith-filled heart. Even more remarkable, God can give that gift to *anyone*.

What one person do you consider least likely to receive God's gift of a trusting heart? Are you willing to let God use you in that person's life? If so, make contact, ask questions, listen with patience and grace. . .and ask how you can pray.

Experience shows that listening is the new loving. Even tough guys respond to such unobtrusive love.

The greatest miracle you'll experience this year could be right around the corner.

MORNING: IT'S ALL IN THE ASK / *God said to Solomon, "Because your greatest desire is to help your people, and you did not ask for wealth, riches, fame. . .I will also give you wealth, riches, and fame."* 2 Chronicles 1:11–12 NLT / What you ask for often determines what you live for. King Solomon asked God for wisdom and knowledge so he could do the work God assigned.

If he were living today, young Solomon would be countercultural. His request was not for money and prestige. Instead, he asked for things that would make his work for God prosper.

Do you ever ask God for help loving your coworkers, reaching out to your neighbors, and assisting widows, orphans, or latchkey kids?

So much of the meaning in life, after all, is in the asking.

EVENING: KEEP BLUSHING / *"Were they ashamed when they committed abomination? No. . .they did not know how to blush. Therefore. . .they shall be overthrown," says the LORD.* Jeremiah 6:15 ESV / This evening's verse was a sobering warning for those who had committed abominations (vile acts) so often that they no longer even knew how to blush. As a result, they were to be counted as unbelievers.

First Timothy 4:1–2 says that people who devote themselves to deceitful spirits end up with a "seared" conscience. It's like lacking feeling in your arm, so when you set it against a hot grill, you don't realize you need to remove it. The effects would be devastating.

Similarly, when you stop fighting against your sinful nature, you'll slowly lose the ability even to feel guilty. Never allow yourself to get to that point.

MORNING: A FAITHFUL GOD / *Remember his covenant forever—the commitment he made to a thousand generations. This is the covenant he made with Abraham and the oath he swore to Isaac. He confirmed it to Jacob as a decree, and to the people of Israel as a never-ending covenant.* 1 Chronicles 16:15–17 NLT / Israel brought the ark of God to the special tent that David had prepared for it. After the priests presented offerings and sacrifices, it was time for worship. Today's verses contain lyrics David gave to Asaph and his fellow Levites to sing during that time of worship.

One of the best ways to remain unshakable in your faith is to do what David did—worship the Lord while remembering His faithfulness to a thousand generations. God was at work in people long before you were born and will continue to be after you have entered into glory.

EVENING: MEEK AIN'T WEAK / *"Blessed are the meek, for they shall inherit the earth."* Matthew 5:5 NKJV / History trumpets the names of men who have tried to conquer the world: Genghis Khan, Alexander the Great, Napoleon Bonaparte, Julius Caesar, Attila the Hun, Charlemagne, Adolf Hitler. As you read their names and recall their character, does the word *meek* come to mind? Probably not.

Had they been men of gentle temperament, they wouldn't have violently trodden so much turf and shed so much blood. And to what end? A grave beneath the earth they sought to rule!

One day, Jesus will create a new heaven and a new earth (Revelation 21:1–3). The militant and megalomaniacal will have no part of it. It is the inheritance of the meek—the followers of Jesus.

MORNING: A GENTLE DEFENSE / *But sanctify Christ as Lord in your hearts, always being ready to make a defense to everyone who asks you to give an account for the hope that is in you, yet with gentleness and reverence.* 1 Peter 3:15 NASB / We welcome instances when someone genuinely inquires about our faith, asking for an account of the hope they see in us. But even during genuine inquiries, conversations can sometimes go off track.

Charles Spurgeon explained, "If they wish to know why you believe that you're saved, have your answer all ready in a few plain, simple sentences; and in the gentlest and most modest spirit make your confession of faith to the praise and glory of God. Who knows but what such good seed will bring forth an abundant harvest?"

God can use our gentle, reverent response to great effect.

EVENING: LIFE-GIVING GOOD NEWS / *When the non-Jewish outsiders heard this, they could hardly believe their good fortune. All who were marked out for real life put their trust in God.* Acts 13:48 MSG / Things didn't end well after Paul's second sermon in Pisidia—antagonistic Jews contradicted what he said and blasphemed the name of Jesus.

At that point, Paul and Barnabas publicly declared their intention to continue preaching the good news to the Gentiles. That news, coupled with the prophetic words of Isaiah 49:6, provoked an immediate, positive response from their non-Jewish listeners.

For the remainder of the book of Acts, Luke repeatedly shows this same pattern of Jewish rejection—and Gentile reception—of the message of salvation in Jesus Christ.

Be grateful for the universal offer of salvation, and the fact that God has drawn you into His family.

MORNING: SHARE YOUR TESTIMONY / *Let the redeemed of the* LORD *say so, whom he hath redeemed from the hand of the enemy.* Psalm 107:2 KJV / The enemy often tempts believers to stay quiet about their faith. He knows that if he is successful, then not only will those around us not turn to us for spiritual answers but our hesitation to declare Christ's redeeming power will weaken our own faith. Today's verse is a call for the Lord's redeemed to speak up.

In what ways are you brightening the sphere of influence God has placed you in? Are you praying for such opportunities each morning?

You have been redeemed from the hand of Satan. It's time to tell other captives about the freedom they can experience in Christ. As you do, you'll find that your faith becomes more and more unshakable.

EVENING: REBUILD THE ANCIENT RUINS / *They shall build up the ancient ruins; they shall raise up the former devastations; they shall repair the ruined cities, the devastations of many generations.* Isaiah 61:4 ESV / In 2019, a West Palm Beach church took over a former strip club with plans to open in 2020. The reverend of NewSound Church said the former facility was being transformed into a church building that would hold six hundred to seven hundred people.

"I don't mind being in a building that was a strip club any more than I mind somebody walking in our doors that had at one time in their life been a stripper," the pastor said in a CNN story. "I believe that God is opening up some doors that a twenty-month-old church can't open by themselves."

That's an example of rebuilding ancient ruins. What might you repair and restore?

MORNING: INTERNAL BATTLES / *He that is slow to anger is better than the mighty; and he that ruleth his spirit than he that taketh a city.* Proverbs 16:32 KJV / For a split second, just before you react to something that makes you angry, you have the opportunity to restrain yourself rather than blow up. If you zoom past that internal check, it shows an inability to rule your own spirit.

Being slow to answer shows emotional fortitude, the kind it would've required to conquer a city back in the day. How so? The person who took a city overcame men and machines—maybe even the weather—to succeed. Meanwhile, the person who rules his spirit has won a major internal battle.

The next time you're tempted to lash out, obey that internal check you feel. It's truly a gift from God.

EVENING: FOLLOW GOD'S WORD WHOLEHEARTEDLY / *There was no king to compare with Josiah—neither before nor after—a king who turned in total and repentant obedience to GOD.* 2 Kings 23:25 MSG / Having called all his people to Jerusalem, King Josiah read aloud from the book of the law. Josiah gave the people God's Word, and then he gave them the powerful example of his own zeal and obedience. With the words of the law still ringing in their ears, the people watched as their king lived it out, loving the Lord his God wholeheartedly.

No one can force another person to love and obey God. Yet when a man gives the Word of God to others and lives it out before them, God uses this example to draw others to Himself.

MORNING: BEYOND PEAK EXPERIENCES / *Thou art my God, and I will praise thee: thou art my God, I will exalt thee.* Psalm 118:28 KJV / Who is your favorite band? Can you remember how you felt the first time you heard their music?

Songs can fill our minds and thrill our hearts. But even their pleasure can fade over time. A number one hit song, heard too often, may ultimately just get on your nerves.

How good it is to know that our God will never grow old or stale. As the infinite Creator, His wisdom and power and goodness go on and on, through all eternity. And we can be sure we'll have an ongoing joy in discovering new things about Him.

He is definitely worthy of praise and exaltation.

EVENING: EVERYTHING'S BACKWARDS! / *You have wearied the* LORD *with your words. "How have we wearied him?" you ask. By saying, "All who do evil are good in the eyes of the* LORD*, and he is pleased with them."* Malachi 2:17 NIV / If you're not careful, you might start to think you're crazy for following Jesus. This world is so backwards that it calls sin good. Biblical righteousness is called evil. But that's nothing new. Seven hundred years before Jesus was born, Isaiah wrote, "Woe to those who call evil good and good evil, who put darkness for light and light for darkness" (Isaiah 5:20 NIV). And four centuries before Christ, Malachi noted that his culture was saying, "All who do evil are good in the eyes of the LORD, and he is pleased with them"!

Of course, that wasn't true then and it isn't true now. No matter how backwards things get, you know the truth—the plain standards of God's Word.

MORNING: WHOLEHEARTED DEVOTION / *"And you, my son Solomon, acknowledge the God of your father, and serve him with wholehearted devotion and with a willing mind, for the LORD searches every heart and understands every desire and every thought."* 1 Chronicles 28:9 NIV / "Christians can never sin cheaply; they pay a heavy price for iniquity," wrote Charles Spurgeon in his *Morning and Evening* devotional. "Transgression destroys peace of mind, obscures fellowship with Jesus, hinders prayer, brings darkness over the soul."

David seemed to understand that truth when he spoke to his son Solomon, encouraging him to serve the Lord wholeheartedly with a willing mind. A mind and heart that are harboring sin are unable to serve God completely.

What does the Lord see right now when He searches your heart, your desires, and your every thought? If He sees any darkness, confess it to Him right now.

EVENING: THE PLAN, GOAL, AND PURPOSE / *Keep your eyes on Jesus, who both began and finished this race we're in. Study how he did it.* Hebrews 12:2 MSG / When a runner is beyond tired, it's the finish line that inspires him to finish strong. When a singer gets invited to perform his first solo, it's the audience that instills courage. When an entrepreneur dreams up a brilliant idea, it's the launch of his product that gives him his first real sense of hope.

Some days, the Christian life will be hard. Our adversary will distract us and offer the equivalent of a recliner, detour, or false promise. That's when you must keep your focus on Jesus. Learn who He is, how He lived, and what He wants.

Feeling weary? Spend time with His story. Regain your focus, get your second wind, and press on.

MORNING: GENUINE REPENTANCE / *That is why the Lord says, "Turn to me now, while there is time. Give me your hearts. Come with fasting, weeping, and mourning. Don't tear your clothing in your grief, but tear your hearts instead."* Joel 2:12–13 NLT / Joel had just spoken of a coming day of judgment when everyone should tremble in fear. "Who can possibly survive?" he asked (Joel 2:11 NLT).

God calls those who wish to escape the judgment to come with fasting, weeping, and mourning. But He goes even further, saying that He's not interested in mere outward repentance. Instead, He wants godly sorrow to seep inside, all the way to the heart.

If your heart is broken over your sin, then you've fully grasped Joel's message. If you haven't experienced such a broken heart, ask God to help you repent and find forgiveness.

EVENING: GOD'S HOLINESS AND JUSTICE / *Mighty King, lover of justice, you have established fairness. You have acted with justice and righteousness throughout Israel. Exalt the Lord our God! Bow low before his feet, for he is holy!* Psalm 99:4–5 NLT / When God imagines a future with righteousness and holiness, justice is always part of the mix. But God's concern doesn't just stop with personal conduct—the righteousness of systems and laws also matter a great deal to Him.

As you worship the Lord today, keep in mind that He cares both for your personal holiness and the justice that you personally experience. That care is also extended to your neighbors and people around the world.

Has anyone you know experienced injustice? If so, how can you be present in that person's pain? A holy and just God prompts His people to listen well to those who have suffered.

MORNING: REMOVE THE FILTH / *"Hear me, Levites! Now consecrate yourselves, and consecrate the house of the LORD, the God of your fathers, and carry out the filth from the Holy Place."* 2 Chronicles 29:5 ESV / After a sixteen-year-reign by his wicked father, Ahaz, Hezekiah radically changed the direction of Judah. In his very first month as king, Hezekiah cleansed the Lord's temple and restored biblical worship there.

Think about your own spiritual lineage. Did your father or grandfather walk in spiritual darkness, making decisions that displeased the Lord?

If not, great! But if so, become a Hezekiah in your family. Consecrate yourself and your household, remove any filth, and enter into a time of rejoicing because of the Lord's subsequent provision—much as Hezekiah and the people experienced in 2 Chronicles 29:36.

It's never too late to change direction.

EVENING: A BETTER DAY COMING / *The Sovereign LORD will wipe away the tears from all faces; he will remove his people's disgrace from all the earth.* Isaiah 25:8 NIV / Have you ever gone through a difficult time and had a friend try to encourage you with a meaningless platitude like, "Just hang in there! Things will get better."

It often seems like our difficulties will never end. But amazingly, God promises that a day will come in which every earthly difficulty becomes a thing of the past. No more pain, no more death, no more tears. . .only a joyful eternity in our heavenly Father's presence (Revelation 21:4).

On this earth, it's hard to imagine such a time. But it's God's promise to His people, and that can get us through our most challenging life experiences.

MORNING: FULLY COMMITTED / *And he did what was right in the eyes of the LORD, yet not with a whole heart.* 2 Chronicles 25:2 ESV / King Amaziah started strong during his twenty-nine-year reign in Judah, bringing his father's killers to justice and building a mighty army. But then he fell into idolatry. After striking down the Edomites, he brought back the gods of the men of Seir and set them up as his gods and worshipped them. His whole heart hadn't been with God, and it led him astray.

Today, Christian men don't bring back false idols from battle, but they sometimes worship other things—like power, wealth, or sex—that appeal to the flesh with false promises.

Don't allow that to be your story. Make a full commitment to the Lord and follow Him all the days of your life.

EVENING: PURSUING GODLY AMBITIONS / *My ambition has always been to preach the Good News where the name of Christ has never been heard, rather than where a church has already been started by someone else.* Romans 15:20 NLT / You probably have several ambitions—maybe to get a promotion, become a better leader in your home, or work on taking care of yourself. But what about your spiritual ambitions? Where do those passions lie?

After his conversion, the apostle Paul had his sights set on preaching the gospel in places where the name of Jesus had never been heard. He spent the rest of his life doing so.

Do you have such clarity of thought? You don't need a "calling" to pursue most of your godly ambitions. You simply need to acknowledge that they exist and then prayerfully seek ways to live them out.

MORNING: LOVING THOSE WHOM JESUS LOVES / *A third time he asked him, "Simon son of John, do you love me?" Peter. . .said, "Lord, you know everything. You know that I love you." Jesus said, "Then feed my sheep."* John 21:17 NLT / Peter had committed what he felt was the ultimate betrayal. Facing the prospect of torture and death alongside Jesus, he'd denied even knowing his Lord. How could he ever recover? Well, Jesus restored Peter by offering him chances to affirm his love. Then He instructed Peter to care for other believers.

In order to serve others, you may need to make sacrifices or changes, looking beyond your own well-being to care for the people Jesus loves.

As often as you care for one of the least of these, you do the same for Jesus Himself.

EVENING: COUNTED AS RIGHTEOUS / *He staggered not at the promise of God through unbelief; but was strong in faith, giving glory to God; and being fully persuaded that, what he had promised, he was able also to perform.* Romans 4:20–21 KJV / Abraham fully believed that God would make his name great, and that all the families of the earth would be blessed through him, just as God promised in Genesis 12:1–3. As a result, it was "counted unto him for righteousness" (Romans 4:3 KJV).

What does that mean for you today?

Consider the object of your faith. Are you trusting in your own ability to keep the law, in your church attendance and Bible reading, or in the God who raised Jesus from the dead?

God's promise to you is eternal life. Don't stagger at His promise by believing in the wrong things. He is faithful, even when you are not.

MORNING: HERE AM I! / *Also I heard the voice of the Lord, saying: "Whom shall I send, and who will go for Us?" Then I said, "Here am I! Send me."* Isaiah 6:8 NKJV / Do you ever find your heart breaking over the hurting and needy people in your neighborhood, nation, or world? Do you wonder how you can reach them with the message of salvation through Jesus Christ?

If you answered yes to one or both of the above questions, God may be preparing you for some kind of service—just like He did the prophet Isaiah.

God had purified Isaiah and made him ready to speak to His hard-hearted people (Isaiah 6:1–6). Similarly, God has given you the gifts you need to do what He's calling you to do. Your part in that is to pray, like the prophet Isaiah, "Here am I! Send me."

EVENING: GOD'S PATIENCE ISN'T APATHY / *Don't you see how wonderfully kind, tolerant, and patient God is with you? Does this mean nothing to you? Can't you see that his kindness is intended to turn you from your sin?* Romans 2:4 NLT / Although Paul had plenty of reasons to praise the church in Rome, the people were still in danger of misunderstanding a key attribute of God's character: His patience.

Perhaps you grew up hearing about either God's wrath or His mercy. Both perspectives can misconstrue God's aim to lead you toward spiritual health. You certainly need to obey Jesus' two greatest commandments—loving God and loving your neighbors—yet God is patient and kind in leading you away from sin.

It may be a messy, time-consuming process, but in God's eyes, you are worth the wait.

MORNING: FINDING JOY IN THE LORD / *Even though the fig trees have no blossoms, and there are no grapes on the vines; even though the olive crop fails, and the fields lie empty and barren; even though the flocks die in the fields, and the cattle barns are empty, yet I will rejoice in the LORD!* Habakkuk 3:17–18 NLT / Habakkuk saw a time of drought in which the trees, vines, and crops would fail, and most of the livestock would be dead. Yet, in a preemptive strike against his own soul, Habakkuk vowed to rejoice in the Lord.

Have you ever prayed like this? If the economy takes a downturn and you're laid off, are you prepared to find joy in the Lord anyway? He is able to place you in a new position, but will you praise Him during the interim time of uncertainty?

EVENING: WHOM ARE YOU TRYING TO PLEASE? / *Then Pilate tried to release him, but the Jewish leaders shouted, "If you release this man, you are no 'friend of Caesar.' "* John 19:12 NLT / Pilate, facing the unenviable task of judging an innocent man before an angry crowd, found himself at the mercy of the mob. He was so busy looking at the shouting mass of people that he overlooked Jesus' words: God had handed over the power of life and death in that moment to him.

When you're faced with a difficult decision or conflict, it's easy to lose sight of what God has entrusted to you. A moral compromise that appears to be for the greater good today can have disastrous consequences in the future.

Often, doing the right thing requires a leap of faith, trusting that the truth will win out and God will ultimately honor your faithfulness.

MORNING: SIX-HOUR WORSHIP SERVICES / *They remained standing in place for three hours while the Book of the Law of the L*ORD *their God was read aloud to them. Then for three more hours they confessed their sins and worshiped the L*ORD *their God.* Nehemiah 9:3 NLT / After Israel rebuilt the temple and walls of Jerusalem, Ezra read from the Book of the Law for seven successive days, followed by a solemn assembly. A few weeks later, they assembled again to confess their sins and fast. Then, for the next six hours, they heard from God's Word, confessed more sin, and worshipped the Lord.

How does this practice compare to your attitude about worship? Do you check your watch throughout the service, or are you fully engaged?

If your heart hasn't been fully present during worship, the coming weekend is the perfect time to change.

EVENING: GOD'S DECLARATION OF LOVE / *Let him lead me to the banquet hall, and let his banner over me be love.* Song of Solomon 2:4 NIV / If you drive around most any city, large or small, you're likely to see banners that boldly advertise political candidates, products, or social causes.

Similarly, God has raised a banner for those who follow Jesus, and it communicates His love loud and clear. As David wrote, God has raised this banner as a loud proclamation of His devotion to His people: "You have given a banner to those who fear You, that it may be displayed because of the truth" (Psalm 60:4 NKJV).

There's no better place to be than under God's banner of love. There, we find security and rest from the world as God gives us strength and perseverance in even the most trying times.

MORNING: A CHANGE OF HEART / *If you will turn (repent) and give heed to my reproof, behold, I [Wisdom] will pour out my spirit upon you, I will make my words known to you.* Proverbs 1:23 AMPC / God's wisdom cannot be bound. It seeks you out, commanding you to repent. As you submit and repent, it will be readily available to you moving forward. Have you found this to be true?

Has reading the Word, listening to a sermon, or talking to a friend ever revealed a sin that you needed to repent of? And after repenting, did you notice that you were given wisdom from on high?

God uses rather ordinary means to get the believer's attention, but His call to repent is always clear. There's no better time for God to make a change in your heart than the present.

EVENING: TEST QUESTIONS / *Jesus said to them, "Very truly I tell you, it is not Moses who has given you the bread from heaven, but it is my Father who gives you the true bread from heaven."* John 6:32 NIV / Experts will tell you that for a man to be properly nourished, he needs a complex mixture of proteins, carbohydrates, dietary fats, vitamins, and minerals.

Nourishing your soul, however, is simple—all it takes is knowing Jesus Christ, the Bread of Life sent directly from heaven, in a personal way.

When God the Father sent His Son to this world to live, die, and rise from the grave, He provided you with everything you need—both to live a life on earth that pleases Him and to be fitted for eternity in His presence.

Let Jesus nourish your soul, this evening, tomorrow, and every day.

MORNING: WARNING SIGNS / *Solomon made an alliance with Pharaoh, the king of Egypt, and married one of his daughters.* 1 Kings 3:1 NLT / Solomon was praised as an obedient and wise king who loved the Lord. However, by allying himself with Pharaoh and marrying his daughter, Solomon violated God's commands and sowed the seeds of his future fall into sin.

Are there warning signs that you've been ignoring that could spell trouble in the future? Perhaps your faith is wavering, or maybe you simply can't trust God to provide for your needs.

If a man with Solomon's wisdom disregarded serious warning signs, it's likely that, at times, *you* may need a spiritual reminder from God—or a godly friend—to wake up and take action.

Every believer, no matter how wise, needs help and support. Are you willing to accept it?

EVENING: BEARING WITH FAILURE / *We who are strong have an obligation to bear with the failings of the weak, and not to please ourselves.* Romans 15:1 ESV / This evening's verse calls for the strong Christian—the man who is deeply rooted in gospel truth—to bear with the failings of his weaker brother.

Examine yourself today. How well are you bearing with a weaker brother's misunderstandings? Are you quick to try to correct him, feeling good about the fact that you are stronger? If so, recall your early days as a Christian. Weren't you glad when a stronger brother gently listened to you and guided you in the right direction?

Become that brother. Care more about the weaker brother's sanctification—which is a process, not an event—than you care about being right.

DAY 316

MORNING: FEAR OR LOVE? / *The fear of the* LORD *is the beginning of wisdom, and knowledge of the Holy One is understanding.* Proverbs 9:10 NIV / A man who'd always enjoyed an amazing relationship with his earthly father once said, "My father never had to punish me to make sure I stayed in line. I loved him so much that I was afraid to do anything that would disappoint him."

That's a pretty good illustration of the fear of God, isn't it?

God doesn't want us to view Him as a cruel tyrant or dictator. Rather, He wants us to love Him so deeply and reverentially that we won't want to do anything to displease Him.

Once we understand that this kind of fear doesn't conflict with love, we can find joy and the strength to endure as we walk with God.

EVENING: REPENT AND REJOICE / *Then he said to them, "Go your way. Eat the fat and drink sweet wine and send portions to anyone who has nothing ready, for this day is holy to our Lord. And do not be grieved, for the joy of the* LORD *is your strength."* Nehemiah 8:10 ESV / When the returned exiles heard the law and realized how far they'd strayed from the Lord, they mourned. Yet as they repented and wept, Nehemiah urged them to celebrate their recommitment and to let the joy of God be their strength.

When you're starting over after a time of struggle and unfaithfulness, you may wonder, *How can I possibly recover and begin again?* The answer is to repent and then rejoice.

Guilt and shame won't help you move forward. Yet rejoicing in God's mercy will draw you to obedience and renewal. In the Lord's joy, there is hope for tomorrow.

MORNING: THE MIGHTY POWER OF GOD / *Finally, be strong in the Lord and in his mighty power. . .so that you can take your stand against the devil's schemes.* Ephesians 6:10–11 NIV / A scheme is a calculated plan for reaching a specific goal. Scheming often involves devious plans with intent to bring about an evil result.

The devil schemes to bring your life to ruin, and he employs time-tested methods such as hatred, fear, lust, covetousness, addictions, and so on. Man's interests and "the will of the flesh" (John 1:13 KJV) often parallel Satan's will, because both are selfish.

So how do you become "strong in the Lord. . .so that you can take your stand against the devil's schemes"? Simple. "Submit yourselves. . .to God." Then you will have spiritual strength to "resist the devil, and he will flee from you" (James 4:7 KJV).

EVENING: SPIRITUAL EARS / *"My sheep hear My voice, and I know them, and they follow Me. And I give them eternal life, and they shall never perish; neither shall anyone snatch them out of My hand."* John 10:27–28 NKJV / When the Jews asked Jesus if He was the Christ, He spoke plainly to them, also telling them that they were not of His sheepfold. If they were part of His flock, they would know His voice—it has a ring of truth to it for the converted heart.

The voices around you might be loud, making demands on your time. You hear all of them and often respond accordingly. But do you still hear Jesus' voice when He whispers to you?

If you aren't tuned in to His Word, it's time to set aside some time to focus on Him above all else.

MORNING: HOLD EVERYTHING LOOSELY / *"Naked I came from my mother's womb, and naked shall I return. The Lord gave, and the Lord has taken away; blessed be the name of the Lord."* Job 1:21 ESV / In his book *Living above the Level of Mediocrity*, Chuck Swindoll recalls a conversation he had with the late Corrie ten Boom, who had lost family members in Nazi concentration camps. She said, "Chuck, I've learned that we must hold everything loosely, because when I grip it tightly, it hurts when the Father pries my fingers loose and takes it from me!"

This is what the transformed life looks like. It doesn't deny heartache, nor does it fail to mourn when the situation warrants. But it also sees life through the lens of the kingdom and is willing to accept whatever happens—because God is in control.

EVENING: YOU DON'T HAVE TO BE CLEVER / *For Christ didn't send me. . .to preach the Good News. . .with clever speech, for fear that the cross of Christ would lose its power.* 1 Corinthians 1:17 NLT / What makes ministry effective today? It's easy to think that a great ministry requires extremely talented people with extensive training. However, the power of God, displayed in Jesus on the cross and shared through the Holy Spirit, undermines the systems and rules that many hold dear.

The truth is you can accomplish great things through your inadequacy—because that's where you will find God's presence and power.

If you can't think of anything clever to say, that only ensures that you will depend on the Holy Spirit to give you the words you need.

MORNING: AN EXAMPLE TO OTHERS / *Be an example to all believers in what you say, in the way you live, in your love, your faith, and your purity.* 1 Timothy 4:12 NLT / This verse may seem like a tall order. You might struggle with bitterness, doubt, and daily battles with lust. You may even feel like saying, with Peter, "Depart from me; for I am a sinful man, O Lord" (Luke 5:8 KJV).

But Jesus *didn't* depart. He continued to work in Peter's life for the next three years. And even after all that time, Peter denied Jesus during a time of testing. But the Lord had seen that coming too, and He said, "I have pleaded in prayer for you, Simon, that your faith should not fail. So when you have repented and turned to me again, strengthen your brothers" (Luke 22:32 NLT).

If there's hope for Peter, there's hope for you.

EVENING: BEFORE ABRAHAM / *Jesus said to them, "Most assuredly, I say to you, before Abraham was, I AM."* John 8:58 NKJV / In this evening's verse, Jesus makes the ultimate claim. He uses the phrase "I AM"—words the Jews would have been familiar with as meaning, "Even from everlasting to everlasting," John Wesley writes in his commentary. "This is a direct answer to the objection of the Jews, and shows how much greater he was than Abraham."

You've probably heard people claim that all paths lead to heaven, no matter the belief system. But as soon as you point out that Jesus claimed to be God in the flesh, many will accuse you of being intolerant.

Proclaim it anyway.

Jesus has indeed always existed, and He's the only way to heaven (John 14:6). Hold on to those truths.

MORNING: SET FREE FROM SIN / *"If the Son sets you free, you will be free indeed."* John 8:36 NIV / It's tough to argue with the truth that you sin (Romans 3:23). But unlike those who dredge up your old sin to use as a club against you, God takes an entirely unexpected course. He forgives and forgets (Psalm 103:12). God offers freedom, but Christians often remain incarcerated by choice. You may not feel ready to forgive yourself, but you can accept His forgiveness and discover the freedom your soul has always craved.

God has an incredible future awaiting you, but you won't experience it by living in the past and recalling the failure that God has already forgotten.

Jesus shared His plan for your life in John 10:10 (NIV): "I have come that they may have life, and have it to the full." Believe today for true freedom.

EVENING: UNSHAKABLE CHARACTER / *Let him kiss me with the kisses of his mouth—for your love is more delightful than wine. Pleasing is the fragrance of your perfumes; your name is like perfume poured out.* Song of Solomon 1:2–3 NIV / "Your name is like perfume poured out." Since the word *name* often refers to character, the young bride in the Song of Solomon desires to be kissed because of her husband's intoxicating character.

How does a man develop this kind of character? By obeying the God of whom the psalmist sang, "Surely the righteous will praise your name [character], and the upright will live in your presence" (Psalm 140:13 NIV).

Having a name that is kissable, "like perfume poured out," involves obeying God. Read scripture and Christian books. Pray. Serve others. Forgive.

Keep up the good work. You're well on your way!

MORNING: INTIMIDATED BY GIANTS / *"There we saw the giants. . .and we were like grasshoppers in our own sight, and so we were in their sight."* Numbers 13:33 NKJV / When Moses sent twelve spies into Canaan, ten of them returned with this conclusion: "We are not able to go up against the people, for they are stronger than we" (Numbers 13:31 NKJV). Their negative report so discouraged the Israelites that they were afraid to invade Canaan, even though the Lord had promised He'd help them.

Does this ever happen to you? You're initially excited about a project, knowing God has promised to be with you. But when it comes time to launch out, you allow yourself to become discouraged by naysayers.

It's the default setting of the natural mind to exaggerate problems. But with God's help you can overcome them, no matter how big they are.

EVENING: WORDS OF LIFE / *"It is the Spirit who gives life; the flesh profits nothing. The words that I speak to you are spirit, and they are life."* John 6:63 NKJV / As Jesus taught His disciples (not just the Twelve or the Seventy, but a larger group) that they must eat His flesh and drink His blood to have spiritual life, many of them rejected this shocking teaching.

Jesus' teachings were spiritual, not literal, but these halfhearted people were unwilling to dig deeper to unpack what He was saying. They weren't committed followers.

When you encounter a hard teaching in the Bible, how do you react? Are you quick to dig deeper, or do you reject it like these shallow followers did?

Jesus is still speaking to His disciples. But it takes careful examination of scripture to truly grasp His words of life.

MORNING: ENJOY WHAT BLESSINGS HE GIVES YOU / *I perceived that there is nothing better for them than to be joyful and to do good as long as they live.* Ecclesiastes 3:12 ESV / God's cure for the restlessness of modern society is to patiently wait for His work while enjoying what you have.

If you trust God to work in you, the outcome He brings about will be a source of rest and comfort. Being grateful for these blessings will blunt the temptations of greed, overwork, and comparison to others, enabling you to be fully present among the people and situations in your life.

God wants you to slow down, do good, and enjoy your family, friends, and community.

EVENING: CONSPIRACIES / *The LORD. . .said, "Don't call everything a conspiracy, like they do, and don't live in dread. . . . Make the LORD of Heaven's Armies holy in your life."* Isaiah 8:11–13 NLT / Conspiracy theories—whether they involve media organizations or secret government operations—are nothing new. That's why the Lord warned Isaiah not to become consumed by the latest news instead of focusing on Him.

Paul also struggled with the prevailing opinions and political pressures of his day, but he reminded the people of God that he and other disciples "depended on God's grace, not on our own human wisdom" (2 Corinthians 1:12 NLT). He had learned like David to replace panic and paranoia with trust: "Let me hear of your unfailing love each morning, for I am trusting you. Show me where to walk, for I give myself to you" (Psalm 143:8 NLT).

And you can too.

DAY 323

MORNING: EMBRACING THE ENORMITY OF GOD'S CALLING
/ *So teach us to number our days, that we may gain a heart of wisdom.* Psalm
90:12 NKJV / Few men know which year, month, or day they will die. Then
again, would you really want to?

God alone appoints the day of our death, and His calling always extends
beyond our lifespan. That's why we must always keep eternity in view.

As pastor and author A. W. Tozer said, "Life is a short and fevered re-
hearsal for a concert we cannot stay to give. Just when we appear to have
attained some proficiency we are forced to lay our instruments down.
There is simply not time enough to think, to become, to perform what the
constitution of our natures indicates we are capable of."

Only by embracing the eternality of God's calling can we face death
with nobility.

EVENING: STANDING STRONG / *When Saul realized that the LORD
was with David and that his daughter Michal loved David, Saul became still
more afraid of him, and he remained his enemy the rest of his days.* 1 Samuel
18:28–29 NIV / Saul set his bride price for his daughter, Michal, at one hundred Philistine foreskins, believing David would perish in his attempt to
get them. Not only did David survive, but he returned with twice as many,
causing Saul to realize that God was mightily with David—and bolstering
David's own faith as well.

Are you currently facing a situation in which some authority might
not have your best interests in mind? Based on your response, does that
person see that God is with you? If not, what can you change to help make
that a reality?

MORNING: WAITING FOR GOD'S RESTORATION / *The people who walked in darkness have seen a great light; those who dwelt in a land of deep darkness, on them has light shone.* Isaiah 9:2 ESV / As the people of Israel waited for God to return and to restore them, they had no idea how Jesus would reveal the kingdom among them. Some were ready for the Lord's return, while many others were not.

As you wait on God and seek His direction, you may not know the timing or the details. You can only wait, often without the answers and resolution you crave.

During these seasons, perhaps the best you can do is to *remember*. Remember that even though you can't predict the details, you can rest assured that the Lord will come.

At the right time, the Lord will provide joy and His transforming presence.

EVENING: UNSHAKABLE EVIDENCE / *But thanks be to God, who always. . .uses us to spread the aroma of the knowledge of him everywhere. For we are to God the pleasing aroma of Christ among those who are being saved and those who are perishing.* 2 Corinthians 2:14–15 NIV / Paul uses a "smell" metaphor to echo the sentiment of those who choose to see only hypocrisy in the church. These people say, "Those Christians are all the evidence I need." But Paul's meaning is antithetical: Christians who follow God as He leads are the evidence that *everyone* needs.

Whether or not people believe in Jesus, believers are the "pleasing aroma of Christ" to them. They cannot help but wonder at the way His followers live and love. Everywhere, their "aroma" transforms any social stench into a satisfying scent.

Does the scent of your life stand as unshakable evidence of God's goodness?

MORNING: LOVE YOUR ENEMIES / "Love your enemies, bless those who curse you, do good to those who hate you, and pray for those who spitefully use you and persecute you." Matthew 5:44 NKJV / This morning's verse is about more than just loving our enemies; it's a remarkable summary of how we should love in all relationships. When we're cursed, Jesus says, "Bless!" When someone says bad things about us, we say good things to them.

Maybe we'd rather blast than bless. Maybe we take pride in our quick, biting one-liners. But scripture says, "Don't repay evil for evil. Don't retaliate with insults when people insult you. Instead, pay them back with a blessing. That is what God has called you to do, and he will grant you his blessing" (1 Peter 3:9 NLT).

Speak good to others. Bless, and don't curse.

EVENING: PROCLAIMING TRUTH / *John bore witness of Him and cried out, saying, "This was He of whom I said, 'He who comes after me is preferred before me, for He was before me.'"* John 1:15 NKJV / John the Baptist knew his calling. He was simply a forerunner to Jesus—one born to be a witness for Christ, and he freely admitted it. He knew Jesus was preferred over him and, judging by his admission that Jesus was *before* him, understood that Jesus was the preexisting Messiah, the eternal "Son of Man" (Daniel 7:9–10, 13–14 NKJV).

It's easy to become preoccupied with building our own kingdom, all while staying quiet about the kingdom to come. Let's be like John the Baptist, excited to point people to the Messiah, God's Son, knowing that we must decrease so that He can increase.

MORNING: WHY DO YOU SERVE GOD? / *We serve God whether people honor us or despise us, whether they slander us or praise us. . . . Our hearts ache, but we always have joy. We are poor, but we give spiritual riches to others. We own nothing, and yet we have everything.* 2 Corinthians 6:8, 10 NLT / Some people expect to be highly regarded for following Jesus, advocating for God's justice on earth, or holding others accountable. Those who have such hopes will surely be disappointed sooner rather than later.

Take Paul, for instance. His life was filled with pain and suffering, and he certainly didn't own many possessions. Yet he had riches that no man could touch: the joy of God and the comfort of His presence.

Whether you are wealthy, poor, healthy, or sick, you can share this joy with others freely without reservation or limit.

EVENING: FAITH IN A GOOD GOD / *Job. . .was blameless and upright, one who feared God and turned away from evil.* Job 1:1 ESV / Job persevered when he was told to give up. He hung on when he was told off. He trusted God when told he'd been abandoned. Job endured because he was faithful to God.

Sometimes, the need to endure arises because of our own choices. Other times, it's caused by the choices of others. But the *cause* of our suffering isn't that important—what we must focus on is the *result*.

Just as a weakling will never finish a marathon and an easy quitter will never hold down a job, a backward-facing Christian will never move forward in faith. Those who maintain their faith in a good God, however, will welcome a positive outcome at the end of each endurance.

MORNING: SOBER JUDGMENT / *Do not think of yourself more highly than you ought, but rather think of yourself with sober judgment.* Romans 12:3 NIV / Humility is the opposite of pride. Too often, however, Christians exhibit a false humility, which is just a different shade of pride.

False humility intentionally shares a personal fault with others, begging them to refute it. This side of pride can be even more insidious than blatant pride because it seeks to manipulate others into verbally affirming what you already believe you're good at.

God demands we consider ourselves with sober judgment. This means refusing to think too highly—or too lowly—of ourselves. We're made in God's image, but pride of any shade distorts the family resemblance.

Sober judgment means discovering how God sees you and then refusing to let your opinion of yourself climb higher than it should.

EVENING: GOD DELIVERS / *"Shall I yet again go out to battle against the children of my brother Benjamin, or shall I cease?" And the LORD said, "Go up, for tomorrow I will deliver them into your hand."* Judges 20:28 NKJV / After losing forty thousand men in two successive battles against Benjamin, Israel sought the Lord, asking whether they should do battle a third time. But this time, the Lord promised to deliver Benjamin into their hand—and He did.

Are you experiencing continued defeat on a work project, your family relations, or in personal evangelism? Are you seeking the Lord, asking Him if you should attempt something one more time? If He responds in the affirmative, are you willing to try again?

Israel obeyed God, and He delivered Benjamin into their hands. He can do the same for you.

MORNING: GOD WILL REMOVE ALL SORROW / *He will swallow up death forever; and the Lord GOD will wipe away tears from all faces, and the reproach of his people he will take away from all the earth, for the LORD has spoken.* Isaiah 25:8 ESV / Sorrow and death are a reality on earth. However, this morning's verse assures us that one day, everything will change. Every damaging experience will be relegated permanently to the past.

Of course, such statements don't erase our trials right now—the promise of a painless future doesn't remove the sorrow of those suffering today. This promise, however, does reveal something of God's character: He does not want death and sadness to be the norm in this world.

God knows all is not well, and He has come to bear your burdens with you until you're home with Him.

EVENING: A QUEEN'S VOICE / *For how can I endure to see the evil that shall come upon my people? Or how can I endure to see the destruction of my kindred?* Esther 8:6 AMPC / When Queen Esther heard of Haman's plan to wipe out her entire race, she knew what she had to do: make an unscheduled (and potentially fatal) visit to the king.

Have you ever determined to no longer endure evil and destruction among people you know—including your own family? Have you sought justice for the oppressed? Have you ever prayed for God to help the defenseless? Have you ever felt righteous anger on behalf of those who are hurt without cause?

Today, don't be afraid to speak up for what you know is right. God is with you, just as He was with Esther.

MORNING: WHY ALL THE R-RATED STORIES? / *"I took my concubine, cut her into pieces and sent one piece to each region of Israel's inheritance, because they committed this lewd and outrageous act in Israel."* Judges 20:6 NIV / The first seven books of the Bible all contain stories that make good men wince: Murder. Rape. Slaughter. Incest. Pillaging. Prostitution. Annihilation. Gang rape. Mutilation.

One of the disturbing stories is found in this morning's Bible passage. The book of Judges repeatedly shocks, and one repeated statement explains why: "In those days Israel had no king; everyone did as they saw fit" (Judges 17:6 and 21:25 NIV).

In this case, the moral of the story is obvious: if you do whatever seems right in your own eyes, there is no limit to how depraved you can be.

Why is the Bible so honest? For very good reasons, indeed.

EVENING: WHOSE AUTHORITY? / *"Tell us by what authority you are doing these things," they said. "Who gave you this authority?"* Luke 20:2 NIV / As Jesus was speaking, the teachers of the law, the chief priests, and the elders gathered thick around Him, questioning His authority. He had, after all, just thrown the entire temple into an uproar by driving out the corrupt merchants. How dare He? As if only *He* had the right and authority to be there!

You may find yourself doubting the authority of Jesus over your finances, your thought life, or your pleasures. As the culture around you tells you things different than Jesus says, you may wonder who's correct.

Doubt no more. Jesus is God incarnate, and His authority is from on high. Whose authority will you submit to today?

MORNING: HOW GENEROSITY CHANGES YOU / *Honor the L*ORD *with your wealth, with the firstfruits of all your crops; then your barns will be filled to overflowing, and your vats will brim over with new wine.* Proverbs 3:9–10 NIV / Generously giving your best to God recognizes that wealth, reputation, and worldly security are mirages set to pass away.

In fact, it would be a severe tragedy to hold back from giving your wealth to God. Jesus frequently warned that being rich puts people in danger of hell, in part because wealth can become a *de facto* deity—a source of false comfort, security, and provision.

Only when you've learned to give money away reliably will you be prepared to handle greater amounts of money. God doesn't prioritize your comfort—rather, He wants to ensure that you are secure in Him alone.

EVENING: OVERWHELMING SADNESS / *When I heard this thing, I tore my garment and my robe, and plucked out some of the hair of my head and beard, and sat down astonished.* Ezra 9:3 NKJV / Ezra was a dedicated student of God's Word. He'd learned what God commanded and told His people to avoid. When Ezra saw that the people were violating God's rules, he mirrored the Lord's broken heart, tearing his clothes to show his profound grief and pulling out some of his own hair in frustration. He sat down, astonished and undone.

How does the reality of your own sin affect you? Is it troubling? Or have you endured sin for so long that grief seems strange?

Ezra took sin seriously, as does God. Let's do the same.

MORNING: CONFIDENCE, STEADFASTNESS, AND TRUST / *They will have no fear of bad news; their hearts are steadfast, trusting in the LORD.* Psalm 112:7 NIV / In Journalism 101, students are told there is no such thing as "good news." Instead, there are only occasional "brights" to slip into the midst of all the bad news of the day.

The reality is that no "bright" can change the reality of the bad news that precedes it. It's enough to make you discouraged, distressed, even depressed. . .unless your heart is steadfast, trusting in the Lord.

Psalm 112:1–9 tells us that godly men don't lose sleep over bad news. We don't deny that we live "in the midst of a crooked and perverse nation" (Philippians 2:15 KJV), but we do trust the God who's so much bigger than society.

His infinite power, wisdom, holiness, and love keep us strong and steady, no matter what.

EVENING: WHAT AM I DOING WRONG? / *"You have planted much, but harvested little. You eat, but never have enough. You drink, but never have your fill."* Haggai 1:6 NIV / Hard times don't always indicate you're doing something wrong. Read Job's story for confirmation of that truth.

But sometimes difficulties *do* point to sin—or at least misplaced priorities—in our lives. Haggai's prophecy indicates that.

God's exiled people had returned to Jerusalem. They quickly improved their own homes but left God's temple in ruins. So the Lord not-so-gently defined their problem. "You expected much, but see, it turned out to be little. What you brought home, I blew away. Why? . . . Because of my house, which remains a ruin, while each of you is busy with your own house" (Haggai 1:9 NIV).

When life is hard, ask God, "What am I doing wrong?" If He shows you something specific, confess and change it. If there's nothing obvious, God may just be drawing you closer to Himself.

MORNING: FOR YOUR GOOD / *As obedient children, do not conform to the evil desires you had when you lived in ignorance.* 1 Peter 1:14 NIV / Dads know it takes time, patience, and plenty of reinforcement to get children to learn to make good choices.

Similarly, God wants to grow His children from babies who don't understand much to mature believers who value godly wisdom. He knows how easy it is for us to slide back into spiritual infancy, which is why He demands personal maturity. Hebrews 5:14 (NIV) says, "Solid food is for the mature, who by constant use have trained themselves to distinguish good from evil."

Just like braces transform a smile, obedience transforms a life. God doesn't want you to stay in ignorance. He wants you to grow up.

It's for your own good.

EVENING: TRUSTING IN GOD'S STRENGTH / *Gideon and his 300 men headed toward the Jordan River. They were exhausted when they crossed it, but they kept pursuing the enemy.* Judges 8:4 GW / This is probably the greatest example of Gideon's newfound trust in God: he had only three hundred starving men and was chasing a Midianite army of fifteen thousand (Judges 8:10). So what did Gideon and his men do? Quit? No, they continued pursuing the Midianites—and defeated them!

Sometimes, God will bring you into a desperate situation where you find yourself at your weakest. No one would blame you if you simply gave up and returned home.

Or. . .you can press on, trusting in God's strength. He once told the apostle Paul, "My power is strongest when you are weak" (2 Corinthians 12:9 GW).

God can give amazing victories if you trust Him.

MORNING: GOD'S CHILD, NOT HIS SLAVE / *And because we are his children, God has sent the Spirit of his Son into our hearts, prompting us to call out, "Abba, Father." Now you are no longer a slave but God's own child. And since you are his child, God has made you his heir.* Galatians 4:6–7 NLT / As a Christian, you should live as a child of God, seeking the Spirit's confirmation of the Lord's presence and acceptance. If you are seeking to obey God out of duty or fear, you have unintentionally demoted yourself from child to servant.

Today is an invitation to be reoriented by the Holy Spirit. Every other priority, possession, and goal pales in comparison to the identity Christ gives you as an heir in God's family.

Gladly accept your new identity and live in it today.

EVENING: LIVE THE ENCOURAGEMENT / Be joyful in hope, patient in affliction, faithful in prayer. Romans 12:12 NIV / During the dark days of World War II, the ten Boom family secretly harbored Jewish men, women, and children in their home. When it was discovered what this family had been doing above their clock-making shop, they were arrested. Eight hundred people had been saved, but four ten Boom family members died for their display of Christian love.

Corrie ten Boom, however, survived the concentration camps.

She could have been bitter and angry with God. Instead, she found joy in the hope that God could rescue from such terrible circumstances. Each day, she patiently and faithfully prayed for her family and other victims of persecution.

For decades after the war, this evening's verse was revealed in Corrie ten Boom's life—and her story has encouraged millions.

MORNING: TRUST GOD, THEN ACT / *When he saw them, he said, "Go, show yourselves to the priests." And as they went, they were cleansed.* Luke 17:14 NIV / When a group of ten lepers cried out for Jesus to have mercy and heal them of their disease, Jesus told them to go and show themselves to the priests. This was what people usually did *after* they'd been healed of leprosy (Leviticus 14:2–32). But they believed Jesus would heal them, so they went anyway. . .and were healed.

Do you need God to do a miracle in your finances, health, or marriage? Perhaps you need to take steps of faith, acting as if you already possess what He's promised to do for you.

You can't always expect God to act immediately, but you can expect Him to act.

EVENING: GOD'S SPIRIT / *Walk by the Spirit, and you will not gratify the desires of the flesh.* Galatians 5:16 NIV / Maybe you've heard it said that if you're looking for answers, look deep inside yourself. This saying is only true if you have God's Spirit living within you to provide the answers you seek. Trying to come up with the right answer apart from God's Spirit always leads to disaster (Galatians 6:8). But when you allow God to direct your steps, He'll make sure you have the right guidance (Proverbs 3:6).

God sent His Spirit to be your partner in purpose, your companion in commission, and your sidekick in support. Never buy into the lie that you're alone.

MORNING: DRAWING A BULL'S-EYE AROUND YOUR ARROW
/ *Jeroboam appointed his own priests to serve at the pagan shrines, where they worshiped the goat and calf idols he had made.* 2 Chronicles 11:15 NLT / Facing a divided kingdom and the possibility that his subjects would desert for his rival's land in order to worship, Jeroboam came up with a "good enough" solution: he created idols and appointed his own priests rather than worshipping in the way God commanded. You could say Jeroboam drew a bull's-eye around wherever his arrow landed.

The easy way out may save some headaches today, but it will eventually lead you—and probably others—astray from God's purpose.

This morning, pray that God will give you the strength and courage to do what He says, the way He says it.

EVENING: HOLINESS / *God's will is for you to be holy, so stay away from all sexual sin.* 1 Thessalonians 4:3 NLT / When the phrase "God's will" is applied to biblical thought, it's part of His plan. In this case, God wants you to be holy. *But*, you might wonder, *how does sexual purity connect with God's will for personal holiness?*

While God established sexual relationships within marriage, men sometimes take what He meant for their benefit and use it to subvert His plan. This doesn't honor God's plan because it substitutes an enduring expression of intimacy and love for a momentary satisfaction of lust. And it doesn't show genuine love to the other person because it's merely physical desire.

It's not always easy to resist sexual temptation. But it's well worth the cost of refraining from sin to enjoy an unbroken spiritual relationship with God. . .and a truly intimate, faithful relationship with your wife.

MORNING: GOD GIVES THE VICTORY / *"But I gave you victory over them. . . . It was not your swords or bows that brought you victory."* Joshua 24:11–12 NLT / Shortly before he died, Joshua assembled the Israelites and told them how God had done miracles for them in conquering the Amorites and Canaanites. Though they'd been required to fight with swords and bows, God wanted them to realize that they hadn't conquered the enemy all on their own.

God may have performed outstanding miracles in your life. He has almost certainly worked unobtrusive miracles on your behalf, answering your prayers, empowering you in your work, and blessing your efforts. And like He told the Israelites, He wants you to remember: "Not by might nor by power, but by My Spirit" (Zechariah 4:6 NKJV).

EVENING: NO CONSOLATION PRIZE / *In him you also. . .were sealed with the promised Holy Spirit, who is the guarantee of our inheritance until we acquire possession of it, to the praise of his glory*. Ephesians 1:13–14 ESV / Game shows offer a "consolation prize" if contestants don't win. But God doesn't offer consolation prizes. If you choose Him, you get everything—if you don't, you get nothing. When you believe Jesus is the only way, and accept God's rescue, you will be saved. The benefits? You can expect grace (access to God when you did nothing to earn His interest), mercy (not being punished for something you deserve), forgiveness, the companionship of God's Spirit, and eternal life with God in heaven.

With rewards like these, why would anyone want to settle for a consolation prize?

MORNING: LOSE THE PROFANITY / *But now is the time to get rid of anger, rage, malicious behavior, slander, and dirty language.* Colossians 3:8 NLT / The great Hall of Fame basketball coach John Wooden, who coached the UCLA Bruins to an amazing ten NCAA championships between 1963 and 1975, once said, "I had three rules for my players: No profanity. Don't criticize a teammate. Never be late."

It might surprise some Christian men to hear this, but God has implemented the first rule for us today. Speaking through the apostle Paul in this morning's verse, He tells believers to "get rid. . .of dirty language."

Foul language can be a problem area for many Christian men, especially those who come from rough backgrounds. But with the Holy Spirit's help, you can have victory over bad language—and make yourself a better witness for Jesus Christ.

EVENING: DON'T BE GULLIBLE / *The men of Israel looked them over and accepted the evidence. But they didn't ask God about it.* Joshua 9:14 MSG / Appearances can be deceiving. And that's what the Hivites from the nearby city of Gibeon were counting on. When they arrived in the Israelite camp, they pretended to be ambassadors from a far-off city. They were wearing worn clothes and had moldy bread in their packs as "proof" that they'd traveled a long distance. But had Joshua and the Israelites prayed, God would have unmasked this deception.

In a similar way, we must thoroughly check out any marching orders we believe came from God in order to be certain they're not really instructions from our spiritual enemy.

God will sometimes ask you to trust Him based on slim evidence—that's why you should always pray and check things out against scripture to make certain.

MORNING: FAILING GOD'S TEST / *"My people are foolish, they have not known Me. They are silly children, and they have no understanding. They are wise to do evil, but to do good they have no knowledge."* Jeremiah 4:22 NKJV / God called the people of Israel foolish, silly, and without understanding. They knew the right answer but chose what caused them to fail God's test over and over—and over again.

It was as if these people had received a master's degree in wickedness—they understood sin and knew how to apply it to their lives and relationships.

Sin is common, so you never need to think that you're the only one who struggles with—and occasionally gives in to—temptation. But you must always remember to confess that sin and start over.

EVENING: TOO FAR GONE? / *"So I will restore to you the years that the swarming locust has eaten, the crawling locust, the consuming locust, and the chewing locust."* Joel 2:25 NKJV / In the 1980s, Michael Franzese, a former New York mobster, earned millions of dollars weekly for the Colombo family. At one point, his criminal activities made him a billionaire. That all ended, however, when he was indicted on fourteen criminal counts and later imprisoned for ten years. Now a free man, Franzese no longer serves the Colombo crime family. Instead, he serves Jesus Christ as a public speaker and author.

If you were to tell Michael Franzese that someone is so far gone that they can never turn to Jesus for forgiveness, he'd likely offer his own life story to prove otherwise.

When Jesus Christ died, He died for the sins of *all*. Nobody is "too far gone."

MORNING: WE'RE ALL SINNERS / *But he said to me, "My grace is sufficient for you, for my power is made perfect in weakness."* 2 Corinthians 12:9 NIV / Many of the Bible's greatest heroes had faults. Jacob was a cheater. Peter was impetuous. Paul was a murderer. God didn't choose His disciples because they were perfect. He chose them as they were—imperfect and unworthy sinners.

The grace of God covers all faults and impurities. But many people still shy away from Him because they think they've somehow done too much to be forgiven. Nothing could be further from the truth—His hands are always wide open.

Think today of all the terrible sinners Jesus has forgiven throughout history. The Lord wants to wash away *your* sins too—all you have to do is ask. Don't miss out on His grace.

EVENING: NO TRADE / *"Take my instruction instead of silver, and knowledge rather than choice gold, for wisdom is better than jewels, and all that you may desire cannot compare with her."* Proverbs 8:10–11 ESV / If you had a choice between God's instructions for life and a few bars of gold, which would you take?

You probably said God's instructions—after all, it's expected, right? The truth is, we'll all sometimes seek to trade God's wisdom for something far less valuable. It's okay to admit that. But so we never think such a trade is worthwhile, God reminds us, "All that you may desire cannot compare."

When you struggle, be honest with God. But remember: trading the mind of God for anything is worse than swapping your brand-new luxury car for a plastic toy.

MORNING: THE GOLDEN RULE / *"Whatever you want men to do to you, do also to them."* Matthew 7:12 NKJV / These words capture the essence of the Christian life—in every situation, we should treat others as we ourselves want to be treated. This is indeed the Golden Rule of civilized humanity.

Tragically, the human heart is anything but golden. In fact, it's deceitful above all things (Jeremiah 17:9) and therefore incapable—apart from God—of living by this rule. Anticipating the betrayal of other hearts, it rewrites the rule to say, "Do to others *before* they do to you."

The Spirit, however, enables us to follow God's ways instead. So, "let us not become weary in doing good, for at the proper time we will reap a harvest if we do not give up" (Galatians 6:9 NIV).

How can you apply the Golden Rule in your life today?

EVENING: THE LOVE OF MONEY / *But those who desire to be rich fall into temptation and a snare, and into many foolish and harmful lusts which drown men in destruction and perdition.* 1 Timothy 6:9 NKJV / It's not difficult to find proof of the Bible's statement "the love of money is a root of all kinds of evil" (1 Timothy 6:10 NIV). All it takes is a quick skim of the news to see how many crimes are committed in pursuit of wealth.

Money, in and of itself, is not evil. It's just a tool you can use to care for your family, build yourself a better life, or bless others. But you put yourself at serious risk when you make the acquisition of material wealth your life's focus.

Possessing riches is okay—just don't let them possess you.

MORNING: BEARING YOUR BURDENS / *Blessed be the Lord, Who bears our burdens and carries us day by day, even the God Who is our salvation.* Psalm 68:19 AMPC / Sometimes we feel that we have a heavy load to bear—and the Lord has left us to carry it alone. One day, as Moses felt the full weight of all the Israelites upon him, he complained to God, "Why did you tell me to carry them in my arms like a mother carries a nursing baby?" (Numbers 11:12 NLT).

God, however, cares immensely, and He wants to carry not only your burden but *you* as well. He promises, "Even to your old age. . .will I carry you: I have made, and I will bear; even I will carry" (Isaiah 46:4 KJV).

God has, in fact, been carrying you all along. So never stop trusting Him.

EVENING: NO ROOM / *Don't fret or worry. Instead of worrying, pray. Let petitions and praises shape your worries into prayers, letting God know your concerns.* Philippians 4:6 MSG / Fear is a natural response. When you're in an uncertain situation, it's normal to be afraid. But God doesn't want you to be "normal." He wants to transform what keeps you up at night into a willingness to let Him take care of things.

Imagine getting a new appliance, plugging it in, and finding it doesn't work. What do you do? You call the appliance store. Prayer is like that: When concerns, anxiety, and fear show up uninvited and suggest life doesn't work, all you have to do is make the call.

Wherever faith is found, fear is forced to leave. It has no choice—when you absolutely believe God has taken care of your future there's no room for concern.

MORNING: PROPERTLY MOTIVATED PRAYERS / *And we are confident that he hears us whenever we ask for anything that pleases him.* 1 John 5:14 NLT / You've no doubt seen social media posts promising amazing financial blessings from God if you'll just click on "Share."

If you haven't already given that blessing plan a try, here's a little secret: it doesn't work. That's not the way God answers prayer. Your heavenly Father, as good and generous as He is with His blessings, isn't like an ATM. He grants your requests only when you ask for what pleases Him.

The apostle James put it very simply: "When you ask, you do not receive, because you ask with wrong motives, that you may spend what you get on your pleasures" (James 4:3 NIV).

Stop to consider your motives when you ask God to bless you. Ask yourself if what you're seeking will please Him.

EVENING: ENGAGED FOR LIFE / *Set your minds and keep them set on what is above. . . . For [as far as this world is concerned] you have died, and your [new, real] life is hidden with Christ in God.* Colossians 3:2–3 AMPC / When you engage in new-life living, expect to be misunderstood. Your thinking and decision-making will change. To your friends, and maybe your family, you will no longer seem like the person they've always known.

And they're right! Because you've put old-life living to death, it's normal when old friends don't understand (1Corinthians 2:14).

Your new life acts as a megaphone to those who see the difference—and they may want to know more about the change that can make *them* new too.

MORNING: STANDING FOR TRUTH / *Everyone who wants to live a godly life in Christ Jesus will suffer persecution.* 2 Timothy 3:12 NLT / The great prime minister Winston Churchill, who led Great Britain through the darkest days of World War II, has been credited with saying, "You have enemies? Good. That means you've stood up for something, sometime in your life."

In today's world, many Christians seem more concerned with being accepted than they are about standing for godly principles. Jesus, however, told His followers, "If you belonged to the world, it would love you as its own. As it is, you do not belong to the world, but I have chosen you out of the world. That is why the world hates you" (John 15:19 NIV).

Are you speaking the truth in love to those who desperately need to hear it? If not, today is the perfect time to start.

EVENING: TRUSTING GOD IN A STORM / *"Where is your faith?" he asked his disciples.* Luke 8:25 NIV / One day, Jesus' disciples were sailing across the Sea of Galilee as Jesus slept in the boat. Suddenly, a squall swept down upon them, churning up the sea and placing them in danger. The disciples woke Jesus, terrified that they would drown. Jesus rose, rebuked the wind and the waves, and the storm abruptly ceased.

Throughout your life, you are certain to face many crises that will seem as serious as this long-ago storm. So if your faith is small now, pray—like Jesus' disciples did—for God to increase it (Luke 17:5).

Trouble is bound to come, so prepare for it.

MORNING: GOOD MOTIVE? / *As for you, brothers, do not grow weary in doing good.* 2 Thessalonians 3:13 ESV / Many people think Christianity is a religion of people trying to do good things. Yet doing good because you feel obligated makes you feel resentment, and resentment makes you want to stop doing good things.

You don't work harder to make God like you. Instead, the work you do opens doors to expressing other parts of your transformed life. You can express kindness and love, but you can also express good news by helping someone who is open to learning more about Jesus. The act of helping may be less important than what others learn from your willingness to help.

Paul's encouragement in this morning's verse should spur us on to make sure we never miss an opportunity to introduce others to God.

EVENING: SPIRITUAL JUNK FOOD / *But solid food is for the mature, who by constant use have trained themselves to distinguish good from evil.* Hebrews 5:14 NIV / Over the past few decades, Americans have become increasingly aware of the importance of a good diet.

But what about the "spiritual food" you consume daily? Living in the early twenty-first century, you're bombarded nearly every waking hour with images, music, television shows, movies, and even a number of "Christian" broadcasts that will stunt your spiritual growth.

Without a finely honed sense of spiritual discernment, it's nearly impossible to maintain a healthy spiritual diet. But you can better your chances by employing these two tests: (1) Does what I'm watching or listening to build me up in my relationship with the Lord? and (2) Does this line up with the truths God has revealed in His Word?

MORNING: EVIDENCE VS. UNBELIEF / " *'The Lord your God carried you, as a man carries his son, in all the way that you went until you came to this place.' Yet, for all that, you did not believe*" Deuteronomy 1:31–32 NKJV / After spending forty years in the desert for their unbelief, Moses emphasized the reason the people had been wandering so long: stubborn unbelief despite clear evidence of God's power.

The ones who rebelled had died in the wilderness, so Moses was speaking to the younger generation. Many of them hadn't actually witnessed the great deeds God had done on their behalf. Did they fully understand this moment? Would they be as slow of heart to believe as their parents?

This morning, stop and consider the evidence of God's love and caring in your life. What He's done should lead you to greater belief, trust, and hope.

EVENING: KNOW WHAT YOU BELIEVE / *He must hold firmly to the trustworthy message as it has been taught, so that he can encourage others by sound doctrine and refute those who oppose it.* Titus 1:9 NIV / Many Christians aren't terribly excited when they hear the word *doctrine*. However, sound biblical doctrine is important—it's central to living the Christlike life and to explaining your faith to others. After all, you can't follow instructions you don't understand, let alone explain them to others.

If you want to understand good doctrine, go straight to the source: God's Word. The Bible contains everything you need to come to the faith, understand the faith, and share the faith with others.

Learning good doctrine is well worth your time. Ultimately, it helps you to know and love God more deeply.

MORNING: SPEAK UP / *"God sent me to preach against both this Temple and city everything that's been reported to you. So. . .change your behavior. . . . Maybe God will reconsider the disaster he has threatened."* Jeremiah 26:12–13 msg / The prophets and priests were at their wit's end with Jeremiah. He'd been warning them about impending judgment from God, and they eventually called for him to be put to death.

People who speak unpleasant truths are rarely appreciated. But as a Christian, this is your calling. Matthew 5:14 (msg) says, "You're here to be light, bringing out the God-colors in the world. . . . We're going public with this, as public as a city on a hill."

In what ways is your faith in Christ public? Do you say the hard but truthful thing when the situation warrants it? If not, pray for the courage God is happy to give.

EVENING: WHAT GOD CAN'T DO / *Why do you look the other way? Why do you ignore our suffering and oppression? We collapse in the dust, lying face down in the dirt. Rise up! Help us! Ransom us because of your unfailing love.* Psalm 44:24–26 nlt / Your perceptions of God and reality can appear difficult to reconcile when life begins to fall apart. But God's presence doesn't always mean your problems will be solved. This tension goes back centuries, and there's no reason to expect that our generation will finally figure it out.

This evening's psalm, however, leads you to the only place where you can find rest. When you feel beaten down by life and struggle to rise up from where you have fallen, remember that because of His unfailing love, God *can't* turn away from you or ignore you.

Even at your lowest point, you are always loved.

MORNING: CHRIST'S AUTHORITY, YOUR FREEDOM / *"A star will come out of Jacob; a scepter will rise out of Israel. He will crush the foreheads of Moab, the skulls of all the people of Sheth."* Numbers 24:17 NIV / When Balak, king of Moab, summoned the prophet Balaam to curse the Israelites, the prophet ended up pronouncing a blessing over them multiple times, in accordance with God's command. In his last blessing, Balaam announced that "a star" would come and "a scepter"—a Savior—would fulfill God's words spoken in the Garden of Eden: "I will put enmity between you and the woman, and between your offspring and hers; he will crush your head, and you will strike his heel" (Genesis 3:15 NIV).

Today, Jesus' authority as the risen Son ensures your new life of freedom. As Jesus Himself said, "If the Son sets you free, you will be free indeed" (John 8:36 NIV).

EVENING: SAVED BECAUSE OF HIS MERCY / *He saved us, not because of righteous things we had done, but because of his mercy.* Titus 3:5 NIV / You've probably heard people say that as long as they do lots of good and not too much bad, then they're okay with God—they'll go to heaven when they die. All that volunteering at the soup kitchen and giving to charity has to count for something, right?

However, there is nothing anyone can do to earn God's salvation. It's purely a gift from a generous, loving, forgiving God.

Don't put down the soup ladle. Don't stop writing checks to your favorite ministry. But keep in mind that you do those things because you've been saved, not because you think they will save you. God has already taken care of that!

MORNING: FINDING UNITY / *Let there be no divisions in the church. Rather, be of one mind, united in thought and purpose.* 1 Corinthians 1:10 NLT / There is no shortage of issues that Christians can be divided over. So how in the world can Christians ever hope to find unity?

The apostle Paul's appeal for unity isn't just wishful thinking. He wants his readers to respond based on the authority of Christ. However, Jesus' authority isn't a top-down decree. Rather, it comes from His Spirit dwelling within believers. He unites us together as His body.

All Christians should aim to reach the same goals of knowing God, thinking of His love and salvation, and sharing His compassion with others. In your worship and your actions, you can find the unity that a doctrinal statement may never achieve.

EVENING: SPIRITUAL EYES AND EARS / *"So! You who are going to destroy the temple and build it in three days, come down from the cross and save yourself!"* Mark 15:29–30 NIV / To those who weren't listening with spiritual ears or seeing with spiritual eyes, many of Jesus' claims seemed outrageous. His statement that He could rebuild the temple in three days, for example, referred to His death and resurrection (John 2:20–22). This happened right before their eyes, yet they couldn't see it.

Likewise, the most prestigious religious leaders couldn't see that "this Messiah" was indeed bringing salvation on the cross. They were "blind guides" (Matthew 15:14 NIV) even as they watched the scripture being fulfilled.

Is it possible that God is fulfilling a promise in your life in a way that you're missing? Stop for a moment to refocus your spiritual eyes and ears, asking Him to let you see His reality.

MORNING: WHEN NO ONE LISTENS / *"But when I speak with you, I will open your mouth, and you shall say to them, 'Thus says the Lord GOD.' He who hears, let him hear; and he who refuses, let him refuse; for they are a rebellious house."* Ezekiel 3:27 NKJV / Not everyone you talk with about the Lord is going to eagerly receive what you have to say. Some may be genuinely interested, but many others will politely listen before excusing themselves from the conversation.

Does that mean you should give up? Of course not! On the contrary, God calls you to continue speaking the message and then let Him do the work within people's hearts.

Always be ready to share what Jesus Christ has done for you and what He can do for others. Remember: it's your job to speak, even when people aren't listening.

EVENING: GOD HASN'T ABANDONED YOU / *"No, I will not abandon you as orphans—I will come to you. . . . When I am raised to life again, you will know that I am in my Father, and you are in me, and I am in you."* John 14:18, 20 NLT / Most everyone has a crisis of faith at some point. In fact, Jesus' disciples frequently struggled with doubts and confusion. So if you feel like living by faith each day is a bit beyond you, you're in good company.

Jesus recognized this struggle in His followers and assured them that He would remain closer to them than they could even imagine. Although we don't see Jesus walking alongside us, He is within us much like He and the Father are one.

This union with God will one day save your faith—if it hasn't already.

MORNING: CLOUD AND FIRE TRAINING / *The cloud of the Lord was over the tabernacle by day, and fire was in the cloud by night, in the sight of all the Israelites during all their travels.* Exodus 40:38 NIV / God offered to give the people the promised land, but their refusal to accept it meant that more than a million people would live as nomads for four decades. Even then, however, God led them, using a cloud by day and a pillar of fire by night.

For forty years the Israelites watched the sign in the sky. When it moved, the people moved. They learned to trust God and follow Him.

Do you ever feel like you've blown opportunities God had for you? Rest assured: He's still leading. Your real destination has always been toward His plan. You're closer today than you think.

EVENING: BECAUSE HE LIVES / *Because Jesus lives forever, his priesthood lasts forever. Therefore he is able, once and forever, to save those who come to God through him. He lives forever to intercede with God on their behalf.* Hebrews 7:24–25 NLT / In the Old Testament system of sacrifices, the priest's role was to serve as a mediator, bridging the gap between God and sinners who wanted His forgiveness. In that system, people would bring their sacrifices to the priest, who would present them to God. It was an imperfect system, but one that foreshadowed what was to come.

Jesus came to be the perfect priest. He serves as the one true mediator between His perfect heavenly Father and sinful human beings. What's more, while all Old Testament priests died, Jesus lives forever and stands before the Father pleading your case.

Because Jesus lives, you too can live—forever!

MORNING: STAY FAITHFUL / *"The Lord God is my strength; He will make my feet like deer's feet, and He will make me walk on my high hills."* Habakkuk 3:19 NKJV / This morning's scripture is the high point of Habakkuk's prophecy. But this positive picture follows a whole lot of negativity. God condemned His people for violence, drunkenness, and idolatry, threatening them with punishment. Habakkuk couldn't argue with God's assessment, so he simply promised to stay faithful. "Though the fig tree may not blossom, nor fruit be on the vines; though the labor of the olive may fail, and the fields yield no food; though the flock may be cut off from the fold, and there be no herd in the stalls—yet I will rejoice in the Lord, I will joy in the God of my salvation" (Habakkuk 3:17–18 NKJV).

Let's choose to be like Habakkuk. Make the conscious choice to honor God first. *Then* we'll climb the mountains.

EVENING: WHAT SHOULD THE WEARY DO? / *Then Jesus said, "Come to me, all of you who are weary and carry heavy burdens, and I will give you rest."* Matthew 11:28 NLT / When Jesus calls you to Himself, He doesn't demand any particular action or mindset. He knows full well that you're weary, so the invitation is spare and simple: come as you are.

Isn't that a relief? Rather than telling you to get your act together or to wait until you're ready for a greater commitment, He tells you to come at your worst, promising rest.

Weariness and burdens are perfect "qualifications" for coming to Jesus for rest and restoration. Perhaps you'll only be prepared for transformation if you first come to the end of yourself.

MORNING: YOUR HEART COULD BE WRONG / *When the people saw how long it was taking Moses to come back down the mountain, they gathered around Aaron. "Come on," they said, "make us some gods who can lead us."* Exodus 32:1 NLT / God invited Moses to come and speak with Him on the mountain. While Moses was gone the people struggled to continue trusting the Lord or Moses. Finally, they urged Aaron to make a god of gold they could follow instead. Surprisingly, Aaron complied.

The people of Israel stopped trusting God and decided they needed to follow their own hearts. Neither God nor Moses were amused.

Don't settle for words that make you feel better about sin. Seek God's words. Discover the ways you're breaking God's law. Trust that He forgives and can help you in all future decisions.

EVENING: DISTRACTED DRIVING / *Let your eyes look straight ahead; fix your gaze directly before you.* Proverbs 4:25 NIV / Have you ever been in a car driven by a distracted driver? While his hands are busy with a cell phone or the radio, yours are gripping the armrests. While he's looking anywhere except the road, you see every potential accident ahead.

The same thing can happen with your relationship to God. You may start your day in devotions and prayer, then get distracted by the concerns of the day. Soon you're looking anywhere except where God wants your attention to be.

How can you be more mindful? Maybe set an alarm to remind you to pray. Fast from a certain activity, and then when you find yourself wanting to do that thing, check in with God.

Whatever you do, do it intentionally with your eyes fixed on the Lord.

DAY 353

MORNING: GOD IS COMMITTED TO YOUR RESTORATION / *"Yet I will remember the covenant I made with you when you were young, and I will establish an everlasting covenant with you."* Ezekiel 16:60 NLT / After listing the shocking sins and transgressions that the people of Judah committed against the Lord, Ezekiel offered a message of consolation: God had planned something incredibly good. His covenant with them was not contingent on their faithfulness.

Perhaps you aren't shocked by God's mercy in the past, but you may have a hard time accepting it for yourself in the present. Is God really that merciful? The answer is *yes!*

God allowed the people of Israel to start over again—and then start over again after that. You can only miss out on God's mercy if you walk away from it.

EVENING: TEND YOUR LAMP / *"Outside the curtain that shields the ark of the covenant law in the tent of meeting, Aaron is to tend the lamps before the Lord from evening till morning, continually."* Leviticus 24:3 NIV / In the early 500s, Benedict of Nursia went to Rome for educational purposes. After encountering a dark culture there, he fled to the forest, where he became a monk. He believed that a peaceful, consistent, structured life would help keep faith's flame alive during the beginning of what is now known as the Dark Ages.

Similarly, Aaron was charged with tending the lamps in the tent of meeting from evening until morning. The symbolism in this passage is hard to miss, isn't it?

Your church, your family, *you* are called to be the light of the world, just as Jesus said in Matthew 5:14. Shine for Him.

MORNING: MADE FOR GOOD WORKS / *We are his workmanship, created in Christ Jesus unto good works, which God hath before ordained that we should walk in them.* Ephesians 2:10 KJV / After God created the heavens, earth, light, darkness, sun, moon, and animals, He declared it to be good. Then, on the final day of creation, God made man and woman in His own image. Genesis 1:31 (KJV) says, "God saw every thing that he had made, and, behold, it was very good."

Since you've been made in God's image, and He is the original doer of good works, you have been made for good works too. When your relationship with Him is right, your good works make it possible for others to see His reflection in you.

Can people see God's image reflected in your works?

EVENING: SPORTS SUPERSTITIONS / *Every man is stupid and without knowledge; every goldsmith is put to shame by his idols, for his images are false, and there is no breath in them.* Jeremiah 10:14 ESV / The world of sports is rife with superstition. For example, in the 1991 French Open, Andre Agassi realized too late that he had forgotten to pack underwear for his match, so he played without them. When he won, he attributed his good fortune to this missing item of clothing, and he kept competing commando-style all the way to his fourth Grand Slam title.

Such superstitions, silly as they may be, are just another form of ancient idol worship. After all, only God has the power to change the world.

Don't hope for good luck. Pray for God's blessing, believing that He'll take care of you. God didn't promise you'd win games, but He did promise that He will win the final battle.

MORNING: FAITH ISN'T JUST FOR TODAY / *Then the L*ORD *took Abram outside and said to him, "Look up into the sky and count the stars if you can. That's how many descendants you will have!"* Genesis 15:5 NLT / Some days, it's hard to see beyond today's challenges and trials. However, Abram's story pulls you out of the present so that you can see God at work in you for the long term.

If you're feeling overwhelmed by your circumstances or a particularly difficult relationship, step outside, look at the stars, and ponder the vastness of God's power. Think about the generations who will follow you. Then ask yourself, *Years from now, after I'm dead and gone, will my grandchildren remember my faith?*

How you trust God today will affect the impact of your life. Faith isn't just for today.

EVENING: PERSPECTIVE CHECK / *Then the L*ORD *asked Moses, "Who makes a person's mouth? . . . Is it not I, the L*ORD*? Now go! I will be with you as you speak, and I will instruct you in what to say."* Exodus 4:11–12 NLT / On one hand, it's okay to admit anxiety and doubt to God; in fact, He tells you to (1 Peter 5:7). On the other hand, doubt can betray a lack of trust in God's ability to keep His promises. Moses, for example, made it clear that he wasn't up to the task God was calling him to do. In return, God made it clear that that was the point.

God knows your shortcomings and will help you to overcome them. After all, He equips those He's called.

Do you trust Him enough to obey?

MORNING: GET DRESSED / *Above all, clothe yourselves with love, which binds us all together in perfect harmony.* Colossians 3:14 NLT / Polonius, from Shakespeare's Hamlet, advised his son Laertes to pay attention to how he dressed because he knew people often judged a man by his clothes: "Costly thy habit as thy purse can buy, but not express'd in fancy; rich, not gaudy; for the apparel oft proclaims the man."

In a way, Shakespeare was making a biblical point.

In Colossians 3:12, 14 (NLT), Paul writes, "Since God chose you to be the holy people he loves, you must clothe yourselves with tenderhearted mercy, kindness, humility, gentleness, and patience. . . . Above all, clothe yourselves with love, which binds us all together in perfect harmony."

Clothes don't make the man, but dressing in God's apparel can show the world what does—God's love.

EVENING: NEW LIFE WHERE THERE'S NO HOPE / *Out of the stump of David's family will grow a shoot—yes, a new Branch bearing fruit from the old root. And the Spirit of the* LORD *will rest on him.* Isaiah 11:1–2 NLT / When the people of Israel believed that they were cut off and as good as dead, much like an old tree stump, the Lord promised new life and even fruit from this stump. How? Through the Spirit of God.

While you can't make new life spring forth from the barren parts of your life, you can trust that the Spirit is more than capable of changing you. With His resurrection, Jesus Himself embodied this story of new life springing from death.

As He unites Himself with you, you too can partake in that story of new life, wisdom, and awe-inspiring knowledge of God.

MORNING: A RETURN TO CLARITY / *And he built an altar there and called the place El Bethel, because there God appeared to him when he fled from the face of his brother.* Genesis 35:7 NKJV / After a disastrous, spiritually barren episode in his life (Genesis 34), Jacob was in dire need of clarity. He returned to Bethel, the place where God had revealed His presence and where Jacob had come alive spiritually. There, God reminded him of His protection and provision (Genesis 35:7–14).

To be fully available to God, you must truly recognize your need and His presence in your life. Clear away the cobwebs of cluttered thinking (and schedules). Remind yourself of what you know to be true about God. Make time to worship, thanking and honoring Him with your words and actions.

Once you do, you'll have your own Bethel moment as well.

EVENING: IMITATION / *You became imitators of us and of the Lord, for you welcomed the message in the midst of severe suffering with the joy given by the Holy Spirit.* 1 Thessalonians 1:6 NIV / Imitation, it is said, is the highest form of flattery.

When Paul wrote to the church in Thessalonica, he encouraged his fellow believers to imitate both him and Jesus in a very specific way. This evening's scripture says the church "welcomed the message in the midst of severe suffering with the joy given by the Holy Spirit."

As Paul had joy in his suffering, the church had joy in theirs. They held fast to the truth of Jesus' resurrection, knowing their trials were temporary and their reward was everlasting. Since their joy didn't come from the world, the world couldn't take it away.

Instead of avoiding suffering, embrace it as an entryway to the Spirit's joy.

MORNING: GOD DELIGHTS TO BE AMONG YOU / *"The Lord your God is living among you. He is a mighty savior. He will take delight in you with gladness. With his love, he will calm all your fears. He will rejoice over you with joyful songs."* Zephaniah 3:17 NLT / During the Christmas season, we often consider how God is with us. Just think how wonderful that message truly is. Besides coming to earth for your salvation in the person of Jesus, God also takes great delight in you. You aren't just a reclamation project. His deep joy in you prompts Him to respond to you with His generous love and kindness.

Jesus spent much time healing and sharing meals with His people, not out of obligation but out of delight. And this same attitude is also why He's present for you today.

EVENING: STAND FIRM / *So then, brothers and sisters, stand firm and hold fast to the teachings we passed on to you, whether by word of mouth or by letter.* 2 Thessalonians 2:15 NIV / When faced with big questions, people are apt to believe sources that sound plausible—even if they aren't true.

This is the problem Paul addressed in 2 Thessalonians 2:1–2 (NIV): "Concerning the coming of our Lord Jesus Christ. . .we ask you, brothers and sisters, not to become easily unsettled or alarmed by the teaching. . . asserting that the day of the Lord has already come." Paul instructed his readers not to be shaken by rumors but rather to cling to the truth they knew.

When you hear something troubling, you should definitely ask questions. But you should also test the answers against God's Word.

A man of unshakable faith stands fast on the truth.

MORNING: THE ETERNAL GOD'S BIRTHDAY / *"I am the Alpha and the Omega," says the Lord God, "who is and who was and who is to come, the Almighty."* Revelation 1:8 ESV / When you think about it, celebrating the birthday of the eternal God is odd. God exists outside of time. He has always been, always is, and always will be. Does it even make sense to celebrate His birthday?

Yes!

Due to His eternal nature, Jesus Christ's birth is *doubly* worth celebrating. God, because of the love He has for us, humbled himself by entering into our world as a frail human baby and ultimately sacrificing Himself for us.

We celebrate the birth of Christ because it shows us the lengths God is willing to go for the world He created. Today, give thanks that the eternal Lord was willing to be born so that you could be born again into His love.

EVENING: LIKE A GOOD SOLDIER / *Join with me in suffering, like a good soldier of Christ Jesus.* 2 Timothy 2:3 NIV / Militarily speaking, a good soldier is the courageous one who expects hardship and suffering to be a part of the job.

The apostle Paul lived in a time and place where being a Christian often meant intense persecution—even death. That's why Paul encouraged a young preacher named Timothy to "join with me in suffering."

Here in the West, Christians don't face that much suffering for their faith. But in some parts of the world, believers often are treated just as badly as Christians were in the first century.

Would you be willing to suffer for following Jesus?

If so, then you are more likely to stand steadfast should persecution become a part of your life of faith.

MORNING: A MAN WHO MATTERS / *Neither before nor after Josi* *was there a king like him who turned to the* Lord *as he did—with all* *heart and with all his soul and with all his strength.* 2 Kings 23:25 NIV / Af 'a painful series of kings who woke up each morning thinking only abo how to please themselves, Josiah ascended the throne.

His passion for doing right honored God so distinctly that the peo around him began to stop serving themselves and start loving God a their neighbors. He was a man who mattered to the people of God, a his life echoed Psalm 104:33 (NIV): "I will sing to the Lord all my life; I w sing praise to my God as long as I live."

Are you striving to be a man who matters?

EVENING: THE ORIGINAL HERO / *In your majesty ride forth victo* *ously in the cause of truth, humility and justice; let your right hand achie* *awesome deeds.* Psalm 45:4 NIV / Think of a hero who fights for truth a justice. If your first thought is of a man in a skintight outfit with a red ca you need to get your head out of the comic books. The concept of heroi is much older than any "Man of Steel."

The origin of the word *hero* is likely related to pre-Greek words "protector." In Psalm 45, the psalmist paints a portrait of God as the ultim. hero who fights evil, wins the loyalty of His beloved, and is remember by the nations for His awesome deeds.

How can you praise God as the hero He is? By reflecting His priorit in the world He came to save.

MORNING: WHERE TO TURN WHEN TIMES ARE TOUGH / *The LORD is good, a refuge in times of trouble. He cares for those who trust in him.* Nahum 1:7 NIV / On their road to spiritual maturity, some Christians find themselves disappointed that their life in Christ isn't the rose garden they thought it would be. Mature believers, however, understand that God never promised an easy life for those who trust in Him. On the contrary, Jesus Himself taught, "In this world you will have trouble" (John 16:33 NIV).

But you can find comfort in the second half of Jesus' statement about troubles in this world: "But take heart! I have overcome the world."

When you're going through difficult times, believe that God cares for you and is fully aware of your suffering. Even better, you can count on Him to bring something good out of what you're enduring.

EVENING: READY, WILLING, AND ABLE / *"Then you see how every student well-trained in God's kingdom is like the owner of a general store who can put his hands on anything you need, old or new, exactly when you need it."* Matthew 13:52 MSG / God does things in unexpected ways, at unexpected times, and through unexpected people. He tends to turn conventions upside down, accomplishing His plans through what seem to us like the most difficult and convoluted methods. God uses this strategy so that He gets His rightful glory each time.

The key to working with an unpredictable but always victorious God is to make yourself available. Then, as Matthew 13:52 suggests, you must stock your shelves with the right supplies—and the Bible is your chief supplier.

Make sure you're filled with God's Word daily; that way, you'll be available for His purposes at any given time.

MORNING: DIFFERENCE MAKING / *For I have kept the ways the Lord and have not wickedly departed from my God.* Psalm 18:21 A / Martin Luther King Jr. dreamed of a day when people would be judg not by their skin color but by their character. This isn't an excuse to ign people's ethnicity and experiences but a reminder that, in God's eyes, people are on the same footing. God, being just, sees and condemns but God, being merciful, also provides a Savior who unites all people as children, regardless of background or politics or any other worldly divisi

As a Christian, you're in a unique position to move beyond dream of a better day—you can actually make it happen! This revolution happe one heart at a time, as people realize their brokenness and need and tu to God for help. Will you be a difference maker today?

EVENING: SEEING THINGS AS THEY TRULY ARE / *Steph full of the Holy Spirit, gazed steadily into heaven and saw the glory of G and he saw Jesus standing in the place of honor at God's right hand. A* 7:55 NLT / As the religious authorities stoned Stephen, he saw Jesus ruli in the place of honor at God's right hand.

Filled with the Holy Spirit, he also saw things as they truly were. A as he trusted his life to God, Stephen expressed great compassion for executioners. He pleaded with God to not hold their sin against them.

When you see yourself under God's rule, you recognize your great ne for His mercy. You won't harbor illusions about what you deserve or yc superiority to others. You'll see that your life depends on God not holdi your sins against you.

MORNING: WALKING WITH GOD / *The LORD has told you what is good, and this is what he requires of you: to do what is right, to love mercy, and to walk humbly with your God.* Micah 6:8 NLT / Taking a walk with someone is a good way to get some exercise—but also to enjoy that person's company.

The Bible contains two examples of people who "walked with God": Enoch (Genesis 5:21–24) and Noah (Genesis 6:9). These men walked with God in the sense that they could fellowship with Him as closely as if they literally went for a stroll together, sharing their hearts and allowing Him to share His with them.

What about you? Maybe "walking" with God through prayer and listening this morning could enhance and strengthen your relationship. Why not try that now?

EVENING: GOD'S ECONOMY / *There is one who scatters, yet increases more; and there is one who withholds more than is right, but it leads to poverty.* Proverbs 11:24 NKJV / Compared to worldly views of wealth, God's economy seems built on paradoxes: to get, you must first give, but you shouldn't give to get (Luke 6:35). If this line of reasoning makes you scratch your head, you're living in the world's economy, not God's.

Remember, God's business is seeing as many as possible receive the gift of salvation. Christ purchased a gift for you that you can never earn or purchase; the only thing you can do is share it through your words, deeds, and resources.

No other religion has Christianity's track record of helping; your involvement carries on that great tradition.

MORNING: DONE WITH SIN / *Therefore, since Christ suffered in his body, arm yourselves also with the same attitude, because whoever suffers in the body is done with sin.* 1 Peter 4:1 NIV / When you're sick for a prolonged period, your suffering strips you down to the bare basics of existence. You no longer care to indulge in pleasurable activity. Pain and suffering loom so large in your mind that you can think of little else.

When you lose your tight grip on all your ambitions and dreams, you finally begin to grasp what Jesus meant when He said, "Whosoever will save his life shall lose it: and whosoever will lose his life for my sake shall find it" (Matthew 16:25 KJV).

As difficult as it is to go through prolonged suffering, that's often when God works in your life the most.

EVENING: SOLOMON'S BIGGEST SIN / Now King Solomon loved many foreign women. 1 Kings 11:1 NLT / Everyone knows Solomon's "original sin": loving an unending string of foreign wives. Unlike his father, Solomon's sin was deeply rooted, blatant, prolific, all-consuming, and unconfessed—to the very end. The man renowned for his wisdom and wealth ended up causing the collapse of his kingdom and began practices for which both the kingdoms of Israel and Judah would be punished.

However, by comparing this evening's verse with 1 Kings 3:1 and 14:21 and 14:31, it becomes apparent that Solomon loved foreign women even *before* he became king. Solomon's sin began in his youth and ran its full course unabated, despite God's best efforts to persuade him to quit.

Is there any sin, perhaps long entrenched and scarcely recognized, that still embraces your heart? If so, don't be like Solomon—make a change today.

DAY 365

MORNING: GOD IS THERE FOR YOU / *The righteous cry out, and the Lord hears them; he delivers them from all their troubles.* Psalm 34:17 NIV / Attempts to find a scriptural promise of a trouble-free Christian life will end in frustration. In fact, Jesus promised quite the opposite: "In this world you will have trouble. But take heart! I have overcome the world" (John 16:33 NIV).

Yes, in this world, we're going to face times of trouble. But there is one promise God has made repeatedly in His written Word for believers facing those times of difficulty. Time and time again, He says, "I'll be there for you."

God is both our loving heavenly Father and a devoted friend. He is there for us in our times of greatest trouble. With a friend like that, who needs anything else?

EVENING: CLOSING THE DOOR ON THE PAST / *He who was seated on the throne said, "Behold, I am making all things new."* Revelation 21:5 ESV / New Year's Eve is a great time to reflect on your walk with Christ over the last year. Have you been consistent in studying the Bible? Has your prayer life been more of a conversation with God than a stream of requests? Do you trust God more today than you did a year ago? Have you prioritized fellowship with God's people? Have you shared His love with others?

If your self-examination turns up areas in your life that still need work, it's time to close the door on your past failures and allow God to renew you. Let every day be New Year's Eve and resolve to let Him work through you. Daily renewal is the key to spiritual endurance.

Go, be new!

SCRIPTURE INDEX

SCRIPTURE VERSION CREDITS